W9-BCF-075

Modern Critical Views

Modern Critical Views

ASIAN-AMERICAN WRITERS

Edited and with an introduction by
Harold Bloom
Sterling Professor of the Humanities
Yale University

CHELSEA HOUSE PUBLISHERS
Philadelphia

© 1999 by Chelsea House Publishers, a division of
Main Line Book Co.

Introduction © 1999 by Harold Bloom

Printed and bound in the United States of America

10 9 8 7 6 5 4 3 2 1

∞ The paper used in this publication meets the minimum
requirements of the American National Standard for
Permanence of Paper for Printed Library Materials,
Z39.48-1984

Library of Congress Cataloging-in-Publication Data

Asian-American Writers / edited and with an introduction by
Harold Bloom.
        p. 249   cm. — (Modern critical views)
    Includes bibliographical references (p.) and index.
    ISBN 0-7910-4787-3
    1. American literature—Asian American authors—
History and criticism.   2. Asian-Americans—Intellectual
life.   3. Asian Americans in literature.   I. Bloom,
Harold.   II. Series.
PS153.A84A84   1998
810.9'895—dc21   98-15463
                                               CIP

Contents

Editor's Note

This collection of fifteen critical essays cannot be wholly representative of Asian-American imaginative literature and its interpretation, largely because that literature is very flourishing and the commentary devoted to it is still at an early stage, in my judgment. Still, here are reflections and meditations upon American writers of Chinese, Japanese, Filipino, Korean, Vietnamese, and Indian origin or ancestry. My Introduction, rather than seeking a conspectus upon this highly diverse company of writers, centers instead upon only one, Maxine Hong Kingston in her *The Woman Warrior* (1976).

Dorothy Ritsuko McDonald begins the critical sequence with an account of the protagonist's quest for self-acceptance in John Okada's novel, *No-No Boy*, after which Amy Ling explores the novelist Diana Chang's sense of Chinese American dual identity.

The story writer, Hisaye Yamamoto, and the playwright, Wakako Yamauchi, who shared internment during World War II, are contrasted by D.R. McDonald, in her second appearance here, and Katherine Newman.

S.E. Solberg reflects upon Edith Eaton, the first Chinese American writer of fiction, while Amy Ling returns with a brief account of Winnifred Eaton (Edith's younger sister) and her novels.

N.V.M. Gonzalez, the Filipino novelist, is seen by Richard R. Guzman as benignly mythic in his handling of time, after which Zenobia Baxter Mistri brings us back to Hisaye Yamamoto and her rendering of the ordeal of internment.

Shirley Geok-lin Lim meditates upon the maternal experience as represented in the writing of Monica Sone and Joy Kagawa.

The Filipino story writer Carlos Bulosan, best known for his personal narrative, *America Is in the Heart*, is warmly celebrated by Elaine H. Kim, while Qui-Phiet Tran studies the fortunes of Vietnamese Americans in the fiction of Tran Dieu Hang.

Ruth Y. Hsiao reflects upon tensions that result from patriarchal repression in Louis Chu's novel, *Eat a Bowl of Tea*, after which Oscal V. Campomanes considers the particular contours of Filipino American writing as a literature of exile.

The works of three Korean American authors—Ronyoung Kim, Theresa H.K. Cha, and Younghill Kang—are studied by Chung-Hei Yun, who sees their writing as a literature both of despair and of hope.

Inderpal Grewal centers upon Bharati Mukherjee's novel, *Jasmine*, finding in it a somewhat problematic representation of the women of India.

Maxine Hong Kingston, the subject of my Introduction, also concludes this volume in Jeanne Rosier Smith's essay on the trickster character in Kingston's work.

Introduction

I have written once before about Maxine Hong Kingston's "No Name Woman," which is part of her famous fictive autobiography, *The Woman Warrior* (1976), and I return to it here to consider again the question of ambivalence towards ancestral tradition in Asian American writing. Ambivalence, marked by its simultaneous negative and positive reactions to a violent past, one that generally featured paternalistic repression of the individual, pervades the work of the authors who are the subject of this volume. Since Kingston, at this time, remains the most widely read of all Asian American writers, her own representation of ambivalence towards an Asian family heritage is likely to remain influential, perhaps more among the general public than among her fellow creators of narratives, lyrics, and plays.

Wallace Stevens remarked that the final belief was to believe in a fiction, with the nicer knowledge of belief, which is that what one believes in is not true. That is probably more ambiguously fictive than Kingston's transformation of her mother's story about a long-dead, nameless aunt, but it may suggest how much the telling (and retelling) of a story always involves imaginative distortions that are essential if anything fresh is to come into being. Kingston writes of "a girlhood among ghosts," and ghosts (unless you believe in them) are fantasies, mostly inherited from others. "No Name Woman," being a fantasy (whatever its basis in family legend) is perhaps best read backwards, starting with the third paragraph from the end, where first Kingston quotes her mother, and then adds her own element of supposed guilt:

> "Don't tell anyone you had an aunt. Your father does not want to hear her name. She has never been born." I have believed that sex was unspeakable and words so strong and fathers so frail that "aunt" would do my father mysterious harm. I have thought that my family, having settled among immigrants who had also been their neighbors in the ancestral land, needed to clean their name,

and a wrong word would incite the kinspeople even here. But there is more to this silence: they want me to participate in her punishment. And I have.

It is difficult to judge whether this is altogether legitimate, in a strictly literary sense. Kingston certainly seems to be appealing to ideological fashions, very strong twenty years ago, and only starting to wane now. With a great fantasist like Kafka, whose spiritual and literary authority is overwhelming, we have to yield to his dread apothegm: "Guilt is never to be doubted." But with Kingston, I am somewhat more resistant: I want some justification for that "And I have." Rereading the two final paragraphs of "No Name Woman" has not provided me with that justification, whether I consider either Kingston's implicit moral stance or her attempt to elevate her style to a negatively sublime conclusion:

> In the twenty years since I heard this story I have not asked for details nor said my aunt's name; I do not know it. People who can comfort the dead can also chase after them to hurt them further—a reverse ancestor worship. The real punishment was not the raid swiftly inflicted by the villagers, but the family's deliberately forgetting her. Her betrayal so maddened them, they saw to it that she would suffer forever, even after death. Always hungry, always needing, she would have to beg food from other ghosts, snatch and steal it from those whose living descendants give them gifts. She would have to fight the ghosts massed at crossroads for the buns a few thoughtful citizens leave to decoy her away from village and home so that the ancestral spirits could feast unharassed. At peace, they could act like gods, not ghosts, their descent lines providing them with paper suits and dresses, spirit money, paper houses, paper automobiles, chicken, meat, and rice into eternity—essences delivered up in smoke and flames, steam and incense rising from each rice bowl. In an attempt to make the Chinese care for people outside the family, Chairman Mao encourages us now to give our paper replicas to the spirits of outstanding soldiers and workers, no matter whose ancestors they may be. My aunt remains forever hungry. Goods are not distributed evenly among the dead.

> My aunt haunts me—her ghost drawn to me because now, after fifty years of neglect, I alone devote pages of paper to her, though

not origamied into houses and clothes. I do not think she always means me well. I am telling on her, and she was a spite suicide, drowning herself in the drinking water. The Chinese are always very frightened of the drowned one, whose weeping ghost, wet hair hanging and skin bloated, waits silently by the water to pull down a substitute.

"Reverse ancestor worship" is a curious oxymoron; doubtless it seeks to redefine ambivalence, but its irony is too diffuse to persuade a dispassionate but still attentive reader. The fiction that the nameless aunt must beg and fight for food from other ghosts has more artifice than pathos: "My aunt remains hungry" is something of a pistol that does not fire. Kingston's final metaphor, with its implication that her aunt's ghost is a menace to her, waiting silently to pull her down into the well of the past, scarcely sustains investigation. The ghost is no menace at all, but a useful fiction to end a narrative. What guilt may exist (and humanly one doubts it) is more than compensated by the fairly successful exploitation of a family legend, a metamorphosis of ambivalence into popular narrative, where it entertains, but perhaps only for a time. Period pieces have their own charm, and the no-name woman, with a story, is likely to attain that status.

DOROTHY RITSUKO MCDONALD

After Imprisonment: Ichiro's Search for Redemption in No-No Boy

It is a curious experience to read John Okada's *No-No Boy* today. When we read of Ichiro Yamada, his family, and others of Japanese ancestry being unjustly incarcerated in relocation camps during the Second World War, Ichiro's double-negative response to questions regarding his loyalty and willingness to serve in the armed forces is understandable. It is difficult to see it as the shameful, treasonous act which most Japanese-Americans then thought it to be. How would a person today under similar circumstances—deprived of home, property, and family, and moved into a barren desert against his will—reply to the questions: "Are you willing to serve in the armed forces of the United States in combat duty wherever ordered?" "Will you swear unqualified allegiance to the United States of America and faithfully defend the United States from any or all attacks of foreign or domestic forces, and forswear any form of allegiance or obedience to the Japanese Emperor, to any other foreign government, power or organization?" Probably "No-No."

But even under these oppressive circumstances, thousands of Japanese-Americans willingly served and fought for their country to prove that they were Americans; the 442nd Combat Team emerged as the most decorated in the armed forces. As Okada says, "For each and every refusal based on sundry reasons, another thousand chose to fight for the right to continue to be Americans because homes and cars and money could be regained but only if

From *MELUS: The Journal of the Society for the Study of the Multi-Ethnic Literature of the United States*, Vol. 6, No 3 (Fall 1979). © 1979 by the University of Southern California.

they first regained their rights as citizens, and that was everything" (p. 34). Okada himself answered the questions affirmatively, joined the U.S. Army, and was discharged in 1946.

The preface of Okada's novel reveals his ironic attitude towards "the removal of the Japanese from the Coast, which was called the evacuation, and . . . [the] concentration camps, which were called relocation centers" (pp. x–xi). As if in answer to the second question (stressing loyalty to the Emperor), the central figure of Okada's preface is not Ichiro but a Japanese-American soldier, patterned after the author himself, who is stationed in the Pacific and flying regular reconnaissance flights from Guam to Japan as an interpreter. A lieutenant, a "blond giant from Nebraska," upon learning of the mandatory evacuation declares that, had that happened to his family, he wouldn't fight for America: "What the hell are we fighting for?" he asks. The Japanese-American soldier tersely answers, "I got my reasons," and thinks with sympathy of a friend who "was in another kind of uniform" because of the government's refusal to let his father rejoin his mother and sisters (pp. x–xi).

It is doubtful that the imprisoned friend is Ichiro whose refusal to serve is more complex. But the preface sets a tone of sympathy of white and Japanese-Americans alike for those who had said "No-No." For his refusal, Ichiro spends two years in jail, during which time he regrets his action, believing indeed that he had committed treason and that society—his Japanese-American world and the larger world of America—would never accept him again. After the war, upon his return to Seattle, facing his own self rejection and that of his peers, he is assured by two friends who could transcend the historical moment that time would be healing—that in time there would be no difference between those who had served and those who had not.

This is essentially Okada's perspective, and it is tinged with the ironic conviction that racism is here to stay. The two friends, Gary and Kenji, believe that, despite the demonstrated patriotism of the Nisei, the attitude towards them has not truly changed and that the No-No boys for an indefinite present are merely the scapegoats of the Japanese community. The dying Kenji, a war hero, advises Ichiro to remain in Seattle: "The kind of trouble you've got, you can't run from it. Stick it through. Let them call you names. They don't mean it. . . . They don't know what they're doing. The way I see it, they pick on you because they're vulnerable. They think just because they went and packed a rifle they're different but they aren't and they know it. They're still Japs." Kenji goes on to speak of the white opposition against the Japanese-Americans' return to the West Coast after the war: "name-calling, busted windows, dirty words painted on houses" (p. 163). He thinks the cruel rejection by the veterans is due to their belief that the No-No boys were responsible for this situation. Similarly, Gary, a No-No boy at peace with himself, says much later in the novel: "Reality will make them (the veterans) lose some of their cocksureness. They'll find that they still can't buy a house in Broadmoor even with a million stones in the bank. They'll see themselves getting passed up for jobs by white fellows not quite so bright but white. . . . When they find out they're still Japs, they'll be too busy to be mean to us. . . . You and I are big, black marks on their new laundry" (pp. 227–228).

The idealistic Kenji, weary of the hatred among the races and ethnic groups of the world, and believing the Japanese tendency to group themselves into communities to be inherently dangerous, bitterly tells Ichiro that after he (Ichiro) has resolved his conflict with his peers, he should go "someplace where there isn't a Jap within a thousand miles. Marry a white girl or a Negro or an Italian or even a Chinese. Anything but a Japanese. After a few generations of that, you've got the thing beat" (p. 164).

But Kenji's momentary cynicism is balanced by his friend Emi who preaches forgiveness and love to Ichiro. The government, she says, "made a mistake when they doubted you." But it was generous enough not to kill him. "They made a mistake when they made you do what you did and they admit it by letting you run around loose. Try, if you can, to be equally big and forgive them and be grateful to them and prove to them that you can be an American worthy of the frailties of the country as well as its strengths" (p. 96).

But it is not heroism that Ichiro desires. Even before his meeting with Kenji, he thinks that in time he might lead a normal life. "I will buy a home and love my family and I will walk down the street holding my son's hand and people will stop and talk with us about the weather and the ball games and elections" (p. 52). These are essentially Okada's values, for in his brief autobiographical sketch, he speaks of his love for his family: "Normal feelings for a normal husband and father, one might say, but I choose to think that my family is quite special. Perhaps I have been endowed with a larger capacity for normalcy than most people" (pp. 259–260).

However, Ichiro's family is far from normal. His conflicts with his parents are most intense at the book's beginning, for he blames them—especially his mother—for having said the fatal words that made him a social outcast. Through these conflicts and the accompanying internal monologues, we become aware of the feelings of a Japanese-American at the advent of the Second World War when "being an American is a terribly incomplete thing if one's face is not white and one's parents are Japanese of the country Japan which attacked America. It is like being pulled asunder by a whirling tornado . . ." (p. 54).

Although noting that Asian immigrants could not by law become citizens (pp. 51–52), Okada is nonetheless critical of their rigid lack of understanding of their American children; and this rigidity he pushes to the ultimate degree in portraying the madness of Ichiro's mother who insistently believes that Japan has won the war and lives only for her family's eventual return to their homeland. Her rock-hard, unloving, destructive dominance is intensified by the weakness of Ichiro's father who fearfully accedes to his wife's madness, takes to drink to escape its reality, and, in a very untypical Japanese fashion, assumes the feminine role in the family. Ichiro, despite his innate love for his father, feels contempt for him, striking him once in anger and calling him a stupid fool. This is shocking behavior for a Japanese son. Taro, Ichiro's younger brother, is alienated from all of them and can hardly wait until his eighteenth birthday to join the army, even while knowing that his action might kill his mother. "It is the war and camp life," says his father of Taro's sullen independence. "Made them wild like cats and dogs" (pp. 18–19). But Ichiro knows that Taro wants to make up for his shameful No-No status; later Taro, in an act of fraternal betrayal, leads him out of the Club Oriental to be beaten up by his friends.

What we see then is the dramatic disintegration of the Yamada family as a result of the war. But Ichiro's mother is proud that he had not fought against Japan: "You are my son, Ichiro," she says. "No," he says to himself. "There was a time when I was your son. There was a time that I no longer remember when you used to smile a mother's smile and tell me stories about gallant and fierce warriors who protected their lord with blades of shining steel and about the old woman who found a peach in the stream and took it home and, when her husband cut it in half, a husky little boy tumbled out to fill their hearts with boundless joy. I was that boy in the peach and you were the old woman . . ." (p. 15). Okada is essentially retelling the popular, ageless myth of Momotaro (Peach Boy), a Japanese hero, about whom anyone familiar with Japanese culture knows.

That Ichiro could identify himself with the Peach Boy is not without meaning, for it underlines his feelings of estrangement: he is not truly the son of his parents but someone miraculously born of the American experience and nurtured by an infertile and alien couple. He continues his monologue: "There came a time when I was only half Japanese because one is not born in America and raised in America and taught in America . . . without becoming American and loving it. But I did not love enough, for you were still half my mother and I was thereby still half Japanese and when they came and they told me to fight for America, I was not strong enough to fight you and the bitterness" which had overcome him. He realized too late that he was wholly American and now because of his deed, he has been dispossessed: "I am not your son and I am not Japanese and I am not American" (pp. 15–16).

It is strange, moreover, that the tiny Yamadas could have had a son husky and tall enough to have played high school football and basketball.

Okada, indeed, in creating his hero has used white American standards, for in the opening chapters of the book, he is at pains to note the small stature of the Japanese people Ichiro encounters, something he need not have mentioned at all. Recall, for instance, "the blond giant of Nebraska" whose protest against the evacuation gives added credence to its injustice and justification for Ichiro's No-No status. This equation of size with ideality is found also in Kenji's Americanized father who, unlike Mr. Yamada, is the beloved and respected companion of his children: "a big man, almost six feet tall and strong" (p. 117). The heroine Emi is likewise atypical: she is taller than average, "with heavy breasts and her long legs were strong and shapely like a white woman's" (p. 83). Ichiro, her lover, is worthier than her escapist husband Ralph whose clothing is somewhat small for him (Ichiro). Conversely, Freddie Akimoto, a No-No boy who is Ichiro's foil because of his frantic escape from his own inner conflicts is called "Shorty" early but not later in the novel, as his fate becomes more tragic.

In struggling with his conflicts, Ichiro, like Momotaro, the Peach Boy, is dependent on friends for help. Momotaro, while in his teens, leaves his parents, and with friends encountered on his journey—a monkey, pheasant, and spotted dog—conquers the demons of a distant isle and returns home with their treasure. Ichiro, in his search for completeness, also attempts to conquer his own demons, but while Momotaro's friends had been given gifts of millet dumplings made by his foster mother, Ichiro's friends appear as if by grace to help him. For John Okada was a Christian, and Ichiro expresses his own inner torment and feelings of emptiness in Christian terms, a fact which further emphasizes his Americanization and alienation from his parents. His short, round, and stubby father is described as a "benevolent Buddha" (p. 9), and his mother's funeral is a Buddhist one whose incomprehensibility disgusts Ichiro and perhaps even the author.

But it would be wrong to assume because of his Christianity and his acceptance of white physical standards that Okada is an assimilationist. The bitterness of Kenji's advice of genocide through marriage cannot, as Emi says, be taken seriously. She herself exudes Christian charity with regard to the evacuation. But even more, to Okada, Christianity is an unrealized ideal in this world. Thus, in this imperfect world, a majority culture, dedicated in theory to human rights, can blindly jail an entire group of people for racial reasons. This imperfection is underscored when, while working in the beetfields of Idaho during his relocation years, Ichiro is persuaded by a friend, Tommy, to attend a Christian church, only to be shouted at afterwards by a passing white motorist, "One Jap is one too many. . . . Two Japs today, maybe ten next Sunday. Don't come back" (p. 230).

Subsequently Tommy finds another church which accepts them. They are even regularly invited by a family for dinner. But the congregation one Sunday quietly and insultingly rejects a black. Enraged, Ichiro never returns to that church. "The ways of the Lord are often mysterious," says Tommy. "There are some things which we cannot hope to understand. You will feel better by next Sunday." "Save the holy crap for yourself," Ichiro replies. "Seems to me like you goddamned good Christians have the supply spread out pretty thin right now" (pp. 230–231).

Okada's Christian perspective is apparent at the book's beginning when, upon Ichiro's return to Seattle after his imprisonment, feeling "like an intruder in a world to which he had no claim" (p. 1), he is recognized at the bus stop as a No-No boy by an old acquaintance in a U.S. Army uniform. Despite his heroic size, the guilt-ridden Ichiro absorbs the hatred of Eto: "The hate-churned eyes with the stamp of unrelenting condemnation were his cross and he had driven the nails with his own hands." Eto spits on him; Ichiro does not retaliate: "The legs of his accuser were in front of him. God in a pair of green fatigues, U.S. Army style. They were the legs of the jury that had passed sentence upon him. Beseech me, they seemed to say, throw your arms about me and bury your head between my knees and seek pardon for your great sin" (pp. 3–4). At home, in a moment of self pity, he blames his loss of self entirely on his mother: "It was she who opened my mouth and made my lips move to sound the words which [gave me] . . . an emptiness that is more empty and frightening than the caverns of hell" (p. 12). "Was there no hope for redemption? . . . People forgot and . . . forgave." But his hope was "swallowed up by the darkness of his soul, for time might cloud the memories of others but the trouble was inside of him and time would not soften that" (pp. 51–52). "I have made a mistake and I know it with all the anguish in my soul. . . . [Is it] not just then that, for my suffering and repentance, I be given another chance?" (p. 81)

Unconsciously he takes a bus ride to the University of Washington where, before the war, he had spent two happy years as an engineering student with his slide rule, a white "sword of learning" at his side (p. 53). But he is treated indifferently by a former teacher, and he blames himself for this indifference, for he had forfeited his right to this wonderful life. He leaves the university that for him is paradisal "with its buildings and students and curved lanes and grass which was the garden in a forsaken land" (p. 57).

But then, immediately afterwards, by pure chance or grace, he meets Kenji Kanno, a dying war hero with only one good leg but a whole man within—while Ichiro "was strong and perfect but only an empty shell" (p. 60). Kenji befriends him; and it is Kenji who saves him from a knifing after the betrayal of his brother Taro. Afterwards Kenji drives Ichiro out of the murkiness of the Seattle ghetto into the cleansing air of the country to meet

Emi, a woman whose complete acceptance of him furthers the healing within. For are not Kenji and Emi part of the Japanese America in which he must regain his place?

He later goes to Portland with Kenji to escape the tensions in his family; and in his search for a job meets—again by pure chance or grace—Mr. Carrick who not only offers him a draughtsman's position but also accepts his No-No status sympathetically, apologizing in fact for the evacuation: "A big black mark in the annals of American history" (p. 150). Earlier in the novel Ichiro had told himself: "There is no retribution for one who is guilty of treason, and that is what I am guilty of. The fortunate get shot. I must live my punishment" (p. 82). But now with the accretion of positive experiences, he no longer regards himself as treasonous. He sees in the compassionate Mr. Carrick the acceptance of his country for "even the *seemingly* treasonous" and the "real nature of the country against which he had *almost fully* turned his back" (p. 153). He decides to refuse the job and return to Seattle and his family, knowing that if he were "to find his way back to that point of wholeness and belonging, he must do so in the place where he had begun to lose it" (pp. 154–155).

He returns to find his mother a suicide; reality at last had obtruded into her delusions. Drained of his hatred for her, he could now understand her unhappiness and feel some love for her and some peace within himself. Escaping from the elaborate Buddhist rituals of her funeral where the eulogy described a woman he had never known, he goes dancing with Emi who has come to comfort him. Momentarily he loses his self-consciousness, and he realizes in this climactic moment of happiness that there is a place for him in this world. "I've got to love the world the way I used to. . . . I've been fighting it and hating it and letting my bitterness against myself and Ma and Pa and even Taro throw the whole universe out of perspective" (p. 209). Again, by sheer grace, a slightly drunken white man buys the couple a drink—and at last "feeling immensely full," Ichiro wants that moment to last a lifetime (p. 211).

Kenji died in the hospital in Portland; and his place as mentor is taken in the latter half of the book by Gary who works at the Christian Rehabilitation Center as a sign painter. When Ichiro first greets him, Gary is painting in red on a green van the "last *i* in the word Rehabilitation" (p. 221). Gary, too, was a No-No boy but feels no guilt. He had been an aspiring artist before the war but had accomplished nothing. The years in prison were valuable: "I died in prison," he says. "And when I came back to life, all that really mattered for me was to make a painting. . . . During the day, I paint for my keep. At night I paint myself. The picture I want is inside of me. I'm groping for it and it gives me peace and satisfaction. For me, the cup is overflowing" (pp. 223–224). Ichiro carefully scrutinizes his friend for the fear, bitterness, and loneliness that he himself has felt but sees nothing but the peace and fullness for which he has long been searching.

As he leaves his friend, his further progress in self redemption is revealed by his likening of his miserable life and the miserable world to a "shiny apple with streaks of rotten-brown in it." But it is not rotten to the core. No longer is he guilty of treason. "I have been guilty of a serious error," he tells himself. "I have paid for my crime as prescribed by law. I have been forgiven and it is only right for me to feel this way or else I would not be riding unnoticed and unmolested on a bus along a street in Seattle on a gloomy, rain-soaked day."

The rain is appropriate. "After the rain, the sunshine," he murmurs (p. 232). Wiser and stronger from his friendly encounters, he is able in the end to bestow compassion upon his father and upon the other No-No boy, Freddie, who has never faced the emptiness within himself but abrasively lives "in total, hateful rejection of self and family and society" (p. 242). Unlike Ichiro, Freddie knifed Eto when spat upon and is consequently now being hunted by the revengeful Japanese-American "vets." As Kenji had done for him, Ichiro tries to protect his friend from the brutality of others; but when Freddie is horribly killed while trying to escape, his brawny attacker, the self-appointed representative of those who had fought and died for America, weeps like "an infant crying in the darkness." Ichiro shares the sorrow and terrible loneliness of this distressed man and, giving his shoulder a tender squeeze, leaves, thinking of the goodness he had found in an imperfect world:

> A glimmer of hope—was that it? It was there someplace. He walked along, thinking, searching, thinking and probing, and, in the darkness of the alley of the community that was a tiny bit of America, he chased that faint and elusive insinuation of promise as it continued to take shape in mind and heart. (pp. 250–251)

AMY LING

Writer in the Hyphenated Condition: Diana Chang

Americans in the "hyphenated condition," a term Diana Chang coined in a talk at the 1976 MLA convention—and particularly non-Caucasian Americans who are most readily because most visibly distinguishable—live constantly trying to balance on an edge, now slipping over to one side of the hyphen, now climbing back only to fall down the other side. This divided or schizoid self, so well-illuminated in Marilyn Waniek's article, "The Schizoid Implied Authors of Two American Jewish Novels," cannot but be apparent in the work such a person produces. Thus, even if a writer does not write of her own ethnic background, focusing instead on characters from the dominant culture, she may nonetheless reveal not necessarily her own ethnicity but the fact that she is not totally or unequivocally part of the dominant culture.

Diana Chang, author of six novels, numerous poems and articles, is Chinese-American. Born in New York City, she was taken to Peking at the age of eight months by her American-educated Chinese father, an architect, and Eurasian mother (whose mother was Irish). In China she attended American schools. She returned to New York City for high school and college and has lived there since, with a brief period in France. In her talk, "A Hyphenated Condition," Diana Chang spoke personally and frankly about the "bifocalness" of her identity:

From *MELUS: The Journal of the Society for the Study of the Multi-Ethnic Literature of the United States*, Vol. 7, No 4 (Winter 1980). © 1980 by the University of Southern California.

13

I have to confess tentatively, not sure what I'm really saying, that I don't really feel like a minority here. Am I turned around? In China, I know I'd be considered foreign and lost to the tribe. And they'd be right because I'm not translating myself into English. I express myself in English. I've imagined from within the points of view of white Protestant characters, as well as Chinese personae. Am I an American who sometimes writes about the Chinese in her? My imagination, based here since high school, doesn't belong to me. l belong to my imagination. It has its way with me. It's closer to lilacs blooming in doorways than to moon gates and lotus pods. I have not experienced the new China. Yet, I find myself saying, "we Chinese" quite often, which is very Chinese of me. Nice liberal Americans have no grasp of the chauvinism of the Chinese they embrace.

She has studied Walt Whitman rather than Li Po, and yet her features are decidedly Oriental, and were she living in Broken Bow, Nebraska, rather than New York City, she would have the experience of feeling like a minority. English is literally her mother-tongue (she took up the formal study of Chinese only last fall), and yet, "As long as I'm not blonde, leggy, and of Massachusetts, I choose to be myself, with this elusive, confused identity known as Chinese-American, in this country." For her, there is no other choice but the complex hyphenated condition.

In several of her poems, Chang directly explores this split. The lines, "My Chinese body/out of its American head," come from "An Appearance of Being Chinese." In another poem, "Second Nature," she writes poignantly:

> Sometimes I dream in Chinese
> I dream my father's dreams.
>
> I wake, grown up
> And someone else.
>
> I am the thin edge I sit on.
> I begin to gray—white and black and in between.
> My hair is America.
>
> New England moonlights in me . . .
> I shuttle passportless within myself,
> My eyes slant around both hemispheres,

Gaze through walls
And long still to be
Accustomed,
At home here,

Strange to say.

This "strange" longing to be "at home here" in a familiar land is somewhat
resolved in the affirmative stance of "Saying Yes":

"Are you Chinese?"
"Yes."

"American?"
"Yes."

"Really Chinese?"
"No . . . not quite."
"Really American?"
"Well, actually, you see . . ."
But I would rather say
Not neither—nor,
not maybe,
but both, and not only

The homes I've had,
the ways I am

I'd rather say it
twice,
yes

But the conditional mood of the verb, "I'd rather say . . ." still expresses
longing for a situation contrary to fact. These poems and her first novel
The Frontiers of Love (New York: Random House, 1956), are Chang's most
direct expressions of her ethnic identity.

Poetic and moving, filled with richly sensual descriptions and acute
perceptions into character, *The Frontiers of Love* received favorable notices
when it first appeared. Kenneth Rexroth, in the *Nation*, wrote of this book
as well as several Japanese novels in an article entitled, "World Ills in the
Far East":

Yet, of all the novels of the Far East published this season, her
book, at least for me, has most reality. . . . Not very many first
novels are written with as much skill and insight. One chapter, in
which the heroine's Communist lover tries to pump her for
information which she doesn't possess by simultaneously making
love to her and belaboring her for facts which she doesn't have,
is a masterpiece of quiet, mature irony. Whatever we may think
of the merits of the Japanese novelists I have been reviewing,
Diana Chang is one of ours. She should be around in American
literature for some time to come.

The Frontiers of Love focuses on the search for identity and love of three
young Eurasians in Shanghai at the close of World War II. The question of
identity for a Eurasian is even more complex an issue than for the hyphenated person. The latter's conflict is one of cultures, a new one overlaid onto
the old; however, for a Eurasian, the characteristics of both races are distinctive and distinguishable but inseparable within herself. A Eurasian may take
three possible directions: she may choose one parent's racial identity and
make that her own, rejecting or ignoring the other parent; she may vacillate
between the two; or as a hybrid and therefore a member of neither race, she
may go her own way, creating herself and improvising as she goes. In our first
conversation last fall, Ms. Chang remarked, "One's family, one's background
is one's fate; however, in some areas, I feel I'm my own invention."

In *The Frontiers of Love*, the points of view of each of the three main
characters is presented in turn as Chang skillfully interweaves their experiences and contrasts their different reactions to their Eurasian identities. She
begins with twenty-year-old Sylvia Chen, daughter of a Chinese, a cultivated, scholarly, and, therefore, quiet and restrained gentleman, and an
American woman, restless, impatient, outspoken, unhappily detained in
China by the war. Sylvia's lover is Feng Huang, age 26, living with his
passive, unfocused, somewhat cloying English mother, whom his wealthy
Chinese lawyer-father divorced sixteen years ago; and her best friend is nineteen-year-old Mimi Lambert, who has lost both parents in the war—her
"Australian adventurer" father and her "Chinese socialite" mother, "who had
shocked the Peking Hotel populace twenty years before with her décolleté
gowns and tennis-playing paramours" (p. 11).

As contrasts to the three young Eurasians, Chang also presents the
perspectives of two full-blooded Chinese characters: Liyi Chen, Sylvia's
father, and his nephew, Peiyuan. Liyi's situation is somewhat analogous to
that of the three Eurasians because he too is in great conflict with himself: he
has married a foreigner and brought into the world "two children who were

'foreign' to him" (p. 77). Though an admirer of Western ways when a young man, Liyi now finds himself threatened with a labor struggle at the printing plant where he is manager, and, unsure of his position between the European owner and the Chinese workers, he evades responsibility by taking a trip at a crucial time, all the while longing for the repose and elegance of a Chinese scholar alone with his brushes, ink, and scrolls:

> "Do you know anything about labor unions?" his daughter had once asked him and, involuntarily, he had replied, "No, I'm above those things," and moved his arm in an ancient gesture. It seemed he had wanted to fling back a nonexistent silk sleeve. But his shirt cuff merely rested stiffly on his wrist (p. 159)

Peiyuan, on the other hand, is unequivocally Chinese. Filled with the idealism and eagerness of his sixteen years, he is anxious to make his contribution to China, but he is "an unhandsome Chinese boy . . . a bumpkin" (p. 54). His physical appearance and his presence in her house irritate Helen, Sylvia's American mother, and in describing him, Chang lets fly satiric barbs:

> He had the features that Helen found so antagonizing on some Chinese. Such small eyes (What's the matter with you Chinese, having such small black eyes?), the kind of Chinese nose that looked stuffed and adenoidal, and such large uneven white teeth. The cowlick made him look unkempt, indolent, unmannered as only the Chinese could be, what with their spitting out of tram-cars, picking their ears at movies, belching at meals. His whole appearance was slack, except for the activity of his eyes, bright and eager (but they were small, tight-lidded, like Korean eyes), and the mobility of his mouth (hardly ever closing upon those teeth). (pp. 54–5)

Nonetheless, Peiyuan is received with great warmth by Paul, Sylvia's brother, and by Feng Huang for his refreshing singleness of focus and positive energy.

Despite his brown hair and the freckles inherited from his redheaded English mother, Feng Huang has chosen to be Chinese. He has dropped Farthington, the name his mother gave him, and espouses wholly the cause of the Chinese Communist Party. But, perhaps because "he was a Eurasian who could never reconcile himself to being one" (p. 9), "he liked action: it had a double effect. It freed you from yourself and it committed you to reality" (p. 27). Feng Huang is abrasive in his manners, contemptuous of social conventions, Chinese or American, but afraid of Tang, the local

Communist leader. He initially seeks to befriend Sylvia Chen in order to gather information about the management of the printing plant where the Communists are secretly planning a strike, then he falls in love with her, but later sacrifices this love in sacrificing the life of her cousin, Peiyuan, for the good of the party. He also sacrifices his own humanity in his relentless determination to further the common good.

Mimi Lambert prefers the West to China. She never wears Chinese dresses, is allowed more freedom than is usual for young Chinese women, and, furthermore, she chooses a Caucasian lover. Beautiful, passionate, lavish with herself, her love, she is astounded to find herself rejected by Robert Bruno, son of the Swiss owner of the printing plant, when she refuses to abort their child and insists on marriage. Robert, despite his thirty-six years, cannot go against his father's wishes and marry a Eurasian. First disbelieving, then furious, despairing, finally numb, Mimi ends by despising herself so much as to throw herself at any American who can offer what she thinks of as a lifeline: passage out of China.

Sylvia Chen is finally the most fortunate of the three. At the beginning of the novel, her discomfort with herself is manifested in her annoyance with her clothes:

> She waved and left, walking down the dark stairs in her newest dress, and rebelling inwardly against the sedateness of the tight skirt required of her. That was the trouble with Chinese dresses; they expressed a kind of aristocratic demureness. But foreign clothes didn't suit her entirely either. Their full skirts seemed to stand out from her, making her slighter than she was, orphaned in them. I shall have to design my own kind of clothes, a modified Chinese dress, she thought. (p. 4)

She is aware, as she walks down the street, of the eyes of curious people upon her, aware of her brown hair that looks reddish in the sunlight, of the fact that "she walked with all the freedom and impatience of a foreigner, yet in her there was something inescapably Oriental" (p. 5).

Sympathizing with her father, she feels torn apart as her mother rages against Peiyuan and the Chinese in general; yet, she sees her father's ineffectualness and understands her mother's impatience with him. Young and unformed, "she was guilty of not knowing who she was," and is thus attracted to Feng Huang. "He, at least, had chosen to be Chinese. But she was both as American as her own mother, and as Chinese as her father. She could not deny her ambivalence" (p. 19). In loving Feng Huang, she feels "new-born" (p. 148), but she mistakenly looks to him to lead her life. "Sylvia forgot her doubts; she felt only like a photographic plate which was less than nothing unless exposed to light. And Feng's love was her illumination" (p. 183). With her realization of Feng's involvement in her cousin's death at the end of the novel, and the subsequent break-up of her affair with Feng, she is truly re-born. Her reliance on others to tell her who she is has ended: "Like a twig, she had been broken in two, the strong nerve of her attachment and dependency giving way at last" (p. 236). She realizes that what she loved about Peiyuan and Feng was their energy, and she makes the eye-opening discovery that she has energy of her own housed in her own body:

> By residing fully and carefully in her own [body], she would be able to engage her emotions, her mind and her days with pride. Abruptly, she had no longer felt accidental but responsible. She was Sylvia Chen, and she would speak out for herself—an entity composed of both her parents, but ready to act and not merely react, for one individual—herself. She had seemed to take her first breath of life. (p. 237)

On this positive note *The Frontiers of Love* ends, and in her later novels, Diana Chang did free herself from "any narrow chauvinism." With the exception of her fourth novel, *The Only Game in Town* (1963), a slight, farcical piece of political satire, originally intended as a movie script, which concocts a love story between a Caucasian American Peace Corps volunteer and a beautiful Communist Chinese dancer, her four other novels contain no Chinese or Chinese-Americans at all.

The heroine of a *Woman of Thirty* (New York: Random House, 1959 and Frassinelli in Torino, Italy, 1960), set in the publishing world of sophisticated New York City, is a blue-eyed Smith graduate, Emily Merrick. Her lover, blond David Samson, a prize-winning architect, "looked like the youngest son of a long line of stern tories, tormented with rebellion but endowed with discipline" (p. 160). *A Passion for Life* (New York: Random House, 1961, and London: W. H. Allen, 1962) gives a sensitive and moving treatment to a somewhat sensational dilemma: what to do about a pregnancy resulting from a rape at a time when abortions were illegal and the new doctor in a small Massachusetts town was law-abiding. The only "ethnic" characters are a Jewish couple, newcomers to the town. Her latest book, *A Perfect Love* (New York: Jove Publishers, 1978), tells of a passionate affair between middle-aged, emotionally starved, unhappily married Alice Mayhew and a younger man, David Henderson, separated from his wife and sons. The most unusual book because it is a departure from the emotion-filled dramas of the other works is Chang's fifth novel, *Eye to Eye* (New York: Harper and

Row, 1974). In this book, all the characters but one are WASP: the "exotic" is again a Jew.

When asked why she no longer writes of Chinese or Chinese-American characters, Diana Chang replied that "exoticism" can stand in the way of the "universal" which she strives for in her themes, and therefore she's "often subsumed aspects of her background in the interests of other truths." If she writes of white Protestant Americans in *Eye to Eye*, it is because she believes that her theme—creativity—would have been "side-tracked had she—writing and publishing here—used Chinese, Chicano or Norwegian characters."

Ethnicity, of course, does not or should not preclude "universality." Ralph Ellison's invisible man, for example, is undeniably black and suffers all the indignities of his race, but he is also a young Everyman confronted by forces beyond his control, losing his innocence through hard experience, and moving from blindness and invisibility to sight and light. In "The Art of Fiction: An Interview," (1955), Ellison discusses the relationship between "minority" and "universal" themes:

> All novels are about certain minorities: the individual is a minority. The universal in the novel—and isn't that what we're all clamoring for these days?—is reached only through the depiction of the specific man in a specific circumstance.

Though no rule binds those from ethnic minority backgrounds to writing books only about their own people and culture, nevertheless, Chinese-American writers are such rarities that the Chinese-American community looks to the few who are master-manipulators of English to speak for them, to record their history, their hopes, frustrations, and experiences; to give voice to this otherwise silent minority. The community takes pride in published works signed by Chinese names. Thus, the ambivalence of the outspoken playwright Frank Chin is understandable. In a December 1972 letter to Frank Ching, editor of *Bridge* magazine, Chin wrote:

> Now let me recommend someone to you whose work I respect and find fucked up as a thinker, a Eurasian, a Chinese-American, a mind and person, fucked up. Diana Chang. She just had another poem published in *The New York Quarterly* in which she fails to come to grips with her Chinese-American identity, but does repeat the clichés and racist stereotype with a certain style and an occasional nice line. . . . She takes a stand with white supremacy as unconsciously and unwittingly and as sincerely as

any of your writers and brings it off in a tour de force of writing flash and style. She manages to have her own voice and take that white racist rhetoric about universals of art and being an individual instead of white or yellow, and mixing the best of East and West . . . the whole stinking mess . . . and show us accurately, how she's made it work, how she believes it. . . . All that she's trained herself to ignore, the enormity of her deafness, her forced ignorance shows through absences in her work . . . brilliantly. And what she writes consciously is pretty good too.

What Frank Chin ignores, however, is the fact that there is an entire spectrum of Chinese-Americans, ranging the gamut from mostly Chinese with a dash of American, to mostly American with a veneer of Chinese, or as Diana Chang put it, with "an appearance of being Chinese."

Diana Chang belongs to the latter group. Her life is set in the artistic-intellectual circles of New York City and Bridgehampton, Long Island. Out of these worlds comes *Eye to Eye*. As a painter and writer, she is concerned with perception and creativity, with the connection between initial familial relationships and later sexual adjustment, and with the relationship between neurosis and art.

When I asked her about the genesis of *Eye to Eye*, Ms. Chang told me it began when she and a friend were lunching in the cafeteria of the Whitney Museum. The friend had been giving her an account of her unhappy relationship with a sensitive, cultivated man who was unable to relate to her. When they finished lunch, they walked around a stone partition and came upon a three-dimensional scene, a work of art. "I was all eyes, and felt as though I'd been struck by lightning." It was an assemblage of a part of a room by Edward Kienholz, with a hooked rug on the floor, a lamp with a tassled shade, a small table with a framed valentine on it. The furnishings seemed to be of another period, about forty years back, and the entire scene had a nostalgic feeling, a sense of waiting about it. She made a connection between the emotional source of the artist who produced this work and her friend's frustrating situation. "All I can remember is that I knew—in a visceral way—that I was onto my next novel. I was filled with an almost unbearable excitement." To protect her friend, she made her protagonist a man. The initial writing came out in a rush; she worked as though obsessed for thirty-five to forty days. "I felt electrified, as though I were a medium. I was in touch with myself in a way that doesn't occur every day—it is an unforgettable sensation." The rewriting, a slower, more painstaking process, took approximately two months.

Eye to Eye is about perception and artistic creativity, about shaping unconscious drives into actual representations and symbols, about the twists and turns of an artist's route to self-awareness. Its treatment of its subject is richly and pervasively ironic. The plot hinges on a surprising twist hinted at but not revealed to all of the participants themselves until nearly the end of the book. The narrator, George Safford, is a visual artist (like Edward Kienholz), a creator of "scenes," but he is blind to himself and to the source of his emotional problems and his artistic creations. The man who leads Safford to self-awareness is Dr. Emerson, a psychiatrist, who listens but himself doesn't fully understand. Bob Meacham, poet and professor of English, begins by helping his friend George but ends by helping himself to the woman George thinks he is in love with.

Two facts immediately stand out. First, the author is a woman while all the main characters are men (the women in the book play influential but secondary roles); and second, the author is Chinese-American, while all the characters (with the exception of a Jewish woman) are WASP. That Chang meets the challenge of different perspectives as successfully as she does attests to her skill as a writer. Nevertheless, something of Diana Chang herself does emerge as well. As Waniek has pointed out, through studying an author's manipulation of point of view, her selection of detail, choice of characters, and development of characterization, through taking apart all the pieces of a novel and reconstructing them, we discover the "consciousness inherent in the work," the consciousness of "the unlimited author."

The choice of George Safford as protagonist is a good one, for as an artist alienated from himself and to a certain extent from society at large, he may speak as well for a writer in the hyphenated condition. Both are detached in their perspectives and both may be ironic in their stance. Though ethnicity is not an obvious concern of *Eye to Eye*, nonetheless, we find numerous references to Puritan traditions and white Protestant traits. In Chang's exposition of the dominant ethnic group, we find a familiarity, an acceptance, and perhaps even a certain pride; but at the same time we sense a subtly detached or alien perspective as well. What kind of portrait of the white Protestant character does this Chinese-American paint? Most prominent are seven cardinal virtues of the white Protestant tradition.

First, there's hard work. George Safford's "girl Friday, a fiftyish workhorse who is a stenographer-bookkeeperreceptionist" named Miss Price, disapproves of Bob Meacham's leisurely professorial summers (p. 3). "I know Miss Price found him too much, hanging around the way he did," Safford says, "a grown man with time on his hands is almost disqualified from manliness, or so we feel in our culture. Miss Price is an upholder of Puritan tradition. She's an updated spinster. It's a comment on me that I have had her working for me since Party Packages was formed" (p. 70).

George believes in hard work and feels comfortable with prim, loyal Pilgrim spinsters, but, ironically, his work is making trimmings for play.

Secondly, there is charity. Of himself and his wife, George comments, "Like lots of people, we're liberal, versatile, and walking hodgepodges of virtue, applied and applied again" (p. 7). The third virtue is fortitude or self-discipline. Contemplating his initial visit to Dr. Emerson, George brags that he has always faced his fears. "I require it of myself, I am Calvinist in that way" (p. 7). Chastity is a fourth virtue. After he begins his sessions, George hastens to assure the doctor that he is not a "skirtchaser" by nature. "But—perhaps I am a hopeless puritan, deep and dyed. I had to make certain, absolutely certain, he did not think I was having a simple case of lust" (p. 31).

Fifth, there's fairness or justice—"Edith considers unfairness a cardinal sin. My girl's a good scout, and I know our daughter will grow up to be just like her lovely mother" (p. 27); and sixth, punctuality, as illustrated when George was ten minutes early for his first appointment with Dr. Emerson. Seventh, there's frugality; George says of his time in Dr. Emerson's office:

> Being at the analyst's is like being in a cab with the meter going. Every ticking moment is expensive, really expensive. I am a Calvinist, and while I'll buy Edith a deepfreeze or a second car, I don't like to see money wasting to no purpose. (p. 122)

Another passage characterizes a certain kind of middle American lifestyle. To his first appointment with the psychiatrist, George wears sneakers without socks, explaining himself in this way:

> It gave me a resort sensation. White Protestant sports and easy camaraderie, look-ma-no-hands cycling, no strain, no sweat, some give and take, clam bakes, lawn mowing, the paper route, inadequate allowances, showing off, early betrayals, the wounded heart of a ten-year-old—all this I saw in my naked ankle. (p. 28)

This lengthy catalogue, inspired by the single detail of sneakers without socks, also demonstrates George's poetic ability as well as an anxious attempt to appear relaxed by using his clothes as camouflage.

As a man who was blind to himself but now can see clearly, Safford is ebullient and at the same time ironic and somewhat self-mocking in relating his earlier experience. His ironic, satiric tone extends to the implied author's presentation of WASPs as well. Though Chang denies any conscious satiric intent, if we examine the text closely, I believe we find evidence for my claim.

Early in the novel, Edith (George's wife), concerned with her husband's shakes, loss of appetite, sleeplessness (all symptoms of a lovesickness for another woman, which of course he cannot reveal) recommends that he see a psychiatrist, Dr. Yale H. Emerson. George speculates on the doctor's middle initial and comes up with "Dr. Yale Harvard Emerson." Edith asks:

> "How do you know H stands for Harvard?"
> "It just has to," I said.
> "I like Yale Harvard Emerson," she said.
> "Yes, but he may not like me."
> "I mean I like his name . . ."

The couple continue this conversation:

> "Yale is a peculiar first name. Can you imagine calling a son of ours Penn State?"
> "That's not analogous at all," she said. "It's more like calling a girl Smith than City College."
> "Smith Safford sounds rich and beautiful," I said.
> "Let's call our next girl Smith for the old alma mater." (p. 7)

In this brief, witty dialogue, we have our attention drawn to two Ivy League colleges and one of the Seven Sisters schools, to the philosophical, transcendental father of the United States, as well as to high class and status. New England as the cradle of American civilization and tradition is also acknowledged. Later, George makes another Emersonian allusion in speaking to his psychiatrist about his lonely childhood, "I'm an all-round self-reliant American boy" (p. 42).

George's description of his wife, just before this Ivy League conversation, is worthy of note because the word "ordinary" appears so often.

> She laughs easily, readily, delightfully, her rather ordinary face breaking up into new arrangements, as when the colored bits in a kaleidoscope slide a mere eighth of an inch and the parts "smile" into another pattern. By ordinary, I mean white Protestant, like myself. Edith Shaw Safford is five-five, smooth limbed, average full-breasted, blue-eyed dark blond, tans handsomely. She could be from California, and if she were, she'd at once evoke beaches, orange juice and an openness, but not a commitment, to Zen or any other philosophy that was making the rounds. If she were from Kansas, she'd suggest fields of wheat, white shingle houses and music sororities. Actually, she is a born

and bred New Yorker, and I love her because she is quite beautiful in this ordinariness I share with her. She could be the girl
who runs toward you in the commericals with her clean hair
flying out slowly behind her, confident because she's used the
right deodorant. Edith also has an upper-class aura, though she's
middle class. (p. 6)

The ambivalence between "ordinariness" and beauty may mean that either
George is being modest or that the author is being ironic, for the explanation that follows the first instance of the word describes someone not ordinary, but, in fact, rather like the woman who received a 10 in the recent
movie of that name, the woman possessing ideal Caucasian physical traits. A
decided tongue-in-cheek quality comes through in these details about Edith:
confidence coming from the right deodorant, the upper class look, openness
but no commitment to any philosophy that's current.

Of his daughter, a smaller version of her mother, George Safford tells us:

She's a perfect little girl. I call her Puttykins: Edith refers to her
as the daughter; her name is Amanda. She is three and a half now,
long-legged, and looks like both of us, that is, totally correct,
white Protestant and turning into a miniature movie actress. Not
the sex-pot type but the serious kind, Like Eva Marie Saint or a
less flinchingly sensitive Geraldine Page. (p. 7)

It seems strange that a father would think of his three-year-old daughter as
"totally correct." The notion of correctness would more likely occur to one
who has had a life-long consciousness of not fitting that description. Edith
and Amanda, thus, are not representative WASPs, but instead, approach the
ideal Caucasian beauty: the model, the movie star. That they are compared
to movie stars and models seen in television commercials suggests that their
inspiration came not from the author's own intimate experience but from
public images.

Though a paragon of health, wholesomeness, beauty, and devotion,
Edith, because she is so familiar, so conventional, is merely "ordinary" to
George. Instead, he is attracted to Nan, the Jewish writer whose office is
above his Party Packages business and who, for the most part, ignores him
and puts him down. Undaunted, he describes her to his psychiatrist:

She is so voluptuous and yet delicate. Her joints are fragile, and
they make me weak. . . . Her arms are very rounded; her knees
are straight and yet full, like a statue's; her behind is delicious.

Altogether, she's unbelievable. . . .

These details of Nan's anatomy seem convincing as the observations of a man about a woman who is still a stranger to him but to whom he is greatly drawn. He expands on her attractions:

> This girl's a foreign princess, I thought. . . . Her face is hard for me to describe. It's heady, like too much scent. That short hair makes her neck look almost too long for her proportions. Her nose is fine and a bit too long, her eyes are dark, her skin tone pale, her mouth clearly carved and yet soft. She is a beautiful Jewish girl, but that doesn't describe her at all. She makes Edith seem so two-dimensional, so recently made. Nan, on the other hand, looks as if a lot of history went into her, ages and ages of Mediterranean history, and she wears it like perfume. (p. 36)

The transformation of exoticism and history into perfume is particularly striking. To stress the ages and ages of history that have gone into making a Jewish woman could intimate an "exotic," like the author herself, justifying the superior attractiveness of all "exotics." The Chinese, obviously, are another people with a particularly long history.

But it is also psychologically right that George is drawn to the "foreign" because it is the unattainableness of love that has him so desperately hooked. For him, because of the circumstances of his childhood, love is equated with despair. The deficiency shaping George's psyche is his unsatisfied childhood longing for the attention of his mother who, a busy actress, was often absent and almost totally inaccessible. This longing is the inspiration for his masterful "sculpture" or "scene" of an empty house with lights going on and off from the nursery upstairs, down the stairs, through the dining room and living room and out the front door—an effective symbol of leave-taking and absence. George's "scenes" are metaphors from his psyche, "permanent dreams for waking eyes to see" (p. 58). Though George himself does not initially have "waking eyes," his work reveals the reason for his prolonged anxiety attack. Thus, understanding one's own motivations is not necessary to the production of art, for George says:

> Feeling has a compulsive drive to become form, even if you don't understand the source of the feeling. I can't get over how we all create our lives, for better or worse, out of our feelings. In that sense, everyone is an artist. (p. 2)

Diana Chang has created *Eye to Eye* out of her feelings, not only her conscious feelings about being an artist, but also perhaps unconscious feelings about the dominant culture of the United States. These glimpses of an unconscious alienation, indicated in the lightly satiric tone of certain passages in the novel, are minor details, of interest mainly to those searching for and thus sensitive to an ethnic perspective in works by writers from ethnic minority backgrounds, even if those works do not concern themselves with minority ethnicity.

According to Blanche H. Gelfant in *Hudson Review*, *Eye to Eye* "call(s) us to celebration." And indeed it does. Chang's portrayal is extremely witty; her plot well-knit and delightfully surprising; her language scintillating, clever, urbane, poetic. In taking George to task, Gelfant distills some themes of the book:

> For a smart and successful "visual artist," George Safford seems naively blind. Not until his analysis has he seen that the artist and the child are inseparable: the child births the artist; the artist releases to expression the child's fantasies and frightening emotions. Nor has he seen that art creates not only an object but also an identity; art creates the artist as he creates the work.

Identity or "self-ness" and love are the two main preoccupations in Diana Chang's work. The word "love" occurs in two of the titles, her first and her latest, and love is a central topic in all of her books. "By self-ness," she explains, "I mean consciousness, awareness, inferiority, being. The 'I,' the 'me,' the 'myself,' and all the 'you's' and 'thou's' around. You'll find this in *Eye to Eye* and *A Perfect Love* and everything else, too, of mine." Expression of self is indeed the artist's function. Whether this expression is direct as in autobiographies or metamorphosed by imagination into novels, the presence of the puppet master, the implied author, may be felt in the text. In final support of my sense of her subtle, slightly detached point of view, I quote from an article "Why Do Writers Write?" published by Chang in *The American Pen* some years back; in this passage she reveals her creative impulse and its relationship to her identity:

> My ego exploits my self, my experience, in order that my ego may be. With this novel, this play, this poem, this biography, these essays, I purchase my citizenship in this land of life from which I feel estranged. Others claim their rightful place simply by virtue of being born. But I must earn it like an illegitimate child, a stateless person, and so, by some exacting game of

industry and imagination, I create something in order to become all that I was meant to be."

For Diana Chang, as for her protagonist, George Safford, "I produce, therefore I am" (p. 105). In creating a work of art, as Blanche Gelfant has noted, the artist is creating herself. Though the need to create the self may be strongest in those who feel "estranged," "illegitimate," and "stateless," and though these adjectives may be applied to every artist, regardless of ethnic background, alienation may be said to be doubly strong for writers in the hyphenated condition.

DOROTHY RITSUKO MCDONALD
AND KATHARINE NEWMAN

Relocation and Dislocation: The Writings of Hisaye Yamamoto and Wakako Yamauchi

I. Survivors

Two young women, their lives frozen by Executive Order 9066 (Japanese Relocation Act of 1942), became close friends during the long boring months of their confinement in the camp at Poston, Arizona. Fortunately there was a "library" of a few old books and some magazines which, somehow, had traveled to the camp by various routes. Hisaye Yamamoto who "had early contracted the disease of compulsive reading" introduced her younger friend, Wakako [Nakamura] Yamauchi, to Thomas Wolte, James T. Farrell, Marcel Proust, and the *New Yorker.* When they sat on the barrack steps, day after day, they discussed writing, although at that time, Wakako thought of herself as a painter and thought of Hisaye as someone beyond her powers of emulation. Then there was the *Poston Chronicle* and Hisaye wrote for that, and for a Buddhist magazine and for a mimeographed camp magazine, and sent out material to the *New Canadian.*

But beyond literature, deeper than any boredom, was the unremitting tragedy of this confinement. They watched and saw what internment was doing to families whose sons had to decide between fighting for America or being moved to Tule Lake Camp preparatory to shipment to Japan. People who had never been allowed to become American citizens, who had just lost the homes and savings of years, now had to face estrangement from their

From *MELUS: The Journal of the Society for the Study of the Multi-Ethnic Literature of the United States,* Vol. 7, No 3 (Fall 1980). © 1980 by the University of Southern California.

own children. The younger generation, American-born, had to face the betrayal of democracy that had allowed American citizens to be incarcerated without cause. Although not as devastating as the Holocaust or Hiroshima, the "Camp Experience" left a deep wound in the lives of Japanese-Americans. It was a psychological trauma for all of the 110,000 people who were incarcerated, but there were added tragedies for Hisaye and for Wakako: Hisaye's nineteen-year-old brother, having joined the American Army, was killed at Livorno, Italy; Wakako's father died in the very last days of confinement, a victim of the stress of the years at Poston and the shock of the atom bomb and the defeat of Japan. Years later, when her husband and children asked her about her stay in Poston, Hisaye Yamamoto found tears flowing down as the memories came back. And when Wakako was asked to read some poetry written during the Relocation, she prefaced her reading with some explanations:

> The Sansei accused us of not wanting to talk about the evacuation experience. And it's true. I speak for hundreds of Nisei like myself, or perhaps just *people* like myself, who are sometimes overwhelmed by a current of events we can neither understand nor stem. . . .
>
> And when we do see those old photographs of the mass evacuation . . . we can see the mirror of our tragedy. Few of us can hold back the tears that most often smack of self-pity, but maybe somewhere behind those tears we know that this is the event that changed the course of our lives, and though there were those among us who had more insight, more courage, whatever path we chose, we have survived—whole. Maybe that's why so many of us remain silent about our camp experience. Maybe in our silence we ask you to honor us for that—survival. We ask that you not indulge us with pity, neither then nor now. The fact of our survival is proof of our valor. And that is enough.

The friendship between the two women has remained sturdy over the years. Now they are both well established writers, with certain similarities in their work. Both show the deterioration of the family, the changing role of women, the bleakness of farm life, the transformation of Japanese traditions into Japanese-American culture. They make us aware of Japanese-American history, of the thousands of Japanese men who arrived in America to make their fortunes in its "gold-paved streets" and then (they dreamed) to return in triumph to their homeland, there to live in their traditional family structure. But making that fortune was not easy. Some men with families—the families that Yamamoto and Yamauchi usually write about—farmed in the desert valleys of the American West, barely wresting a living during the depression years. The bachelors were migrant farm workers, harvesting fields and orchards, and, in their boredom, gambling and drinking away their wages. Their difficulties in surviving in an entirely alien civilization weakened them, and there are only a few strong male figures in the authors' works.

This is not to say that their women are pure and heroic. But there is the pathos in the stories of arranged marriages that are unsatisfactory, forcing the romantic women into adultery and into longing to return to a beautiful illusory Japan. There is also the pathos of the women born in America and the conflicts they feel as they try to blend the traditions of their parents with those of their own country. There is the pathos of the resultant stress on the traditional family structure, weakened even more by the Relocation. These writers have reproduced a sorrowful society—and their key word is survival.

Their differences are at once apparent in their responses to a formal question: how have Japanese traditions affected their writings? Wakako Yamauchi wrote, stressing her personal involvement with her characters and their stories:

> If I tried to tell you in a scholarly way how my Japanese back-
> ground has affected my writing, it would be a long time before
> you heard from me. I can only say that in my writing I reach
> inside and plunder—I use every experience, everything I know as
> a person, as a woman, as a divorcee, as a mother, and yes, as a
> child of Japanese parents. My childhood and being Japanese
> American is an integral part of the person I am today. I write
> from these experiences and I consider myself an American writer.

Hisaye Yamamoto, on the other hand, moves outward, with a blend of irony, forbearance, and connectedness:

> I'm sure the Japanese tradition has had a great influence on my
> writing since my parents brought it with them from Japan and
> how could they not help but transmit it to us? I even wonder if
> I would have been a writer at all without this tradition to go by,
> since most of the stories seem to deal with this interaction of
> the Japanese tradition with the American experience. And even
> while I have come to look upon the American experience with
> a jaundiced (yellow) eye, I appreciate being able to communi-
> cate in the English language and just plain being alive at this
> time and in this place.

Yamauchi writes totally within the Japanese-American community; Yamamoto sees a world in interaction (though seldom with Anglos in it). They pace off at different distances from their subjects and see them from different perspectic. In short, two women, two friends, two people with similar experiences, are still very different as writers.

II. Hisaye Yamamoto [*DeSoto*]

Yamamoto received her first rejection slip at the age of fourteen and persisted in her aspiration to be a writer until she received her first acceptance from a major periodical when she was twenty-six. In the years between, she completed the program at Compton Junior College, contributed to school, college, and small magazines, and wrote even while she was at Poston. After her release from camp she went to Los Angeles and obtained a reporter's job on the only newspaper that would hire a Japanese: the Negro *Los Angeles Tribune*. She worked there from 1945 to 1948. Her first story, "High-heeled Shoes" appeared in 1948. The following year she was accorded a John Hay Whitney Opportunity Fellowship which enabled her to write without a worry for a year. During this time, in addition to more short stories, she translated the whole of Rene Boylesve's "L'Enfant à la Balustrade" from French into English.

While she was working at the *Tribune*, she had begun to collect copies of the *Catholic Worker*, and so, intrigued that there was a place where "nonviolence, voluntary poverty, love for the land, and attempt to put into practice the precepts of the Sermon on the Mount" were the rules, she finally went East and spent the years 1953–1955 on the Catholic Worker farm on Staten Island. For years after she returned to California, she continued to write for the paper, the *Catholic Worker*, among her most important pieces being on Seabrook Farms, Iva Toguri ("God Sees the Truth but Waits"), and the United Farm Workers.

After the Catholic Worker experience she settled into a career as wife and housewife, then as mother of five kids, and now, also, the grandmother of two, all of whom live in or near the DeSoto home. In short, as she phrases it, she keeps busy "tending her own garden," which means family, flowers, friends, and writing.

During all these years, there has never been a published collection of her work, but her reputation has been kept steadily alive by anthologists. Four of her short stories made Martha Foley's list of "distinctive" short stories for their particular years, with "Yoneko's Earthquake" reprinted as one of the *Best American Short Stories of 1952*. She has been represented in at least twenty anthologies, with favorites being "Seventeen Syllables" and "The Legend of Miss Sasagawara." Runners-up are "Las Vegas Charley," "The Brown House," and "Yoneko's Earthquake." It is noteworthy that between 1949 and 1952, when there was still some hostility and a great deal of apathy about the Japanese, Hisaye Yamamoto published five short stories that won national acclaim.

"High-heeled Shoes" is more essay than story, unlike those that followed, but it has the Yamamoto hallmarks:

1. References to literary materials outside the Japanese-American tradition. This shows her wide reading. In this story, Freud, Ellis, Stekel, Krafft-Ebbing, and Robert Browning are mentioned. In "Epithalamium," she quotes extensively from Gerard Manley Hopkins as well as echoing the Miltonic poem. This strategy lifts her stories into the wider world of European-American culture and adds surprise and new angles of perspective.

2. References to actual events, place, or people. In this story she names Wakako Yamauchi as the friend who has given her the plants from which the narrator is picking pansies in the story.

3. Lists, particularly of foods, flowers, and oddments that give sensory appeal as well as substantiating the reality of the story. In "High-heeled Shoes," she is irritated when the phone rings because she fantasizes that it is a salesman and she does not have money to buy from him. She lists what she would have bought by week's end if she only had money.

4. Soliloquies and imaginary dialogues. Here she has a talk with Gandhi about non-violent responses versus the suffering of women attacked by rapists. Gandhi does not come off well.

The keynote in all of Yamamoto's work is her use of her own mind: she is analytic, meditative, honest, compassionate, and ironic. Whether she uses the first person or a narrator, the final word is usually hers—and it is frequently so open-ended that the reader feels there are stories and meanings as yet unguessed implicit in each tale.

Yamamoto's pervasive love for humanity is found in "The High-heeled Shoes." The protagonist ("I") is confronted with sexual perversions: she receives an obscene telephone call at the story's beginning and this propels her mind into "unlovely, furtive things" about other encounters with men that she and her friends have had. The most startling was the time she caught sight of a pair of legs in black high-heeled shoes sticking out from the open door of a "dustyblue, middle-aged sedan." As she approached and glanced in, she discovered that the shoes were worn by a naked man reclining on the front seat . . . and she was, "with frantic gestures, being enjoined to linger awhile."

The narrator calls on her reading for some understanding of this frightening experience but concludes: "Reading is reading, talking is talking, thinking is thinking, and living is different." However, she regards both incidents as caused by society and does not blame the men, believing that they were part of "a great dark sickness on the earth that no amount of pansies, pinks, or amaryllis, thriving joyously in what garden, however well-ordered and pointed to with pride, could even begin to assuage."

There is a final paragraph: her aunt calls, thus purifying the telephone from the contamination of the obscene caller, and she offers to come over for dinner, bringing food with her. This is the only "Japanese" touch in a story all too universal: "ricecakes with Indian bean frosting, as well as pickled fish on vinegared rice. She has also been able to get some yellowtail, to slice and eat raw." Yamamoto, as narrator, comments, "It is possible she wonders at my enthusiastic appreciation, which is all right, but all out of proportion."

What remains with the narrator is: "Whatever, whatever—I knew I had discovered yet another circle to put away with my collection of circles." A similar personal revelation of the sickness of humankind was revealed in "The Wilshire Bus," a 1950 story, which deals with a Japanese-American woman's fear of being identified as Chinese by a drunken bigot. Shocked at finding this weakness in herself, she lost "her saving detachment . . . and she was filled once again in her life with the infuriatingly helpless insidiously sickening sensation of there being in the world nothing solid she could put her finger on, nothing solid she could come to grips with, nothing solid she could sink her teeth into, nothing solid."

She has written two stories about gamblers: "The Brown House" (1951) and "Las Vegas Charley" (1961). The former has a jocose tone: Mr. Hattori, weary of trying to make a living growing strawberries, seeks out a Chinese house where he can try his luck at gambling. The appearance of the house is whimsical: "recently painted brown and relieved with white window frames. . . . To the rear of the house was a ramshackle barn whose spacious blue roof advertised in great yellow letters a ubiquitous brand of physic."

During the travail, as the Hattoris come to argue and their marriage nearly expires, there are humorous incidents, such as a police raid and the semi-friendship between Mrs. Wu, wife of the manager of the brown house and Mrs. Hattori, who must wait, hour upon hour, in the car with the three little children. The children come to acquire a taste for the Chinese cookies that Mrs. Wu brings to the car and Mrs. Hattori becomes quite attached to the Chinese woman. But Mrs. Wu, looking at them, concludes "she had never before encountered a woman with such bleak eyes." As the story ends, the reader goes back over it and sees that it never was humorous, that human interaction is "a collection of circles."

Las Vegas Charley began life as Kazuyuki Matsumoto, a prosperous young immigrant farmer until the death of his beloved wife in childbirth broke his spirit. Ultimately he has become a dishwasher in a restaurant in Las Vegas, spending his free time gambling. As he grows old, he becomes closer to his son and daughter-in-law in Los Angeles. Finally Charley dies, and the doctor who has attended him, complaining of his own frustrations at seeing his patients die, comments:

> "Well, at least your father had a good time—he drank, he gambled, he smoked; I don't do any of these things. All I do is work, work, work. At least he enjoyed himself while he was alive."
>
> And Noriyuki—who, without one sour word, had lived through a series of conflicting emotions about his father . . . finally, [reaching] something akin to compassion, when he came to understand that his father was not an evil man, but only an inadequate one with the most shining intentions, only one man among so many who lived from day to day as best they could, limited, restricted by the meager gifts Fate or God had doled out to them—could not quite agree.

Yamamoto's honesty also shows through in this story, because she sums up Kazuyuki Matsumoto's reaction, after one son is killed and the other leaves for Tule Lake:

> As for himself, he would be quite content to remain in the camp the rest of his life—free food, free housing, friends, flower cards; what more could life offer. It was true that he had partially lost his hearing in one ear, from standing by those hot stoves on days of unbearable heat, but that was a small complaint. The camp hospital had provided free treatment, free medicines, free cottonballs to stuff in his bad ear.

Obviously the future "Las Vegas Charley" was not of heroic mould, even so his adjustment to camp is, by contrarities, an indictment of it. A story like this in 1961, too, would have sufficient distance in time to arouse little disapproval. This was not the case in 1950 when Yamamoto's story, "The Legend of Miss Sasagawara" was accepted by the *Kenyon Review*. This is probably her finest piece of writing and it is still one of the most evocative of all stories of the camp experience (as Wakako Yamauchi says, people did not want to talk about that experience). It is possible that the success of the story results from the way she controlled her own emotions as she wrote, for this time she used a filtered intelligence of a girl obviously herself to give the story through random glimpses of Miss Sasagawara. The rest of the other witnesses are unreliable: an ambulance driver, a teenaged boy, a hysterical woman, and people who love gossip for its own sake, not realizing the human anguish behind bizarre actions.

Miss Sasagawara, aged thirty-nine, has had no regrets that she has never married because she has traveled "all over the country a couple times, dancing in the ballet. . . . she's had her fun." But now, her mother having died, she is confined in a portion of a barracks with her father, a Buddhist priest. Yamamoto explains how adversely the pursuit of the Buddhist-Nirvana—"that saintly state of moral purity and universal wisdom"—can affect those close to the would-be saint. The daughter is the victim of a man who wished to "extinguish within himself all unworthy desire and consequently all evil, to concentrate on that serene, eight-fold path."

The relocation camp experience ironically freed the Reverend Sasagawara from worldly responsibilities, including those to his daughter. She, however, is filled with admiration of his superior being. But a full explanation comes to the narrator in later years when, in a college library, she finds an old poetry magazine which includes "the first published poem of a Japanese-American woman who is, at present, an evacuee from the West Coast making her home in a War Relocation Center in Arizona."

In other words, this is a poem which Miss Sasagawara wrote in the middle of the war, at the time of this story, before she was permanently committed to a mental institution. In an "erratically brilliant" poem, she questions: would not such a saint be "deaf and blind to the human passions" of another who does not wish to attain this sublime condition and wishes instead to respond to the "passions rising in anguished silence in the selfsame room?" The poet (who is Miss Sasagawara) regards the saint's intense idealism as madness, not seeing that she herself will only find freedom from this Buddhist idealism through her own madness.

The story operates on two levels. The news of the unhappy dancer comes to the reader in sporadic items, but the picture of life in the camp is sustained and highly informative. The young narrator sits on the front stoop with her best friend, using such phrases as "Oooh," and "Wow!" while watching the other people and slapping mosquitoes. We learn that two Army cots pushed together make a double bed for a husband and wife, that an apple crate makes a night table, that people eat in the mess hall by age classification. We have the complete program of the block Christmas entertainment. We can almost taste the boredom. But when the story ends, it is with Miss Sasagawara's own poem, her voice really heard at last, and the details fall into the background of this tragic story of a woman beset jointly by the frustrations of her own culture and by the imprisonment imposed on her by her fellow-Americans.

In a pair of stories, "Seventeen Syllables" and "Yoneko's Earthquake," Yamamoto depicts life on the little tenant farms before the War. So specific is she that the reader even learns about the two days' work and one night's discomfort that girls in Japan were glad to endure in order to have their fingernails "shining with a translucent redorange color." Both of these stories are examinations of unhappy marriages; in one the wife seeks release through the writing of haiku, in the other, through intimacy with the Filipino farmhand after her husband is invalided in an earthquake. In the first, the wife begs the teenaged, blossoming daughter to promise never to marry. Yamamoto's realism hits its own low in the second story when the child, Yoneko, is annoyed by the invalid's threatening to pick his nose and wipe the snot on her and her friends' paper dolls.

Yamamoto selects as her main characters those who are hurt, who have deviated from the norm, who are grasping for some bits of beauty in their desperation: gamblers dreaming of the gifts they will heap on their loved ones when they make the big payoff, a ballet dancer being driven insane by confinement with a religious fanatic, a farmer's wife who writes haiku in the evenings, women who take lovers in order to find the love of which they have been cheated—all those who seek but lose are of interest to Yamamoto, and somehow she wins our understanding, largely through the accepting interpretations of the narrator.

In one late story, however, she goes even further; she makes the female narrator herself neurotic. In "Epithalamium," the woman, Yuki Tsumagari, shows no apparent guilt in her tumultuous love afair with an Italian-American alcoholic seaman at a Catholic community for social rejects on Staten Island. Yuki herself is not a reject; up until now she has been supporting herself and now, at thirty-one, remains unmarried by choice. Though her mother, back in her earlier years, had urged marriage on her, her father had said, untraditionally, to leave her alone. Now an inexplicable love has come. As lovers, the Italian Marco and Japanese Yuki use all the secluded spots near the community, which neighbors a seminary. She even suffers a secret miscarriage; but though the narrator uses such words as "defile," "terrible," and "sordid" to describe their lovemaking, a love for all humanity hovers over the entire story, making it right for Yuki to marry the seaman while he is drunk. In "Epithalamium," Yamamoto is not only forgiving sin; she has her persona, Yuki, embracing it. And in so doing, Yuki is acknowledging the inevitability of suffering and accepting the fact that this marriage will be as much a burden as a glory. On the way back to the Community after they are married, "with Marco slumped heavily against her, Yuki kept remembering Hopkins: "The world is charged with the grandeur of God. . . ." She hopes that this is a sign from God that she has chosen the right way. But her thoughts then ramble on to the missal of the day which had told the story of St. Sabina, a Roman widow who, having become a Christian, was beheaded under the Emperor Hadrian, and secretly buried. . . . "However," the missal had added, "it was not certain whether such a woman had existed at all." Yamamoto thus enigmatically turns the story of a strong love and a sad wedding into, a legend for the bride to ponder—what is God's reality after all?

Yamamoto's most recent publication, "what might be the second chapter of an autobiography," is "Life among the Oilfields." Here are the familiar Yamamoto hallmarks: the contacts with non-Japanese children, the delights of the American candy store, the smells of her mother's kitchen, all the details that bring into near-camera realism the seasons of farming, the frequent moves, the constrictions of poverty—the life of the Nisei a generation ago. There is the self-deprecation (the teacher wonders what to do with "this deluded Oriental shrimp with second-grade pretensions").

But the realism of the story is set off by the epigraph from Fitzgerald and the conclusion. A speeding sports car, coming up the asphalt road in the oilfields, strikes her little brother, tosses him to the side of the road, and keeps on going. The child has not been killed, only badly bruised, to the relief of the sister, the child Hisaye. But the mature woman, keeping her detachment, muses:

> When I look back on that episode, the helpless anger of my father and my mother is my inheritance. But my anger is more intricate than theirs, warped by all that has transpired in between. For instance, I sometimes see the arrogant couple from down the road as young and beautiful, their speeding open roadster as definitely and stunningly red. They roar by; their tinkling laughter, like a long silken scarf, is borne back by the wind. I gaze after them from the side of the road, where I have darted to dodge the swirling dust and spitting gravel. And I know that their names are Scott and Zelda.

Another recent piece reinforces the continuing strand, from oilfields to the present, the determination to appreciate "just plain being alive at this time and in this place.":

Survival
The freeway yonder, deferred
for a time, has at last come
through. At first the razed lots
reminded of war's aftermath but
gradually they merged under tree
and flower and weed to make an
impromptu park where children
stalked one another in hiding
games, where humming bird hovered
over nicotiana, where bumblebee
buzzed the wisteria and hollyhock,
where there was room for gopher,
field mouse, skunk, opossum,
golden garden spider, fat snail,
mating lizards, king snake skating
through the grass, and raccoon
sneaking over here to up-end the trash
in the dark of night.

They must have all gone
somewhere. The neighborhood
owl, giant, and white, has eaten
three kittens of our Manx,
leaving only bloody traces
of intestine smeared on the driveway
where he swooped to dine. Only
the runt of the litter, whom one
would have thought the easiest
prey, remains. It grows
by leaps and bounds, having
now all the milk
to itself.

III

Yamauchi now is fully embarked on a career as a dramatist. Her *And the Soul Shall Dance*, adapted from a short story into a full-length play for the East-West Players of Los Angeles, was also produced at Cafe La Momma in New York, and as a PBS television drama has had several reruns. Then, in May 1980, there was a New York Public Theatre workshop production of another play, *The Music Lesson*. This had an all Asian-American production staff, and the *New York Times* critic was impressed by the revelation of "the barely touched resources" of Asian-American talent. At present, having received her third Rockefeller grant to be a playwright-in-residence, Yamauchi is at work on a new play for East-West Players. She is also the author of several short stories, some of which have appeared in *Amerasia Journal, Yard Bird Reader, Greenfield Review, Aiiieeeee!, Rafu Shimpo*, and the *Bamboo Ridge* (a Hawaiian literary magazine).

Yamauchi cites Hisaye Yamamoto's inspiration as a determining cause of her switch from painting to writing. Another cause was her becoming housebound by the arrival of her daughter. At first, she says, "I was like a cripple in a foot race dragging a gimpy leg." She took a correspondence course in short story writing and improved so much that she had the short story, "And the Soul Shall Dance" completed at the time that the Asian-American "militants" were preparing *Aiiieeeee!* Hisaye Yamamoto recommended the story to Shawn Wong who carried it to Frank Chin, and Wakako Yamauchi was assured of a place among the most respected Asian-American writers.

Afterwards, the artistic director of the East-West Players, Mako Iwamatsu, asked for it as a play, but Yamauchi found the idea preposterous. Once again she was housebound, this time with a broken leg. As she stared at the ceiling, she saw the way to write the playscript, and the play was produced in 1977.

Of her work in general, Yamauchi says, "I write stories of people, stories of hurts, stories of love . . . mostly stories of love. Variations of very ancient themes. . . ." Besides her childhood in the desert valley, her work is influenced by her love for Japan and things Japanese (even though she claims she is not fluent in the literary language) and the devastation caused by her divorce after twenty-five years of marriage.

As the narrator explains in the story, "Makapou Bay," "In spite of the uneven marriage, I had assumed I would always be married to Joe; divorce among Japanese Americans is uncommon and I was not prepared for it." In another short story, "A Veteran of Foreign Wars," the divorced narrator compares herself to a one-legged man in the wheelchair, a veteran of Corregidor, and sees the two of them as "a blot on the Nisei horizon—the two that did not make it past the war and through the subsequent years, did not become wiser, more self-assured, prosperous, snug and secure middle class middle-aged Japanese Americans. The model minority."

Despite her intense pain, the narrator slowly discovers within herself a strength of spirit and becomes more aware of the world around her:

I began to look cautiously out of my window, began to water my front yard again, began to notice the warm sun on my skin, to touch the camellias that somehow survived my neglect and year after year bloomed pure and perfect like the part of me that refuses to lie down and die and continues to peer out from a dung heap expecting a more sufferable world.

Because of the divorce Yamauchi (and her narrators) are forced to push beyond the traditional Japanese belief in the sanctity of the family, reidentify themselves, and embrace the freedom of the American woman of the last part of the twentieth century. "In "Makapou Bay," the narrator reports of telling her daughter:

Some of the old concepts I'd been taught and also imposed on her, of nucleus—one man, one family—were no longer viable for us and we must push on, not necesarily together, but forward to explore and discover workable philosophies for ourselves. I told her I would never withdraw my love and support so that no matter where she stood, she would not be alone and that she should not be afraid to love, that joy was worth the risk of pain. After all, one does not die from pain unless one chooses to. I am witness to that.

The force of Japanese tradition, however, remains in her story, "And the Soul Shall Dance." The unhappily married woman, who had been sent from Japan to replace her dead sister, dreams of leaving her brutal and insensitive husband, but has no means to do so, so she turns to smoking and drinking instead. Her husband beats her and there is, according to the narrator, something masochistic about the way she displays her purple welts. Once, in her desperation she lurched behind a moving truck and was only saved by her stepdaughter. The unnerved driver said to the neighbors, "Never, never had I seen a drunken Japanese woman," to which the neighbor replied, nodding gravely, "Yes, it's unusual."

The title of the story and the play made from it comes from a fragment of a song which Yamauchi has Mrs. Oka sing, a few lines of music which she recalls from her own girlhood and translates for the story (and subsequent play):

Red lips press against a glass
Drink the purple wine
And the soul shall dance.

When, in the course of the play, the visiting neighbors play this tune, the battered woman suddenly appears in a dance costume and shows that she had been trained not to become wife to a peasant farmer in America but to win a husband from high station. She still dreams of a "rescue." But the brutal and insensitive man once had his own dream and has lost it; his first wife had been his helpmate as well as his love, and since her death, he has been unable to send for their daughter. He resents the way his parents-in-law saddled him with her sister, this woman who is sexually "damaged" and yet holds herself from his arms and treats him with contempt.

Yamauchi portrays both man and woman so vividly that the playgoer (or reader) can sympathize with both. In addition, one has some sympathy for the fourteen-year-old girl when, finally, she comes to join her father and stepmother. Totally strange to American ways, she is rejected by the little narrator (a nine-year-old girl) and frightened by the violence in her own home. But like her father, the newcomer is insensitive to Mrs. Oka's plight. It is the neighbor's little girl and her happily married parents who convey the sensitivity and understanding for this unhappy family. Yamauchi writes as though she herself is playing in turn each character of this little tragedy.

Unlike Mrs. Oka, the trapped wife in "Songs My Mother Taught Me," finds a temporary way out by committing adultery. There is irony in the title because the young daughter knows only one song that her mother favors, a song embodying her longing for Japan; it is called in English, "Transient Moon," (Translation by Yamauchi)

> Today too
>   passes in solitude
> The evening sun is distant
>   beyond the rim of the sea
> Who can be calling
>   Who can be seeking me?
> The sea birds
>   Cry from the shore.

The father has lost all hope of returning to Japan, but the mother takes a lover, a handsome young itinerant farm worker whose mandolin-playing reminds her of Japan. The husband resents the vibrations he feels between the two, but while on the farm he keeps the young man on, for he is a good worker. After the young man leaves, the mother has a baby which the farmer thinks is his own child, but the guilt-stricken woman wishes for the baby's death. When, as a result of carelessness, the infant drowns in four inches of water in a tub she cries out: "I've killed him, I've killed him, forgive me, I've killed him!" This is the song the daughter learns, one of extreme human guilt.

One of Yamauchi's protagonists does take the modern way out: she leaves without guilt. In "The Handkerchief," a story significantly written in 1977, the wife asks her husband's permission to go to San Francisco for a month to take care of an ill sister. The wife is needed on the farm—the husband tells her so—but untraditionally he does not command her to remain. "*Katte ni se!* [It's up to you!]," he says. She replies, "it's always like this. Don't you think I need to do what I think is right? Eighteen years I've devoted to you . . . this family. Don't you think I have feelings too? . . . Don't you think I have needs? I'm a person too! How long do you think I can live like this? Stifling everything . . . every feeling. . . ." He replies, "If you want to get out, the door is open! If you don't like it, get out!"

So Mrs. Tanaka does go to San Francisco, leaving her fifteen-year-old Mary in charge of the domestic duties of the family. But one month soon passes, and Mrs. Tanaka writes to say that perhaps she will return the next month. Then the "second month passed and Mama wrote to say she would probably return before school resumed in fall. She was now helping a friend in his restaurant, she said. Just helping out—sometimes in the kitchen, sometimes at the counter—helping and earning a little money besides. This man had been widowed recently and without his wife he was unable to carry on the business . . . just until he got competent help, she said. . . . No word was said about Auntie's condition." Later, she apparently writes to say that she will remain with this man, for Mr. Tanaka bitterly burns the last letter he receives.

Yamauchi says of her own work, "I go into the whole experience; I don't stop until I have seen it through to the end." The human spirit is most boldly revealed in "The Boatmen on Toneh River." Again the key song has been transplanted from the Japanese by Yamauchi:

I am a dying reed by the river bed
As thou, a drying dying reed
Alas, our lives together lie,
Blossomless, on the river bed.

Whether we live, or whether die
Tides will ebb and flow
Come then, thou with me, to dwell
As boatmen on Toneh River.

Here, as in other writings by Yamauchi, all nature seems to be pervaded by a Shintoistic spirit. She does not belong to any organized religious or philosophic group herself, but describes herself as "a religious person verging on mysticism." These qualities are evident in this story of the dying young woman, Kimi Sumida, whose body is apparently lifeless but her mind is holding many memories. She tells her dead mother of the wind spirit that once inspired her: "Though you may not believe it, I've found something here in the arid desert that is gentle and sweet too. I want to ask you about it, but to put it to words or to your critical eye may be to profane it. And now the tall summer reeds bend in the wind, cicadas hum, shadows lengthen, cottonwood leaves catch the last flutter of sunlight, and the lad who pedals down the warm dusty road each evening at this time is passing by, and I am not there. I shall not see the wind move through his black hair, and touch his smooth brown cheeks and fill his blouse with air. I want to be as close to him as that wind. Where he comes from, where he pedals to, I don't know; but when I watch him, I see west winds in the sage, I see tumbleweeds lope across the prairie, and primrose petals fall, and I am moved." As Kimi dies, "her lips [are] twisted in a pain akin to joy as she moves with a wind that carried her out, back to the country road and against the smooth brown cheeks of a lad on a bicycle, and into the blouse that billowed behind him." Death is her freedom and divinity is in the wind.

This story illustrates, probably better than any others, the author's mode of paralleling emotional and earthly landscapes. There is often a sense of the desert, of open spaces, and of souls dancing, yearning—but solitary and silent. The aloneness becomes sorrowful and tragic when such souls are unable to traverse the spaces that separate them. Thus Kimi's regret before her mother's critical eye: "Alas, our lives together lie,/ Blossomless, on the river bed." Her dead mother responds in self-realization:

> When finally my time was up, I counted my fortune. Fifty years of living and what was there to show? Ten thousand nights I lay there remembering my Japan; clear lakes, lonely shrines, the lyric of flowering cherry trees, street vendors' calls, plaintive and sweet as a mother's lullabyes, the sound of a flute on a summer evening. I spent a lifetime waiting to return to these. I thought my happiness was bound to these. I reached too far for what was always here in the dust, in the sunrise, in the sunset, in you.

The parallel "speeches" between the dead and dying demonstrate clearly Yamauchi's statement of her credo: internal action, not interaction. Although this is not true of all her work, this is the active principle in *And the Soul Shall Dance:* each character has his or her own soul, own dreams, own needs, to suffer, to inflict pain, to work, to gain wisdom. Each "dances" to his or her own inner music.

This is true also of *The Music Lesson*, the 1980 drama produced in New York. The plot concerns a widow whose goal is to make her farm profitable for her family during the Depression; her children, particularly her teenage daughter; and the man who comes to work for her, selling himself not only as a farmhand but also a violinist who can give lessons to the children. The widow finds some of her emotional life beginning to surface, others are stimulated by contact with the man, who himself is recovering from a disastrous love affair. He is hoping to make a sober, decent life for himself after years of dissipation but the whole situation explodes when the fifteen-year-old declares herself in love with him. All of them lose their dreams.

The critic in the *New York Times* of May 16, 1980, called *The Music Lesson* "a good memory piece . . . with moments of comedy dominated by sadness." He admired "the authenticity" of the drama, "the quiet evenly modulated level" of the writing, and "the unaffected directness" of the playwright's style.

In the play at which she is presently at work, Yamauchi is doing what she did in both earlier plays: converting one of her own short stories into a full-length drama. This one has the working title of "Cur-de-Sac," and deals with the two main characters in "A Veteran of Foreign Wars," the wheelchair man and the divorced woman. Although they did not communicate in the short story, they do in the play; their creator's name for both of them is "culls," that which is picked out to be rejected because of inferior quality; the Japanese word is *kuzu*, the left-overs, the scraps. Once again she is dealing with people in pain.

Only once has she made a major attempt to convey the "camp experience." Uncharacteristically, instead of showing individuals living intense personal lives, she shows group interaction. In *12-1-A*, a drama that has not been produced as yet, family units move into Block 12 to settle into their assigned barrack positions. The time span is from May 1942 to July 1943. Very little happens on stage. People talk, play cards, and try to help each other understand their situation. One boy leaves on a farm furlough, comes back embittered, and decides to go to Tule Lake. A girl decides to become a nurse. It is all low-key without spectacle or passionate denouement, but at the end, every life has been changed, and the relationships within every family, altered. The reader must empathize with the people involved, their sense of being nothing but puppets with no control over their own lives.

Yamauchi's sorrow for them is the same that she has shown in her stories of pre-war farm life and post-war marriages and divorce. She has a brooding love for humanity and a sense of the inevitability of suffering, but she can also create within her characters some moments and illusions of perfect freedom, as she did with the drunken Mrs. Oka, dancing among the sage in the desert valley. Her mystical belief in the human spirit pervades her work.

But for all her spirituality, Yamauchi is no innocent. The woman narrator of "Makapou Bay" buys a cockleheart paperweight with "all the beautiful colors of the shores of Hawaii, and depending on how I hold it, it is greener or bluer, and sometimes the light catches on the shell and it shines all gold and white and blue and green. Yet if I hold it directly at eye level, it is clearly only a plastic bubble and one can see that the colors are just at the base of the paperweight. I suspect that there is a way to look at things so the truth clearly separates itself from the illusion."

S. E. SOLBERG

Sui Sin Far/Edith Eaton:
The First Chinese-American Fictionist

Both her photographs and her own testimony seem to indicate that Edith Maud Eaton (1867–1914) could have "passed" into the majority society with little trouble. Moreover, although her mother was Chinese, Edith was unacquainted with her mother's native language, except for a few phrases, during her early years; in fact, she had very little contact with Asians or Eurasians, except for her own large group of siblings. Yet when she began to publish stories and articles, she chose to write chiefly about China and Chinese-Americans, and she wrote under the *nom de plume* of Sui Sin Far (occasionally Sui Seen or Sin Fah).

Such public identification with a group which was treated so contemptuously in America (as her autobiography vividly depicts) must be attributed to her allegiance to the principle of Confucius who "taught 'The way of sincerity is the way of heaven.'" Because of her integrity, Sui Sin Far earned the encomium, "one of the first to speak for an Asian-American sensibility that was neither Asian or white American." She was not a great writer; she has only one book (a collection of her stories) to her credit, but her attempts deserve recognition.

She tells us that, after she began to write, she met "some funny people" who advised her to distance herself from reality. She scoffs:

From *MELUS: The Journal of the Society for the Study of the Multi-Ethnic Literature of the United States*, Vol. 8, No. 1 (Spring 1981). © 1981 by the University of Southern California.

Instead of making myself familiar with the Chinese-Americans
around me, I should discourse on my spirit acquaintance with
Chinese ancestors and quote in between the "Good mornings"
and "How d'ye dos" of editors,

> Confucius, Confucius, how great is Confucius, Before Confucius,
> there never was Confucius, After Confucius, there never came
> Confucius," etc., etc., etc.

or something like that, both illuminating and obscuring, don't
you know.

What makes her choice so remarkable is the fact that she had lived in
many parts of the world before she finally settled in Seattle. The public
record is scant, but it is clear that she came from an educated family, very
large yet very close. Out of a morass of contradiction, confusion, and evasion,
a rough sketch can be hazarded. Edward Eaton, her father, came from a well-
to-do English family. As a young man he went to the Far East, apparently to
further family business concerns. While in China he met and married an
Asian woman. Upon returning to England with his wife, he ran into difficulties with his family, both over his marriage and over his determination to
become an artist. The upshot was that he emigrated to the United States.
The family lived for awhile in the New York area, then, after a Japanese
interlude, finally settled in Canada (Montreal or Quebec), living in poverty
in the French district.

Edith, as the eldest girl in a family of fourteen, appears to have taken
over many of the maternal responsibilities for holding the family together.
By her own account, and that of her sister, Edith was never very strong,
suffered from protracted illnesses, yet somehow made her own way into jour-
nalism and stenography from a childhood spent selling lace and her father's
paintings door to door—sales that, she was later to remark, were helped by
her "nationality." Then came, in turn, a stint on a paper in the West Indies,
an advertising contract with a railroad which took her to San Francisco and
later to various stenographic and journalistic positions in Seattle. It was in
these West Coast cities that she became a part of Chinese-American communities, serving at times as spokesperson and partisan.

Again we have her own verification, although in a tantalizingly brief
comment. "My heart leaps for joy when I read one day an article signed by a
New York Chinese in which he declares 'The Chinese in America owe an
everlasting debt of gratitude to Sui Sin Far for the bold stand she has taken
in their defense.'"

To go much further is to become enmeshed in a sticky web of contradictions and confusions. There may be more answers in archives, family and

personal papers, even in obscure printed sources. There are no doubt people still living whose memories could yield information. *The MacMillan Dictionary of Canadian Biography's* reticence in listing sources beyond "private information" would suggest that there may be personal or family objections still standing in the way of any open discussion of antecedents. It takes more than death to release the living from the meshes of prior dissimulations.

In Edith's case, however, the obfuscation was provided by her own sister, for Winnifred Eaton Babcock must have been the one responsible for the *New York Times* obituary of Edith on April 9, 1914. Edith, straightforwardly enough, had described her mother as "English bred with English ways and manner of dress." But this description was evidently too prosaic for Winnifred. The obituary ran:

> Edith Eaton, author, known in the East as Sui Sin Far, the "Chinese Lily," died on Tuesday at her home in Montreal, Canada. She was the daughter of Edward Eaton, landscape painter, an intimate friend of Gen. Gordon, known as "Chinese" Gordon, the English soldier killed at Khartoum in 1885. When a young man, Mr. Eaton received $300,000 and went to the Orient. He became fascinated with the East, and after a year married a Japanese noblewoman who had been adopted by Sir Hugh Matheson as a child and educated in England. Miss Edith Eaton was the oldest girl of their fourteen children. After a number of years the family returned to England.
>
> Financial reverses in that country reduced the family to poverty and Miss Eaton's grandfather made a place for her father in the banking firm of Pardee Matheson & Son. However, Mr. Eaton soon came to this country, where his fortunes varied. At one time he built a church in Jersey City that is still standing; later, on being reduced to poverty, he was forced to obtain assistance from England. Eventually he earned a living by painting landscapes.
>
> Miss Eaton took up literary work at this time and her short stories attracted favorable comment. Her best known book is *Mrs. Spring Fragrance*. One of Miss Eaton's sisters, Mrs. Betram W. Babcock of New York, is an author writing under the pen name of Onoto Watanna.

Edith, being dead, had no more claims in the matter, but Winnifred, engaged in an active and successful writing career, had a great deal at stake. The irony is that the obituary manages to skirt any meaningful summary of

Edith's life in favor of legitimizing family history for Winnifred. Not only is the mother a "Japanese noblewoman"; she has been adopted by an English peer. The family credentials are impeccable, given the necessary truth that must creep in: a solid background in English mercantile life and peerage, yet with a touch of the exotic added to even the father's life through his implied association with "Chinese" Gordon. There is less critisim than truth in saying that obituaries are written to serve the living rather than the dead.

Here Edith's name of Sui Sin Far and the sobriquet of the "Chinese Lily" seem dependent on her father's friendship with an Englishman nick-named "Chinese." Her stories, with such titles as "Her Chinese Husband," "Ku Yum and the Butterflies," or "White Woman Who Married a Chinaman," are not mentioned; they would not give much authenticity to the work of the daughter of a "Japanese noblewoman." Indeed, the "obit-uary" seems to be that of Edward Eaton, not of his daughter.

Perhaps the obituary should be taken as one more proof of the hostility toward Chinese-Americans against which Edith Eaton had fought during her life time. An overview can be cited from the work of Stow Persons, who noted in 1944:

> any summary of attitudes expressed in the California race conflict fails to indicate the depth of hatred for the Oriental and the determination of the native [white] Americans to exclude them. Treaty, legislation and court action were all employed to close the first chapter in immigration restriction.

William Purviance Fenn, in a basic study of attitudes towards Chinese in American literature, suggested that these attitudes might be summed up in four periods, the first three falling into what he somewhat wryly labeled the era of the "Chinese 'Invasion'—1) that of toleration, from 1849 to 1853; 2) that of growing antagonism, from 1853 to 1882; and 3) that of restriction, from 1882 on." The San Francisco fire of 1906 marked the end of that "era," he says, and "the Chinese question dropped into discard as a real issue, making way . . . for the Japanese question of more recent times."

In terms of that periodization, Edith succeeded during the time of restriction in having five publications, one of them in the prestigious *Century* magazine. She had no model to follow; the public taste was for the exotic or for the stereotype. The "funny people" who wanted her to trade on her nationality told her:

> if I wanted to succeed in literature in America I should dress in
> Chinese costume, carry a fan in my hand, wear a pair of scarlet

beaded slippers, live in New York, and come of high birth.

Not only did she repudiate all this; she saw it as ineffectual. She knew that Americans definitely preferred Japanese to Chinese:

> The Americans having for many years manifested a much higher regard for the Japanese than the Chinese, several half-Chinese young men and women, thinking to advance themselves, both in a social and business sense, pass as Japanese. They continue to be known as Eurasian, but a Japanese Eurasian does not appear in the same light as a Chinese Eurasian.

Immediately after this she adds:

> The unfortunate Chinese Eurasians! Are not those who compel them to thus cringe more to be blamed than they?

The question of choice, of being true to one's heritage and family, of selling a birthright for momentary peace in an uncomfortable society are the same questions that have plagued Asian-American writers down to the present.

Further comprehension of her situation, as a Chinese person as well as a writer, can be found in American cultural history and in mainstream literature of her time. Howard Mumford Jones, in an extended discussion of the taste for the exotic in what he calls the "cosmopolitan spirit," makes the provocative suggestion that while the American response to Japan was derived from a taste for the exotic the same was not true of China. "American taste for Chinoiserie descends from the eighteenth century, and aside from vulgar notions about Chinese sexuality, joss houses, and Opium dens, it is problematical whether things Chinese served greatly to quench any thirst for the exotic." While the reasons for this are no doubt complex, central to them would seem to be the simple fact that the Chinese were already present in the United States and most of the popular images derived from that direct contact. The Japanese had, for the most part, the added attraction of being across the Pacific without much danger of the facts of their presence damaging whatever fantasies might be evoked.

While this contrast could be illustrated from many sources, it is suggested in even the works of those great champions of Anglo-Saxon supremacy Jack London and Frank Norris. Note, for example, London's description of Captain West in *The Mutiny of the Elsinore* as a "samurai," or the evocation of a remembered woman in *Martin Eden*: "Japanese women, doll-like stepping mincingly on wooden clogs" as contrasted with his treatment of the Chinese in the short story "Yellow Handkerchief": "What was to happen next I could not imagine, for the Chinese were a different race from mine, and from what I knew I was confident that fair play was no part of their make-up" or, further on, "I was familiar enough with the Chinese character to know that fear alone restrained them."

Frank Norris, in describing Vanamee's vision in *The Octopus*, has the spectre "dressed in a gown of scarlet silk, with flowing sleeves, such as Japanese wear, embroidered with flowers and figures of birds worked in gold threads," while in *Moran of the Lady Letty*, the Chinese crew of the *Bertha Millner* is described in these terms: "the absolute indifference of these brown-suited Mongols, the blankness of their flat, fat faces, the dullness of their slanting, fishlike eyes that never met his own or even wandered in his direction was uncanny, disquieting."

A general pattern had been established, much as in these examples, of the Chinese as mysterious, evil, nearby, and threatening, while the Japanese were exotic, quaint, delicate (or manly, as the samurai), and distant. A verbal equivalent appears in a curious article in the *Bookman* in 1923 entitled "Chinese Characters in American Fiction": "The Chinese resent the popular term *Chinaman*. They prefer to be referred to as *Chinese*, just as natives of Japan are termed *Japanese*. Would anyone ever use the expression Japanman?" While this is not the place to go into the specific stereotypes of Japanese and Chinese that existed at the turn of the century, it is necessary to note the curious way in which the general fascination with the exotic (Japan) was able to transcend racist ideas so long as distance was a part of the formula.

As a Chinese-American writer, then, Sui Sin Far had to find a mode that would enable her to deal with her own experience (as the classic editorial injunction has it), but to do that meant to fall outside the boundaries of any of the "maincurrents" of American writing. She was not a regionalist nor nationalist. If anything, she was an internationalist, but hardly of the Henry James school, though some of what is interesting in her work lies in the subtleties that are apt to be lost on the untrained casual reader. She is not naturalist or local colorist, and her essays at humor, which tend to fall short of the mark in any case, can hardly be looked upon as falling in the Mr. Dooley or Mark Twain "native American" styles. She was trapped by experience and inclination into working within a sub-genre of American prose: what, for lack of a better term, we might call Chinatown Tales. Such classification by subject matter (Chinatown, or more broadly, the Chinese in America) breaks down an established literary form, the novel, into sub-genres defined by content, not form or stylistic skill. Eaton, by choosing to identify with and write about the Chinese, found herself alone in an essentially formless field. There had been fifty years of writing about the Chinese in America, but out of that writing no clear literary form had evolved. As William Purviance Fenn sums it up:

> The impress of Chinese immigration on American literature . . .
> is hard to evaluate. . . . Its influence has been two-fold: first, as a
> problem the discussion of which has resulted in literature;
> second, as a source of subject matter for the literature of local
> color. In the first place, the half century of economic and polit-
> ical discussion resulted in an immense amount of material which
> is still preserved for us in newspaper, magazine, pamphlet, and
> book. Of this, a larger proportion, of course, is of value only to
> the economist, historian, or sociologist; but the heated emotions
> of that struggle occasionally found expression in fiction, drama,
> and verse. Party prejudices and passions, however, are poor inspi-
> ration for anything but cheap propaganda, and it is in the appeal
> of the subject to the sense of justice that we have an approach to
> the fundamental inspirational problems of literature.
>
> In the second place, the existence of a large number of this
> alien race offered an unusual opportunity for devotees of the
> local-color movement; and in the glorious process of exploding
> old myths and of creating new ones, the Chinamen were bound
> to suffer in many a poem, story, and play. . . . They were strange
> and they were enigmatical; their appearance and ways added
> color to already too colorful backgrounds, and the difficulty of
> understanding them piqued the curiosity of American readers.
> The result was a body of fiction, drama, and verse exploiting the
> Chinese as a rich source of local color.
>
> But even of this small body of creative literature, by far the
> greater part was written by amateurs in the field of letters, and
> only a handful of efforts even approach greatness.

Fiction, drama, and verse, each with a sub-genre which exploits the "Chinese as a rich source of color." This gave Eaton little enough to build on, for her intent was certainly not to exploit, but rather to record, explain, and somehow give meaning to the experience of the Chinese in America. Fenn's 1933 summing up is interesting, for he had considered two of Eaton's stories in his summary, though his bibliography does not list her collection, *Mrs. Spring Fragrance.*

Such, then, is the literature of Chinatown—no poems, no plays, but possibly half a dozen short stories worth remembering. And Chinatown will never be adequately described by anyone who fails to see in it something more fundamental than the superficial barbarity and high coloring which have been almost the only appeal so far. . . . The real Chinatown that is worth preserving lies beneath the surface color, among the deeper currents.

I would argue that Edith Eaton as Sui Sin Far did manage to dip into those deeper currents beneath the surface color, but no matter what she saw and understood, there was no acceptable form to shape it to. Had she been physically stronger and had a more sophisticated literary apprenticeship, she might have been able to create that new form. As it was, she was defeated, for in that "glorious process of exploding old myths and of creating new ones," as Fenn puts it, "the Chinamen were bound to suffer."

Fictional stereotypes for the Chinatown tales had been established, and it was difficult for anyone, even of a strongly independent mind, to ignore them. No matter how frank and open Eaton might have been in a memoir such as "Leaves from the Mental Portfolio of an Eurasian," when she turned her hand to fiction the possible was limited by the acceptable. She was modest about her work. In acknowledging permissions to reprint previously published stories in *Mrs. Spring Fragrance* she writes: "I wish to thank the Editors . . . who were kind enough to care for my children when l sent them out into the world, for permitting the dear ones to return to me to be grouped together within this volume."

Even at the outset there were those who appreciated her difficulties and her attempts to create authentic characters. Said the editor of *Land of Sunshine*, a California magazine, in 1887:

[her stories are] all of Chinese characters in California or on the Pacific Coast and they have an insight and sympathy which are probably unique. To others the alien Celestial is at best mere "literary material": in these stories, he (or she) is a human being.

That her contemporaries saw Sui Sin Far's writing as an attempt to speak for Chinese-Americans is borne out by the review of *Mrs. Spring Fragrance* in the *New York Times Book Review* of July 7, 1912.

Miss Eaton has struck a new note in American fiction. She has not struck it very surely, or with surpassing skill, but it has taken courage to strike at all, and, to some extent, she atones for lack of artistic skill with the unusual knowledge she undoubtedly has of her theme. The thing she has tried to do is to portray for readers of the white race the lives, feelings, sentiments of the Americanized Chinese of the Pacific Coast, of those who have intermarried with them and of the children who have sprung from such unions. It is a task whose adequate doing would require well nigh superhuman insight and the subtlest of methods.

The review had more insight than the publisher who inserted an advertisement on the same page; the advertisement reads in part: "Quaint, lovable characters are the Chinese who appear in these unusual and exquisite stories of our Western Coast. . . . Altogether they make as desirable reading as the title suggests." Taken out of context, what does the title suggest? Perhaps the exotic, that could be traded on, at worst, the quaint, but hardly the struggle toward realism that is found in the pages.

The title story of *Mrs. Spring Fragrance* deals with the difficulties of Mr. Spring Fragrance in understanding and coming to grips with his very Americanized wife. While the story is slight, it does allow Eaton to create passages such as the following exchange between Mr. Spring Fragrance and an American friend:

> "Everything is 'high class' in America," he [Mr. Spring Fragrance] observed.
>
> "Sure!" cheerfully assented the young man. "Haven't you ever heard that all Americans are princes and princesses, and just as soon as a foreigner puts his foot upon our shores, he also becomes of the nobility—I mean, the royal family."
>
> "What about my brother in the Detention Pen?" dryly inquired Mr. Spring Fragrance.
>
> "Now, you've got me," said the young man, rubbing his head. "Well, that is a shame—'a beastly shame,' as the Englishman says. But understand, old fellow, we that are real Americans are up against that—even more than you. It is against our principles."
>
> "I offer the real Americans my consolations that they should be compelled to do that which is against their principles."

In the story "The Inferior Woman" an interesting possibility is suggested, then dropped. But the suggestion shows that Eaton knew what she was up against and was somehow trying to warn her readers. The story describes Mrs. Spring Fragrance's interference in the love life of her American neighbor's son, and she helps him to marry the "inferior woman" he prefers rather than the "superior woman" chosen by his mother. As the story opens, Mrs. Spring Fragrance is walking in the garden reflecting upon the possibilities of "a book which she had some notion of writing. Many American women wrote books. Why should not a Chinese? She would write a book about Americans for her Chinese women friends. The American people were so interesting and mysterious." Unfortunately Mrs. Spring Fragrance never writes her book, and we never see her develop the stereotypes of the "mysterious Americans."

"Particularly interesting," says the *New York Times* reviewer, "are two stories in which an American woman is made to contrast her experiences as the wife of an American and afterward of a Chinese." In 1952 the same stories caught the attention of John Burt Foster, and impressed him so much that he speculated: "So intimately does the author write of mixed marriage that one is tempted to believe that she herself married a Chinese and was enabled in this way to get firsthand information."

Yet despite the fascination of many of the stories and their subjects— the problems with Angel Island, the selfprotective aspects of the Chinese community, the Eurasians who in the crunch throw in their lot with the Chinese—the most impressive aspect of the writing is the conviction that environment is more important that heredity, that race is an accident, and, when, as with the Eurasian, there is a question of choice, the individual has the power to make that choice.

The most dramatic statement of the theme of choice is in "Pat and Pan," the story of two children, the boy Caucasian-American, the girl Chinese-American, being raised together in a Chinese household; the Chinese couple has raised the boy from a baby as their own. He speaks only Chinese, has only Chinese playmates, is inseparable from his little "Chinese" sister. Enter the meddling mission school teacher who cannot allow a "white boy" to be brought up Chinese. The child is removed from his Chinese home and adopted by a white family. Slowly he grows away from his Chinese background. On next meeting his little Chinese sister, he is friendly, but in their second encounter after their separation, egged on by his new playmates, he rejects her completely, shouting at her to get away from him. "But when she reached the foot of the hill, she looked up and shook her little head sorrowfully. 'Poor Pat!' said she. 'He Chinese no more; he Chinese no more!'"

While Eaton wrote well, she never acquired the control of style necessary to deal with her subjects in depth or at length. What she wrote were chiefly sketches, vignettes. The task she had set herself was nearly impossible at that time. Trapped in the stylistic conventions of the time, including dialogue in a forced and artificial dialect, she could only try, by selection of her story material, to tell about the real Chinese-Americans she knew.

In 1974, attention was called to her by the editors of *Aiiieeeee!* who were keenly aware of her problem. In their Introduction they point out that in an atmosphere where the Chinese in America was "at best mere 'literary material,' she was forced to work 'within the stereotype of Chinese as laundryman, prostitute, smuggler, coolie'; she was able to do little more than present 'John Chinaman' as . . . a comic caricature, giving him a sensibility that was her own."

What she left was a unique public record of the difficulty of being an individual without racial, national, or group claims. "After all I have no nationality and am not anxious to claim any," she wrote. "Individuality is more than nationality. 'You are you and I am I,' says Confucius." And then she goes on to the bitter heart of her dilemma. "I give my right hand to the Occidentals and my left to the Orientals, hoping that between them they will not utterly destroy the insignificant 'connecting link.' And that's all."

AMY LING

Winnifred Eaton: Ethnic Chameleon and Popular Success

"Somehow or other I cannot reconcile myself to the thought that the Chinese are humans like ourselves," said Mr. K.

"A Chinaman is, in my eyes, more repulsive than a nigger," replied the town clerk.

"Now the Japanese are different altogether. There is something bright and likeable about those men," added Mr. K.

This conversation, from an autobiographical essay by Edith Eaton, Winnifred Eaton's older sister, records the comparative judgment of minorities prevalent among majority Americans at the turn of the century. The Japanese were at the top of the ladder, respected in part because this island nation had won wars against China in 1895 and Russia in 1905, and in part because few Japanese had then immigrated to the United States. The Blacks had long been considered inferior, but they, at least, had the dubious advantage of being familiar. The Chinese, however, were not only regarded as an incomprehensible subhuman species, but with the completion of the transcontinental railroad in 1869, the thousands of Chinese laborers imported for its construction had become a threat to white

From *MELUS: The Journal of the Society for the Study of the Multi-Ethnic Literature of the United States*, Vol. 11, No. 3 (Fall 1984). © 1984 by the University of Southern California.

workers. Anti-Chinese agitation grew to such proportions that the Chinese
Exclusion Acts were passed in 1882, making the Chinese the only nationality in the world named by an act of Congress for exclusion. John Higham
in *Strangers in the Land*, a study of American nationalism and ethnic prejudice, confirms the virulent rejection of the Chinese at the end of the nine-
teenth century:

> No variety of anti-European sentiment has ever approached the
> violent extremes to which anti-Chinese agitation went in the
> 1870's and 1880's. Lynchings, boycotts, and mass expulsions
> still harassed the Chinese after the federal government yielded
> to the clamor for their exclusion in 1882. At a time when the
> Chinese question had virtually disappeared as a political issue,
> a labor union could still refer to that patient people as "more
> slavish and brutish than the beasts that roam the fields. They
> are groveling worms."

S. E. Solberg, in a *MELUS* article on Edith Eaton, also noted the denunciation of the Chinese and a preference for the Japanese: "A general pattern had
been established . . . of the Chinese as mysterious, evil, nearby, and threatening, while the Japanese were exotic, quaint, delicate (or manly, as the
samurai), and distant."

Such was the political and social climate of Winnifred Eaton's childhood. She was the eighth of fourteen surviving children of an English
painter, Edward Eaton (1839–1915) and his Chinese wife, Grace Trefusius
(1847–1922). The Eatons immigrated first to the United States in the early
1870s and then settled in Montreal in 1874, where Winnifred was born,
either in 1876 or 1877. Such interracial marriages being rare, the Eurasian
children received more curious attention than they liked; however, Edith
noted that her ethnicity helped her sell her hand-made lace and her father's
paintings door to door. In later life, ethnicity was to play a major part in the
writing careers of both sisters.

In Edith's case, sensitivity to prejudice against the Chinese took the
form of assertion of her Chinese heritage, despite the fact that her facial
features did not betray such origins. Throughout her career, from 1897 until
1914, under the pen name Sui Sin Far, Edith Eaton defended the Chinese in
numerous articles and stories published in such magazines as the *Canadian
Dominion Illustrated*, *Overland*, *Century*, *Land of Sunshine*, *The Chautauquan*,
Independent, *Good Housekeeping*, *Hampton*, *The Delineator*, and *New England
Magazine*. For her efforts on their behalf, the Chinese set up a special monument on her grave in Montreal, commemorating her work and expressing

their gratitude with the inscription "*Yi bu wong hua*" (literally translated: Righteousness does not forget country).

Winnifred Eaton, however, followed a different route. Calling herself Onoto Watanna, she wrote highly successful popular novels, supporting herself and her four children by her pen alone, producing a novel every year but one between 1901 to 1916, and from 1924-1931 editing and writing movie scripts in Hollywood, rising to the position of head of Universal Studios' scenario department. As far as we have been able to determine, though Edith Eaton's first article on the Chinese, "The Chinese Woman in America," appeared in 1897, her first piece of fiction, a short story, "A Chinese Ishmael," was not published until July 1899; her only book, a collection of her short stories, did not appear until 1912. Winnifred Eaton's first novel, *Miss Numè of Japan: A Japanese-American Romance*, also appeared in 1899, to be followed by seventeen other books and hundreds of short stories. Thus, though Edith has been called "The First Chinese-American Fictionist," the title may by right be Winnifred's. Undoubtedly, Edith Eaton was the first person of Chinese ancestry to write fiction in English about the Chinese in America and a case may also be made for her being a feminist. However, if we put subject matter aside, by the quantity of her work and perhaps also by chronology (for we don't know what month *Miss Numè* appeared), Winnifred Eaton may actually be the first Chinamerican fictionist and something of a feminist also in both her work and life.

Winnifred Eaton's work was extensive and varied. For her first seven novels, she assumed a Japanese persona, set her books in Japan, and romantically entangled Japanese or Eurasian women with English or American men. In 1907, tired of the Japanese theme, she took up an Irish-American persona, writing *The Diary of Delia, Being a Veracious Account of the Kitchen with some Side-lights on the Parlour*, purportedly the diary of an Irish immigrant cook, which she submitted to the *Saturday Evening Post* under the name Winnifred Mooney. *The Post* promptly accepted it but published it serially under her better known name Onoto Watanna. Thus, for the first time in literary history, we had the anomaly of an "Irish" book by a "Japanese," who was actually Chinese/English/Canadian.

Since the entire book was supposedly the diary of an uneducated young Irish woman, the orthography reflected this aspect of her character, as well as her accent, and the unconventional spelling is at times a stumbling block. Though some of Eaton's reviewers complained about her orthography, none gave her deserved compliments on the fidelity of her ear for the Irish accent. It seems very apparent to me that her Irish-American dialect is far superior to her Japanese-American English. For example, she has Miss Numè say to Arthur Sinclair at their first meeting: 'Me? I lig' you. You are big—and thad

you nod lig' poor liddle Japanese womans—still I lig' you just same." This
sounds more like someone speaking with a cold in her nose than with a
Japanese accent, not to mention the fact that such a bold remark would have
been very unseemly for a young Japanese woman. In the *Diary of Delia*,
however, we find lines like these: "Indade, ses I. Then I'll set here till the
24th, but civil a bit of work will I be doing" and "It's an onest gurl I am . . .
and its ashamed I'd be to mix mesilf in any such mess as that." Undoubtedly,
living in New York City, from 1901 until 1917, Winnifred Eaton had much
greater opportunity to hear Irish immigrants speak than any Japanese.

Despite the authenticity of her Irish dialect and the lively story of the
spirited Delia, who cleverly manages to discover which of her two suitors is
only after her money and which loves her for herself, Winnifred Eaton was
advised "to stick to her last." The public was apparently more entranced by
her fanciful Japanese heroines. She then produced two of her better Japanese
romances, *Tama* (1910) and *The Honorable Miss Moonlight* (1912); followed by
a delightful autobiography, *Me*, (1915) published anonymously to protect her
Japanese persona; and *Marion* (1916), the story of an artist's model based on
her sister Sara's life. *Sunny San* (1922) was her last "Japanese" novel and a
departure from the others by being set in the United States. Eaton's last two
novels were set in the Bow valley of the Canadian province of Alberta, where
she and her second husband, Francis Fournier Reeve, had a cattle ranch. In
these two works, she turned for locale to her own experience and for certain
characters, to her father's ethnicity. In *Cattle* (1923) the English "greenhorn,
son of an English lord, one of those odd derelicts that drift over from the Old
Country," is a minor character. In Canada during this time, so-called
"remittance men" were very common; they were often younger sons of
English families sent to the "provinces" with small remittances to make
their way in the world. In *His Royal Nibs* (1925), the hero, an Englishman
dubbed "Cheerio," turns out to be Edward Eaton Charlesmore of Maccles-
field and Coventry (a family name) and also a painter. The heroines are
young, spirited Canadians.

The Japanese persona, however, was undoubtedly the predominant one
in the life and writing career of Winnifred Eaton. We can imagine the young
Winnifred, setting out from the family nest having followed Edith's development from typist/secretary to journalist/story writer, thinking to herself:
First of all, Edith is already going the Chinese route and I don't want merely
to hang onto her skirts. Second, the Japanese are much more highly regarded
in this society than the Chinese. Third, most people can't tell the two nation-
alities apart. Therefore, I'll give myself a Japanese identity, research whatever
basic information I need, rely on my imagination for the rest, and no one will
know the difference. And she was right.

Winnifred Eaton was to play her Japanese part to the hilt. For the frontispiece of her third novel, *The Wooing of Wisteria*, for example, she is photographed in a kimono standing before a screen decorated with wisteria and iris. A vertical scrawl in the corner, vaguely reminiscent of Japanese writing, is identified as the "author's autograph." Edith's obituary in the April 9, 1914 *New York Times*, which Winnifred very likely had a hand in, claims that their mother was "a Japanese noblewoman who had been adopted by Sir Hugh Matheson as a child and educated in England. Various editions of *Who Was Who* still contain the misinformation that Winnifred Eaton was born in Nagasaki of a noble Japanese mother. This fabricated ethnic heritage may have been "an advertising ploy, possibly dreamed up by her publishers" or even her first husband who was also her publicist and agent; however, this supportive background alone could not have accounted for the great success of her books.

Her first novel, *Miss Numè of Japan*, was well received; the *New York Times* reviewer called it "a charming Japanese tale" that gave him "a delightful evening." He found much in it that was "entertaining," praised "the cleverness of incident," and concluded that "it is a well-done piece of writing." Her second book, *A Japanese Nightingale* (1901), was a stunning success. Published by Harper & Brothers, with full color illustrations by a Japanese artist and each page printed on paper decorated with oriental motifs, the book was a visual delight; and the story with its startling twists, its tender emotional subtleties, and mysterious, seductive heroine readily won admirers. *A Japanese Nightingale* (1901) was translated into Swedish, Hungarian, French, and German, was adapted for a Broadway production, competing for audiences with *Madame Butterfly*, and eighteen years later was made into a film and an opera. It won praise from William Dean Howells, who, in an article for *The North American Review* deploring the current romantic trend, made an exception of *A Japanese Nightingale*, noting, "There is a quite indescribable freshness in the art of this pretty novelette . . . which is like no other art except in the simplicity which is native to the best art every where."

Since *A Japanese Nightingale* is representative of Winnifred Eaton's work, which few readers are likely to be familiar with today, a plot summary may be in order here. Both her flaws and certain of her virtues will be apparent. She relies, perhaps, too much on coincidence, but she is skilled at telling a charming story and evoking tender sentiments. The opening paragraph immediately sets the romantic mood:

> The last rays of sunset were tingeing the land, lingering in splendor above the bay. The waters had caught the golden glow,

and, miser-like, seemingly made effort to keep it with them; but, inexorably, the lowering sun drew away its gilding light, leaving the waters a dark green. The shadows began to darken, faint stars peeped out of the heavens, and slowly, unwillingly, the day's last ray followed the sunken sun to rest; and with its vanishment a pale moon stole overhead and threw a seraphic light over all things.

By moonlight, at a teahouse in Japan, two American men are entranced by an unusual dance performed by a beautiful Eurasian, Yuki. One is Jack Bigelow, a recent college graduate, and the other man is a theatrical manager who offers Yuki a contract to tour America. She refuses. Later, a matchmaker offers Yuki in "marriage" to Jack for a high fee. First, he declines but, unable to forget her and realizing that these arrangements are easily broken, he accepts. After a few idyllic days, she suddenly disappears without a word, returning days later without an explanation. She constantly needs money, coaxing and teasing it out of him, until he becomes fearful that he has married an adventuress. Months pass, with Yuki always needing money and periodically disappearing and returning without a word, until his Japanese college friend Taro Burton arrives from the United States. When Taro comes to meet Jack's "wife," he discovers to his dismay that she is his sister. Yuki flees in shame. The men go to Taro's home and learn from his mother that the family finances had deteriorated drastically and that Yuki had "married" in order to have money to keep her brother in school and to earn his passage home. Distraught, Taro falls, striking his head, becoming seriously ill and ultimately dying. Jack affirms his love for Yuki and promises to spare no effort to find his wife. For two years, he wanders all over Japan searching in vain. Yuki, in the meantime, has accepted the offer of a tour in America but, ill and depressed, she is released from her contract. Just before returning to America, Jack pays one last visit to the house where he and Yuki had lived two years before and there, to his great surprise and delight, the lovers meet and are happily reunited.

As Winnifred Eaton's career continued, with each book following the basic structural formula but tremendously varied in its elaborative details, only the critic of the *Independent* sounded a note of protest, complaining of inaccuracies and saying of one of her novels: "In her latest book *Onoto Watanna* she continues her mistaken career as a Japanese novelist." However, Japanese readers themselves found her work praiseworthy. Kafu Nagai, who studied at Princeton and Rutgers Universities between 1871 and 1873, wrote in his diary about *The Heart of Hyacinth*, "This novel is hardly to be counted among the best literary works, but the style is exquisite and its pretty sentiment is well displayed." Katsuhiko Takeda in *Essays on Japanese Literature* devoted an entire essay to Onoto Watanna and concluded that Onoto Watanna was not a long time resident of Japan; however, in her books "Japanese customs and manners [are] . . . properly introduced to the West"; she is on a par with Lafcadio Hearn and Pierre Loti, and "her descriptions of human feelings are more delicate than those of both famous writers." Apparently then, Winnifred Eaton did do her homework, and furthermore, had enough imagination and skill as a writer, particularly enough knowledge of human nature, to compensate for what she lacked in facts about Japan.

The Onoto Watanna romances are all variations on the theme boy meets girl, boy loses girl, boy finds girl again, but then what romances are not? What is interesting is that her heroines are almost always Japanese or Eurasian young women in socially inferior positions (social outcasts, orphans, unloved stepdaughters) while her heroes are generally American or English men in influential positions (diplomats, ministers, professors, doctors, architects). One might initially conclude that Winnifred Eaton thus catered to stereotypes of the female as childlike, flighty, and brainless while the male was invariably strong and powerful. And further, one might argue that her books supported white supremacist views—little wonder she was popular. However, on closer reading, one notes that the heroines of her novels, though Bohemian and socially unaccepted, are intelligent, independent, and strong-willed. They know what they want and they work to get it with whatever means they possess; generally their means are personal charm, beauty, cleverness, and a good-natured sense of humor. While the men in her novels always hold the purse strings, the women hold the men's heartstrings and manage to get their own way. Thus, Winnifred Eaton's heroines are sturdy survivors, a far cry from the stereotype of the shy, deferential, totally self-negating Japanese female.

Of *A Japanese Nightingale*, for example, Howells noted: "The charm, the delight, the supreme interest is in the personality of Yuki." Certainly, Yuki's social position is inferior. The proprietor of the tea house has only harsh words when asked by the Americans who she is: "a cheap girl of Tokyo, with the blue glass eyes of the barbarian, the yellow skin of the lower Japanese, the hair of mixed color, black and red, the form of a Japanese courtesan, and the heart and nature of those honorably unreliable creatures, alien at this country, alien at your honorable country, augustly despicable—a half caste!" (p. 15). And yet, this woman is all reliability and faithfulness in relation to her brother, working for his benefit, making the money he needs through her physical beauty and charm. And though she falls in love with her husband, she runs away, driven by her brother's disdain, and again supports herself independently until her own aching heart brings her home. On the most basic level of physical survival, Tama, another Eurasian heroine of an

Onoto Watanna romance, lives in the wild so remote from the rest of society that she is thought to be a fox spirit, but it is she, though blind, who shows a highly respected American professor how to trap fish and where to find wild fruits and vegetables.

In Winnifred Eaton's romances, we find ourselves in the hands of a skilled story teller, seducing us into suspending disbelief, forgetting reason and unabashedly enjoying our feelings, which are being manipulated very effectively. With every book, in spite of ourselves, we are caught again in the spell. There is something fundamental, something unfailingly (perhaps biologically) satisfying in the ebb and flow of paradise discovered, lost, and regained. But Eaton herself was clearsighted enough to realize her limitations. In 1915, despite her name in lights on a Broadway theater where *A Japanese Nightingale* was being performed, she critically appraised her work and lamented having fallen short of her youthful dreams:

> What then I ardently believed to be the divine sparks of genius, I now perceived to be nothing but a mediocre talent that could never carry me far. My success was founded upon a cheap and popular device, and that jumble of sentimental moonshine that they called my play seemed to me the pathetic stamp of my inefficiency. Oh, I had sold my birthright for a mess of potage. [sic]

Most likely suffering a mid-life crisis, Eaton was extremely hard on herself in this passage. Her books may not be the work of lasting genius; however, they showed more than a "mediocre talent." And in her last two novels, she returned, in a sense, to her birthright, making use of her father's legacy and the world around her. Her work did not have the refinement and complexity of the work of her friend Edith Wharton, with upper class New York society behind her and European culture before, but in her field of the popular novel, Eaton was highly skilled and always entertaining. Furthermore, the path she chose was politically viable and economically necessary if she was to support herself and four children.

From an unpublished memoir written by her daughter, we can readily see that Winnifred Eaton was an extremely resourceful and energetic woman:

> On the ranch my mother found it more difficult to write, for we children were growing, [and] she had all the duties of a ranch wife; and though we always had a housekeeper it was Mamma who put down the pork, made headcheese, canned peas, beans, beets—she always seemed to be canning something—made the butter, candled the eggs, saw to it that the meals at harvest and

threshing time were taken to the men in the fields and that we
children rode our seven miles and back to the country school we
then attended.

Yet, she managed to write three novels in Alberta. Further, Winnifred Eaton
was clever at getting her way, for her daughter remembered that when they
first moved to the "Bow View Ranch," her mother wanted to have the
outside of the house repainted and had bought the paint, but her husband
said the men could not be spared from branding the cattle and that the paint
would have to be returned. "In order to prevent this, my mother drove nails
into the tops of the cans making a hole in each. She then started to paint the
house herself, from the bottom up! At this my Dad gave up, called in the men
and the house was painted, the job taking a couple of days."

This was the independence of spirit, the liveliness that characterizes
her heroines and makes them so appealing. It was also this spirit that took
Winnifred Eaton to Hollywood in 1924, when the ranch was not doing well,
with a letter of introduction to Carl Laemmle, president of Universal
Studios. She was surprised to be immediately hired at a salary of $500 a week,
for that time an astronomical figure. Undoubtedly, Hollywood recognized in
her books Winnifred Eaton's skill in embroidering on a universally effective
formula. In romantic and pleasantly exotic settings, her lovers were always
deserving, the complications were always suspenseful and the endings always
happy. Her heroines were independent and lively, yet non-threatening and
thoroughly lovable. Eaton undoubtedly had her hand on the public pulse, for
the narrative talent that created bestselling books could certainly be put to
the service of creating popular entertaining movies. However, she was not
entirely happy in Hollywood since her work consisted primarily of editing
the work of other writers not under contract. Among the films Winnifred
Eaton Reeve worked on are "False Kisses" (1921), "Undertow" (1930),
"Young Desire" (1930), and "East is West" (1930). Her own original scripts
include "The Mississippi Gambler" (1929) and "Shanghai Lady" (1929),
which was a box office success. She was content to leave Hollywood when
her contract expired in 1931 and to return to Calgary where her husband had
begun a successful oil drilling business. She died on April 8, 1954 in Butte,
Montana, returning to Calgary from a winter vacation in Phoenix, Arizona.
Her papers are now at the University of Calgary, where a building has been
named in her and her husband's honor.

Finally, that Winnifred Eaton could put on ethnicity as a chameleon
changes her color or spots not only testifies to her ingenuity, her daring and
cleverness, but it serves to prove that we are indeed all the same under the
skin. The success of Onoto Watanna or Winnifred Mooney or Winnifred

Babcock Reeve was not due to her knowledge of the Japanese, the Irish, or English/Canadian condition, but to her understanding of the human condition. Whether her protagonist is a Japanese geisha, an Irish cook or an orphan raped by a Canadian cattle baron, they are all, like Winnifred Eaton herself, survivors in a harsh world. That her books were translated into Asian and many European languages attests to her universal appeal. That many of her novels were made into silent films and that she herself became head of Universal Studios' scenario department confirm the fact that this small, extraordinary Eurasian woman achieved the greatest success a popular writer can dream of.

RICHARD R. GUZMAN

"As in Myth, the Signs Were All Over": The Fiction of N.V.M. Gonzalez

Everything, then, can be a myth? Yes, I believe this, for the universe is infinitely fertile in suggestions.

—Roland Barthes

Magellan made his fateful landfall in the Philippines at Cebu on March 16, 1521; and, with the signal exception of his slaying some six weeks later, it has seemed possible to read the bulk of Philippine history as a series of capitulations. Politics became Spanish, religion became Spanish (the Islands were an Archdiocese before 1600), and in 1850 when, to ease tax-collecting problems, Governor-General Narciso Claveria decreed that all indios be given Spanish surnames, even given names became Spanish. One of the Philippines' greatest modern writers, Nick Joaquin, has said:

> . . . there is as great a gulf between the pre-Spanish drift of totem-and-taboo tribes and our present existence as one people as there is between protoplasm and a human creature. The *content* of our national destiny is ours to create, but the basic form, the *temper*, the physiognomy, Spain has created for us.

From *The Virginia Quarterly Review*, Vol. 60, No. 1 (Winter 1984). © 1984 by The Virginia Quarterly Review.

Yet I wonder if even Joaquin believes form and content to be so separable. And what of the Americans, who accomplished in just over half a century a transformation of Philippine culture perhaps more spectacular than Spain managed in just over three and a half?

In 1900 the Partido Federalista, the first political party organized under American jurisdiction, had as one of its planks eventual annexation to the U.S.; and in general Filipinos so embraced American ideals that Americans found it natural to refer to them as "little brown brothers." So far the most successful Filipino fiction writer in America has been Carlos Bulosan, whose 1946 best-selling autobiography was entitled *America Is in the Heart*.

Naturally, then, many Filipino writers have long been haunted by the sense of a buried, perhaps irretrievably lost native past. In the December 1940 issue of *Philippine-American News Digest*, journalist P.C. Morante wrote:

> In myself I am often at a loss to account for the genuine native. To be sure, I have the physical quality of my race; but I feel that the composition of my soul is thoroughly soaked with the alien spirit. Of course . . . a great number of my people . . . are aware that even their virtues are borrowed and that their thinking, their dreams and their aspirations have been influenced so much by American and Spanish ways that the indigenous substance of their true being has been crushed or lost.
>
> . . . My actions and reactions, my thoughts and ideals, even my complexes and inhibitions—all this seems to revolve around a foreign pattern that is easily recognizable as intrinsically of the West.

On the other hand, N.V.M. Gonzalez writes in a recent letter:

> At the moment . . . I'm reading history and a whole ton of it. I can say with some sense of responsibility now that the Filipino today has not changed from the way he was circa 1400!

He is an optimistic man. Born in Romblon, Romblon Island, on Sept. 8, 1915, he turned before his twenties from the study of law to the life of writing, first as a staffer at Manila's *Graphic Weekly*. Some of the early years are recounted in his first novel, the autobiographical *Winds of April* (1940), and his turn to writing in "On the Eve," the story which begins his latest volume, *Mindoro and Beyond* (1980). Believing in the efficacy of storytelling and the power of the past, especially of childhood, Gonzalez has, amid heavy demands also as an influential editor and teacher, produced a body of work that has won all his country's major honors, been translated into several languages, and shown him worthy of being considered among the finest English prose stylists to have come from the Third World. He also makes guitars.

In 1974 he found an old, broken guitar in a junk shop and bought it for $1.50. His account of the incident in a newspaper article titled "Reflections on an Old Guitar" is worth quoting at length.

> Some five hours and a half later, along with a roll of paper towels, a couple of brushes, and a quart of denatured alcohol, the box began to reveal its worth.
>
> To be sure, we recognized its mark, "C.F. Martin & Co." branded on wood in 12-point caps sans serif, followed with "New York" similarly imprinted on the cross grained center lining of the back. A check with the published records of this maker showed that it was the practice of this firm to place its brand name in two places as well: on the block that joins the neck to the body; and on the back, where the heel joins the body.
>
> Our cleaning job revealed that all but the letters "C" and "N" of the firm name, and the "K" in "New York" had been scraped away . . . .
>
> "For this," said the proprietor of a music shop we visited, "I can give you a real classic guitar, and some cash besides." Forthwith, he took from the rack a signed Yairi guitar worth four hundred dollars . . . but of course, we had to decline the offer. . . .
>
> Now the responsibility of owning a gem like this one involves not so much material values but ethical and artistic ones. We decided, for example, to undertake the restoration job ourself. . . . But what were we now to do about being faithful to the guitar's original appearance.
>
> . . . What songs it must have strummed to, no one can tell, but the ivory fingerboard remains to this hour a small monument to perfection. An ambitious repairer had wanted to protect it from wear by varnishing it, which, of course, had been a blasphemy. We had to remove the coat with care, revealing a board on which minor chords had been much favored, judging by the rubbings of the fingertips on the ebony.

Now, the Philippine past is, as it were, the battered guitar. So many things are irretrievably lost, it is true; but Gonzalez' intense, patient devotion to detail and history has seemed to strip so many colonial overlays, to reveal clues—some as subtle as the rubbings of fingertips but powerful enough to impel the ethical and artistic urge to restore. Gonzalez says he has even found a transcendent reason for the Philippine peasant's seemingly easy acceptance of his landlord's usury:

> The acceptance of the practice [of doubling unpaid debts], I now seem to understand, was (and is) not traditional but transcendental. For exactly the same practice was observed in pre-Spanish Philippines, the logic of those times being this: that when a measure of rice was planted, harvest rewarded the effort at the least a hundredfold. The "dublihan" practiced then was actually generous. It is this sense of generosity that appears to have transcended time. . . . Perhaps it is the nobility of the peasantry that has allowed its members to acquiese to the practice . . . and the gentry's sense of guilt that has led it to devise other means of exploitation.

He is, as I have said, an optimistic man. Yet under the continuing scrutiny of sociology, anthropology, and history a unique—and, yes, "transcendent"—Philippine past is rapidly disclosing itself; and the Philippines even possess, after all, a somewhat respectable, if fragmented, revolutionary tradition complete with mystic overtones and fiery, colorful leaders who moved their people to stand against a multitude of foreign indignities. Gonzalez' optimism is not, in short, mere optimism. It, too, is severely tempered by that dark sense of loss and concession that haunts the best Filipino writers. But in most instances Gonzalez is able to balance cultural pessimism and personal optimism so tightly that his works are generally, though not completely, free both from the facile hope and melodramatic romanticism that otherwise plague a literature so obsessed with its people's lost identity. Furthermore, while he is a master of high drama, Gonzalez' very prose style works against the overly dramatic, the imbalanced. "Every volume since Gonzalez's first," writes the American critic Leonard Casper,

> is so noticeably underwritten that he runs the risk of being misread, of having subtleties overlooked, of leaving unmoved those readers used to bathos.

Such restraint is the product of a vision which blends detail and history with pattern and cosmos. Gonzalez' narrative style intends to deemphasize the forward-moving, the linear, in favor of a complex, often near-static time frame, a frame which seems to shimmer gently as Gonzalez moves easily, with minimal transitions, between past, present, and future, between conscious time and the less-metered times of memory, dream, hallucination, or reflection. In turn, this handling of time makes more natural the creation of confluences between the realm of myth and the minutiae of daily living. Besides its restraint and complex timing, what typically impresses the reader of Gonzalez' work first is its abundant and lovingly given detail. More than any other Philippine writer, Gonzalez concerns himself with names, with the building of houses, the catching of fish, the harvesting of rice, the sharpening of knives used in that harvest. Then in the midst of detail will often come a kind of time warp making us realize that certain facts, certain rhythms of action, somehow rise from some ancient memory, some cosmic pattern, and, more important, have the potential of connecting us to those things from which they arise.

Gonzalez' best works are thus significant ventures in mythmaking, or, more precisely, countermythmaking. For a society establishes meaning and interprets its history by dint of its myths, those signs and stories which seem to it to be immemorial; and it is the seemingly timeless, dehistoricized, depoliticized naturalness of myth which creates the illusion of naturalness in any given social order, any given history. Myth, then, is a kind of metahistory, the very premise of historical constructions. In essence, the writer who proposes really to "re-vision" history must offer us a countermyth, must select new facts, images, actions for elevation to a transcendent plain or create narrative contexts in which old material takes on new meaning. It is in countering the myths of the Philippines' irretrievably lost native past, of her people's weakness, of the near-total triumph of the foreign that Gonzalez' fiction is unique. Such countering is most beautifully realized in *A Season of Grace*, his masterpiece, and surely one of the four or five most beautiful novels to have come from the Third World.

II

The novel revolves around the contrasting of two couples who live on the island of Mindoro. One couple is Epe and Tiaga Ruda, the establishment, the supervisors, the people of means to whom others become beholden. The other couple is Doro and Sabel Agnas, poor folk who leave the Rudas' employ to seek a life for themselves on a frontier farm, or *kaingin*. Their life is hard. Crops often fail:

> There was a week when they lived on nothing but mushrooms; and there was the week of the bamboo shoots, which tasted quite

all right, pickled in vinegar that Blas Marte's wife sent over.

Still, can one go on that way? The thought was like a temptation. It said further: Leave the clearing for once! And, mouse-like, it gnawed at Sabel's mind.

Gonzalez does not at all romanticize their hard lives, yet it is impossible not to sense that, because of the sharing among the poor folk and because of their closeness to the earth, people like Doro and Sabel maintain vital connections to those elemental rhythms of life that sustain communion and make them more whole. For the Rudas, especially Tiaga, the story is different. They are *not* portrayed as villains. Rather, because they are unconnected with the earthy rhythms of planting and harvest, they also partake only superficially in real sharing with people. They are lonely, and one notices in Tiaga a growing paranoia which is accompanied by an increasingly frantic rhythm in her movements and speech. In the end, in contrast to Sabel, we also confirm the fact of Tiaga's physiological infertility as we learn, sadly, of her third miscarriage.

A Season of Grace—which consists of a prologue, epilogue, and three long, unnumbered chapters—follows the Rudas, Agnas, and others through just over one cycle of planting and harvest. Yet the feeling of time is expansive, so much so that the *Philippine Free Press* reviewer described the book as

> . . . a poem about an island—and so full of myth-making images that it recovers for Mindoro—poor island with a wondrous name —something of the mystery . . . with which the conquistadores and the early navigators saw it.

This feeling of expansive mythmaking comes largely from those things previously mentioned: Gonzalez' handling of time, his constant recourse to the memories and dreams and reflections of his characters. It comes, too, from a lyricism in the narrative voice and the speech of the Philippine peasant which laces the story with poetry. Thus the first chapter begins:

> Man and woman were walking one morning in the sun down a trail that cut across the bed of the empty river Alag.
>
> The woman carried a baby, using a hammock slung over her shoulder. The cloth was the same piece of chatcha which last night had served as her little one's blanket. The baby whimpered inside the hammock-pack: the woman couldn't seem to make him quiet. The man said:
>
> "Why don't you fix it, Sabel, so that it will not hurt?" He

wanted to add: "Is it heavy like a yoke?" But he realized that she looked pretty enough with that hammock-pack; it was quite an ornament.

"Doro," the woman said, "please have the kindness to wait for us."

Whereupon Doro stopped and looked back. Without either slowing down or hurrying, Sabel lifted her hammock-pack a little and began rubbing the back of her neck with her palm, hoping in some way perhaps to relieve the strain there.

Doro was all the more reminded of the yoke. This had been a carabao's trail. Now it was a man's trail. Ferns raised their arched fronds on all sides and a patch of cogon stood now a little way off to the right, waving bright tassels in the sun.

Or, when Sabel first arrives at a harvest site, we read:

Sabel was about to go when she saw a girl in the hut, seated in the middle of the floor. The girl's dress had been dyed with tanbark so that it was dark brown, like the thatched wall behind her.

Without any shyness, the girl asked: "You are Manang Sabel?"

Surprised, Sabel said: "Yes. How did you know my name?"

"Someone will come from over across the dry bed of the Alag, I was told. Someone with a baby, and she will be called Sabel, they said."

Sabel pondered for a moment. She liked the girl for being talkative.

In the first passage the near-Biblical tone quickly gives way to a scene of domestic friction, which in turn alternates with Doro's reflections, some selfish ("she looked pretty enough"), some which ponder the mythic yoke. We have, too, a restatement of the man-animal-plant hierarchy which Gonzalez had established early in the prologue to give us the feeling, present here, that man and animal make their way through life by the grace of the earth and its vegetation. The color of dress and thatch in the second passage suggests again the man-earth bond, but more noteworthy is the tone of the girl's reply to Sabel. That tone itself, one feels, might send Sabel searching through her memory. Indeed, she does just this shortly. For now, though, she pauses—ponders—on the verge and is quickly called back by a commonplace: she likes the girl's "talkativeness."

Such passages abound in *A Season of Grace*, and most (like the scene of a dream and lovemaking following a day of clearing the fields in chapter three) weave together the domestic and mythic, the memorial and mundane in extraordinarily beautiful and complex ways. In such a stylistic atmosphere so many images become mythmaking, become—or seem on the verge of becoming—transmuted upward into timeless signs that give meaning to history. Whether it is an object (like a coconut), an action (the weaving of buri mats), or a relation (between Filipino manual labor and American mechanical harvesters, for example), one feels in Gonzalez' work a subtle, gentle, yet monumental retooling of signs for different ends. Let us take, for example, the coconut.

For a multitude of historical, commercial, and geothermal reasons the coconut has long been associated with the Islands. My brother, Jose Enrado, was given (for reasons I could not then fathom) the nickname "Coconut Joe." And a recent TV commercial tells us that company X is bringing the coconut halfway around the world—"From the Philippines!"—as a guarantor of moist skin. In *A Season of Grace* its function is less cosmetic.

Early in the novel a coconut is found and planted, and though there are other references to it throughout, it is only near the end of the book that its full meaning becomes apparent.

> . . . [Nay Kare] was standing, her feet wet, not more than ten yards from him. The coconut she had picked up looked small in the crook of her arm. Its husk glistened more than ever now that it was out of the water, a rich dark brown that was the color of one's skin.
>
> Doro walked up to her. "Will that ever grow, Nay Kare?" he asked, although what really crossed his mind was: "What wind and wave have sent it to this shore?"
>
> "Why, yes, of course. You can ask Sabel."
>
> Her patadiong wet against her breast and hips and legs, Sabel stepped out of the water, saying: "Yes, I remember. The one you picked up last time—why, it has sprouts already, I believe. And Doro," she assured him, "we planted it at once and it grew."
>
> "Soaked in salt water as it was?" Doro could not believe her.
>
> . . ."How else do you think can coconuts go from island to island?" Nay Kare said. "Oh, well, let's be on our way."

Because so much of the book has concerned the poor folk going from clearing to clearing, island to island, working in the saltwater sweat of their brows for whatever the earth will yield, one realizes that the coconut is a metaphor for the Philippine peasant's survival and growth—but not only

that. It is a sign meant to re-vision history by joining together certain qualities of a people with certain other historical facts about that people's creation.

Except for the Negritos (themselves relatives of the natives of the
Australian bush), the Philippine people are an amalgam of travelers. A
Philippine village, in fact, is called by a name that suggests not settlement,
but journey: it is *barangay*, the name of a coconut-tough little boat on which
many arrived from Polynesia, Malaysia, Micronesia, China, the Indian
subcontinent. Philippine history, then, is shaped largely by those who arrive.
This includes the white man, too, and thus *A Season of Grace* begins with an
epigraph from *New Voyage Around the World* by the English seaman and pirate
William Dampier (1652-1715). "The 18 Day of Feb." it begins, "we
anchored at the N.W. end of the island of Mindora, in 10 Fathom-Water,
about 3 quarters of a Mile from the Shore. Mindora is a large island. . . ."

"Will that ever grow?" asks Doro. Some travelers come, plant themselves, and grow—some do not, either because they do not really plant, or
because, like the corrupt officials in *A Season of Grace* who take buri mats
from Sabel in the beginning and Clara at the end, they are flagrant robbers.
Those qualities which do spur growth Gonzalez wants to identify as the
spine of Philippine character, the essence of a genuinely native past. They
show most clearly, though certainly not without a great deal of tarnish, in the
generosity, patience, and nobility of the Philippine peasant. The coconut
becomes a mythic sign as it links the qualities of peasant life and the historical origins of Philippine society to its own immemorial travel and endurance
of the salty sea. In many quarters of the Southeast Asian world the coconut
is, of course, an already sacred sign; what Gonzalez adds to it is a new,
pointed historicity. He uses it, that is, to reshape subtly, but significantly, an
old story; and thus the fruit of the palm goes beyond even its more significant meanings, to say nothing of the way it surpasses its other familiar function as a sign of the carefree, exotic tropics, of Coconut Joes and luscious
complexions. It helps make "natural" that generosity, patience, and nobility
which makes more likely the overcoming of the hardships of travel, landing,
and growth—or, more important here, the overcoming of colonialism.

In a recent lecture at the University of Hawaii, Gonzalez speculated
that in terms of the literary imagination the Comic Rhythm might be the
sbest way for the Third World to deal with the historical circumstances of
imperialism; for the Comic Rhythm celebrates community, integration, the
overcoming of fragmenting alien spirits. *A Season of Grace* leaves the Rudas
inclining toward the Tragic Rhythm, toward loneliness and disintegration.
The poor folk, for all their faults and the often desperate straits of their lives,
incline toward the comic. In fact, the novel ends with a joke which involves
not only a sailing ship but rice, one of the book's most crucial, mythic signs.

In the epilogue Tata Pablo, the first villager we meet in the book's prologue, is slowly going blind, and his wife, Nay Rosa, searches an old almanac to find an appropriate saint to pray to:

> Nay Rosa, unused to the weight of paper in her hand, could not keep her arm from trembling. "Tiempo variable, it says," she said. "And after the first quarter of the moon, clear skies with light winds from the southwest."
>
> Tata Pablo blinked his eyes and leaned forward, turning his head a little to one side. "Louder."
>
> "I need better light," Nay Rosa said moving toward the door.
>
> "All right. Go on, though. What does it say about the southwest monsoon?"
>
> "Nothing more, it seems," Nay Rosa said. "Can I look now for a name of that saint?"
>
> "It's now a week since the batel came and loaded Epe Ruda's rajitas."
>
> "Exactly a week. Don't you think it's San Juan?"
>
> "I don't know. 'San Juan for the blind?'—that doesn't sound familiar," the old man said. "Was it a big batel?"
>
> "With two masts," said Nay Rosa. "Maybe, it's San Pablo."
>
> "It seems I can still hear the sound of the pulleys when the men hoisted up their sails," Tata Pablo said. "It was painted white?"
>
> "White, like boiled rice," Nay Rosa said, putting down the *Almanaque Panayana*. "Maybe, it's San Lorenzo."
>
> "You make me hungry—thinking of rice," Tata Pablo said. "Try another saint."

Against the failing of crops, of dreams, even of eyesight, such an attitude is strangely powerful. At its best, Gonzalez' mythmaking moves to this comic rhythm. It is one of the most steady, hopeful rhythms in Third World literature. The native culture will survive, it seems to say, and by an inner strength that antedates colonialism.

III

Until some enlightened U.S. publisher takes it on, *A Season of Grace* is available as an inexpensive import from The Cellar Bookshop (in Detroit at 18090 Wyoming). Now at least the University Press of Hawaii is making available Gonzalez's latest book, *Mindoro and Beyond: 21 Stories*. In part, the book is a retrospective collection culled from 40 years' work. It contains some of the Third World's finest short stories—"Lupo and the River," "Children of the Ash-Covered Loam," "The Sea Beyond," "On the Ferry," "The Wireless Tower," "The Tomato Game"—and Gonzalez has arranged them not only to reflect a growing range of concern (symbolized by the distance between Mindoro and the U.S.) but also to parallel his abiding interest in the act of storytelling itself. (Coincidentally—or maybe not—the stories also fall roughly in chronological order.) In the book's preface Gonzalez reproduces this passage from one of his notebooks:

> It is because of our access to storytelling that the confusions and the incomprehensible realities round and about do not overwhelm us with despair. We find in due course a way of ordering the experience we go through (as, indeed, others do), and somehow come to understanding Reality as we live it—until swamped once more by fresh confusions and perplexities. Then comes a new surge of hope, and, again for him who must give an account of how things are, a search for form.

Several of Gonzalez's characters can be taken as symbols of the artist, the storyteller. Twenty-five years ago Francisco Arcellana singled out this passage from "Lupo and the River" in order to praise Gonzalez's own craftsmanship:

> Lupo taught him [Pisco] how to work the rattan this way and that, never sacrificing pattern for strength, never losing your purpose, and yet taking care to make out of something ordinary a beautiful thing.

Significantly, Sabel, in *A Season of Grace*, is a mat maker whose habit it is to weave the word *Recuerdo* "—Remember"—into the center of her design. As she works with buri, so Gonzalez the writer can be seen working words, weaving on the warp and woof of myth and detail stories which declare to his people that there is indeed some unique past, something worth remembering.

Mindoro and Beyond, then, begins with the semiautobiographical "On the Eve," about a young man's decision to become a writer, and the book ends with an historical essay on Philippine storytelling, followed by an often whimsical glossary of Philippine terms. As "On the Eve" begins, Greg Padua is a proofreader for Commonwealth Publishing Co. His father is a salesman. Says Padua:

> As proofreader, with lines of type before my eyes, or galleys in my hand, my commitment was to the present. It is now rather easy to see things in this light. I stood for the text of the day, Father the pages of tomorrow.

As he moves toward the literary life, however, he realizes, as he says, that "I was transgressing my commitment to the present, that I was in fact making a dubious step to the future, a territory of promises. . . ." One Mr. Campo, as the editor of a company named "Commonwealth" might be expected to do, rebukes Padua's poetic ambitions. Padua quits his job, as well as his night-time study of law, and as the story ends is handing his father a folder of his short stories and poems. His father is uncomprehendingly silent, and Padua tells us: "The Chinese fiddle across the street began once more to wring its heart out. Father and I had changed places."

Very early in the story Padua had listened to that fiddle and told us:

> My untrained ear could not grasp the melody, which resembled tortured cries and yearnings; but I imagined that it told some enchanting story inspired by the exotic aroma of narra wood and the unarticulated patience of the lives round and about. . . .

It seems as if, in this 1970 story, Gonzalez was summarizing the inspiration, mission, and pattern of growth of virtually his entire literary output. The stories in *Mindoro and Beyond*, which are grouped in six sections, may in fact be seen as growing in melodic complexity and evocativeness. "On the Eve" comprises Part One. In Part Two are pieces from the late thirties, some of which are more sketches than fullbodied stories. As melodies they are simple, with a folk song-like depth and transparency. In Part Three, given the growing complexity of Gonzalez' handling of time, the stories begin to resemble a kind of frozen music. And the music darkens. One critic has pointed out that "The Sea Beyond," which ends Part Three, shows how man, though he may overcome the evil in nature, cannot overcome the evil within himself. Part Four consists of the long story "Serenade," which ends with the main character, Pilar, contemplating her new piano,

> a brooding presence that made the moment alive once more with the music that Pilar knew by heart—"Love and Devotion," "Flower Song," "Poet and Peasant"—music with which she must learn to woo the world into being less harsh and, perhaps, less rude.

(The songs here are highly appropriate to themes which span Gonzalez' entire work.) In Part Five, tensions between and within individuals begin merging more noticeably with the theme of tensions between cultures, especially the culture based more upon the Philippine peasant as opposed to one based upon the Americanized, Hispanized "city." Yet Part Five ends with "The Wireless Tower," which paradoxically images both a total breakdown of communication (the tower, a radio tower, has been struck by lightning) and a celebration of the light and dark sides of life—both personal life, and, one presumes, cultural life as well. It is by striving to understand the inextricable entanglements of light and dark, good and evil, victory and concession, that communication might one day be restored. Yet this must surely be the hardest of human tasks.

"Dear Greg" (Greg Padua?), begins "The Tomato Game," the first story in Part Six: "You must believe me when I say that I've tried again and again to write this story."

Two of the six stories in Part Six take place in America, and this setting accentuates virtually every conflict that has appeared thus far in the book. Clearly Gonzalez has had to struggle hard for the momentary victories afforded by art. "As in myth," the writer in "The Tomato Game" says,

> the signs were all over. The wooden bridge, the fork of the road, the large track all around us which earlier had been a tomato field, the rich crop as indicated by the harvesting machine to one side of the field, a menacing hulk. . . . You can see how hard I try.

This passage puts us in direct contact with Gonzalez' effort to re-vision history by creating alternate mythic possibilities. Here the mechanical harvester, so devastating to the manual labor in which Filipinos played so large a part, is reshaped into a sign of technology's inability to eliminate the human factor. It does a bad harvesting job, finally. It is also linked metaphorically to certain unscrupulous Filipinos who engage in bride-selling schemes. Their victim this time is an elderly Filipino who, though victim, rises in character above his conniving compatriots. His generosity, patience, and nobility clearly link him to those people and ancient qualities celebrated in *A Season of Grace*.

It has been Gonzalez' aim to foster such links through art; and he has realized that one of the greatest obstacles to establishing a nourishing relationship with the past is that that past is, in Robert Frost's words, so "unstoried, artless, unenhanced." Or, perhaps, it is just wrongly storied. The problem with the main character in "In the Twilight," the last story in the book, is that he has lived so long remembering a key incident in his life incorrectly. He literally has the wrong story. A fiddle player in his youth in the Philippines, he is now, in America, "Dan," a jazz saxophonist. The character through whom he inadvertently learns the truth was a Philippine guerrilla. Now he is a security guard—Union Carbide, night shift—hoping for U.S. citizenship in three years. Such transformations are jarring; they seem too forced for a story otherwise so delicately crafted. Yet such changes, especially in music, seem common among Filipinos in America. "In the Twilight" is a somber echo of "On the Eve," but even amid darkening sounds and shadows Gonzalez seems to suggest that a more accurate memory of the past would help his people define who they are as a people and thus be less prone to such far strayings and cultural pessimisms. His message is still *Recuerdo*. But facts take us only so far: we live in a world of contending *stories*, of myth and countermyth. What a writer ultimately says is, Remember *my* vision of our past. This is the great artist's privilege and obligation. "Unhappily, the spiritual welfare of this country depends upon the fate of its creative minds," wrote Van Wyck Brooks of the American situation in 1918.

> If they cannot grow and ripen, where are we going to get new ideals. . . . Discover, invent a usable past we certainly can, and that is what a vital criticism always does.

Thoughts like these reach obsessive proportions in the Third World, for there artists and critics face baldly redemptive and recreative relationships to native pasts which have been pressed so hard, sometimes so nearly annihilated, by the colonial experience. Fortunately for the Philippines, Gonzalez' vision—even in its twilight, somber hues—is strong, complex, and daringly hopeful.

ZENOBIA BAXTER MISTRI

"Seventeen Syllables": A Symbolic Haiku

In 1942, the Japanese Relocation Act incarcerated 110,000 Japanese in Poston, Arizona. Born in 1921 of Japanese immigrant parents, Hisaye Yamamoto is a Nisei and one of those who watched closely the effects of that tragic internment. Although there are books, taped reminiscences bound into collections, and a slender handful of films, there is little criticism available that examines the experience of fiction writers who may have been marked by concentration camps like Manzanar, which was the first of ten such camps. The saga of the people who suffered this indignity has been documented by writers. Michi Weglyn, for example, gives a detailed account of this experience in *Years of Infamy: The Untold Story of America's Concentration Camps*.

In the brief biographical information on Hisaye Yamamoto that she provides in *Between Mothers and Daughters* proceeding Yamamoto's short story "Seventeen Syllables," Susan Koppleman writes: "she, along with 110,000 other Japanese Americans, was subjected to relocation and imprisonment. . . . During the war, she moved to Massachusetts for a summer, but returned to camp, and then to California in 1945 where she was employed by the *Los Angeles Tribune*" (161). Confinement seems to have sensitized Yamamoto to the devastating results of a loss of control. In almost all her short stories, her central characters battle overwhelming odds. In "Relocation and Dislocation:

From *Studies in Short Fiction*, Vol. 27, No. 2 (Spring 1990). © 1990 by Newberry College.

The Writings of Hisaye Yamamoto and Wakako Yamauchi" McDonald and Newman accurately assess that she selects characters who are "hurt, who have deviated from the norm, who are grasping for some bits of beauty in their desperation. . . . All who seek but lose are of interest to Yamamoto" (28). This assessment also applies to Yamamoto's much anthologized "Seventeen Syllables." However, despite its popularity, the artistic levels in the tale, as in the others, remain unexplored. Koppleman draws attention to the fact that Yamamoto's stories have been reprinted at least twenty times in one or more of twelve anthologies since 1969. Yet Yamamoto still has not received the critical attention she merits.

Typical of a Yamamoto story, "Seventeen Syllables" offers multiple perspectives which need to be peeled back layer upon layer, for this tale simultaneously records a daughter's—Rosie's—awakening sexuality, and depicts a mother's—Tome Hayashi's—devastating annihilation. The tale's power lies in the vortex created by the mother's stepping outside her traditional Japanese Issei role of farm worker, cook, housekeeper, and wife. The narrative tensions arise out of a seemingly simple interest that Tome develops, haiku. At one level, the story depicts the cultural barrier that haiku creates and reveals among Tome, her husband, and her daughter; at another level, the tale unravels the destruction of a woman who creates independently.

To neglect Yamamoto's artistic achievement in using haiku is to bypass the deeper metaphor for separation which it suggests. To understand the subtle symbolism of haiku, one must understand the complexity of this art form: its simplicity is deceptive in depth of content and in origin. In the Introduction to the first of his four volumes entitled *Haiku*, R. H. Blyth explains that this type of poetry needs to be understood from the Zen point of view. He describes haiku as "a spiritual state of mind in which individuals are not separated from other things, instead remain identical with them while yet retaining their individuality and defining peculiarities" (iii). Obviously, neither Rosie nor Mr. Hayashi is able to understand haiku or the meaning it has for Tome. Both father and daughter lack the undiluted, intuitive understanding necessary, for haiku represents the Eastern world of religious and poetic experience. Japanese traditional roles and the American world seem to have stripped Mr. Hayashi and Rosie of the innate ability to be one and yet separate. Blyth compares the haiku experience to a kind of enlightenment in which the reader sees into the life of things.

During the three months that Tome contributes haiku to *Mainichi Shinbun*, "The Daily Newspaper," she takes the "blossoming name" of Ume Hanazono. In Japanese, the name *Ume* stands for an exquisite flowering tree which blossoms in early spring and bears fruit by the end of spring—that is, in three months. *Hanazono* means "a flower garden." Both names enfold one of the central experiences described in the story: Tome Hayashi's brief awakening into a creative independence which does not include her Japanese husband of "simple mind" or her Nisei daughter who pretends to understand Japanese because she doesn't want to disillusion her mother about the "quantity and quality" (163) of the Japanese she knows. On the other hand, *Tome* ironically signifies "good fortune," or "luck," while *Hayashi* means "woods." In the names, one sees some of the subtle shades of meaning implied in this Nisei, second generation Japanese-American, story.

The number three plays a subtle role in "Seventeen Syllables." Tome's/Ume's brief awakening lasts for *"perhaps three months"* (164; italics mine)—a *season*—as does her namesake tree, Ume, which blossoms and bears fruit in *three* months. The brief three months are echoed by the *three* line scheme—five, seven, and five syllables—used for haiku when it is translated or written in English. Haiku becomes the metaphor for Tome's separateness. After she works in the fields, keeps house, cooks, washes, and serves dinner, she becomes a significant other person; she transforms into Ume Hanazone—a poetess.

The creative pull Ume feels assumes threatening dimensions as she discusses haiku with other males. Tome steps outside her role as an insignificant other and strives for intellectual stimulation and challenges in the process of composing poetry. Essentially, haiku transforms her from a quiet wife into one who becomes in a sense a true Japanese, an "earnest muttering stranger, who often neglected speaking when spoken to and stayed busy at the parlor table as late as midnight scribbling with pencil on scratch paper . . . " (164). Mr. Hayashi now must play solitaire. The gulf between the Hayashis widens each time the family goes visiting. Her haiku makes her forget her traditional role—the submissive, passive working person—for Tome engages in comparing ecstatic notes with visiting poets while her husband entertains "the nonliterary members" (164) or looks at *Life* magazine instead of intuiting *life* through his wife's poetry as would a true lover of haiku or ukiyo-e.

Rosie's emerging womanhood parallels the three months of Tome's poetry writing. Rosie secretly meets with Jesus Carrasco, the son of the Mexican family hired for the harvest. With the first stolen kiss, he awakens her sensuality: "Once he had made her screech hideously by crossing over, while her back was turned, to place atop the tomatoes in her green-stained basket a truly monstrous, pale green worm (it had looked more like an infant snake)" (168). The phallic innuendo is hard to ignore.

Rosie is so wrapped in herself that she fails to see her mother's need for identity, creativity, and approval. Each time Ume reads a poem for approval,

Rosie's response is a refrain: "It was so much easier to say yes, yes, even when one meant no, no" (163). The "yes, yes" she says to placate her mother reflects the cultural vacuum that exists between the mother and daughter as it reflects Rosie's inability to become one with the haiku that Ume writes. However, the language barrier between the mother and daughter pales besides the growing haiku barrier between the parents.

One hot afternoon, "the hottest day of the year," when the creative pull seems to have reached breaking point, the haiku editor of the *Mainichi Shinbun* personally delivers the first-prize award that Ume wins. The Hiroshiges Mr. Kuroda brings subtly echoes the spiritual chasm between the Hayashis, as it affirms the deep relationship of oriental art to haiku. Blyth explains:

> a haiku poet may express his understanding pictorially as well as verbally. . . . It is indirect, in that the pictures he sees teach him how to look at and feel and listen to the world of nature. . . . They show him where the value and meaning of things [are], so he may say in words what the pictures say in lines, concerning that mysterious interplay of the simple and the complicated, the general and the particular. . . . The ukiyo-e of Hiroshige would have no significance, were the scenery of Japan as plain and clear in outline as they. (86)

Like haiku, Hiroshige's famous landscapes evoke emersion and must be intuited. The viewer must feel her feet in the pink clouds he paints and become one of the individuals in the sampans that float near the pines. The gap in understanding is reflected in Rosie's cold, literal description of the Horoshiges:

> Rosie thought it was a pleasant picture, which looked to have been sketched with delicate quickness. There were pink clouds, containing some graceful caligraphy, and a sea that was a pale blue except at the edges, containing four sampans with indica-tions of people in them. (173)

The entire description reflects the failure to see the mysterious interplay among life, the painting and the self. Rosie's inability to imagine the floating world of ukiyo-e or to intuit what the picture suggests reaffirms the barriers between her mother and herself as well as between the Japanese culture and herself.

In the excitement of receiving the prize, Ume takes over from Tome—

the subservient tomato packer—and entertains the illustrious Japanese visitor at tea. Once more cut out from a true understanding, Mr. Hayashi storms in, seizes the prize, takes it outside, and proceeds to smash and burn it.

After the mother and daughter watch the fire die, Tome tells her story to her daughter. "It was like a story out of the magazines. . . . Her mother, at nineteen, had come to America and married her father as an alternative to suicide" (175). At this point, the title "Seventeen Syllables" becomes meaningful. It seems to stand not only for the number of syllables in a haiku but also for the stillborn illegitimate child Tome bore *seventeen years* ago in Japan, a syllable for each silent year she lives in America. The reader then recalls the patience with which Ume had explained haiku: "See Rosie, . . . it was a *haiku*, a poem in which she must pack all her meaning into seventeen syllables only . . ." (163).

The power of this seemingly simple Nisei tale comes from several interwoven themes. The primary one reveals a cultural straitjacket in which a male dominates and destroys a gentle woman who is consumed by an urgent need to create and express herself. Moreover, the narrative suggests another possible female tragedy in Rosie's future. Rosie and Jesus' relationship harbors a potential intercultural conflict, for Jesus is not of her ethnic group or station. Rosie's romance recalls her mother's unfortunate love affair with the young Japanese who was above her social position.

The conclusion of the story echoes the cultural chasm between the mother and daughter also, for Tome asks Rosie, "Promise me you will never marry." Tome receives the same glib agreement Rosie used for haiku—the old lie—"Yes, yes, I promise" (176). Ironically, just as Tome barely understands English, Rosie scarcely understands the mother's suffocating plea. Each is a prisoner, isolated in solitary confinement. Tragically, Tome loses her second child also, this time to an alien culture which does not have an artistic spiritual intuitiveness or the same gender restrictions as the Japanese. Rejected by both husband and daughter, Ume Hanazone is destroyed, no more to be a flowering garden.

Tome's fate is played in counterpoint, as it were, in the story of Mrs. Hayano, who we are told bore four lovely daughters, each named after *one season* (again, *three* months) of the year. Haru, *spring*, is her first-born. The reader is told "something had been wrong with Mrs. Hayano ever since the birth of her first child" (164). Mrs. Hayano, who was reputed to have been the belle of her native village, moves stooped and shuffling, violently trembling, always. Mr. Hayano, we are told, is "handsome, tall, and strong" (168). So Mrs. Hayano has her brief spring like Ume/Tome and is destroyed.

What is the reader to intuit about the female role in this culture? These women blossom/create and pay the price—intense personal jeopardy or annihilation. The duration of their flowering shrinks to the length of almost a season; confined and compressed, their existences recall a sparse seventeen-syllable ephemeral haiku.

"Seventeen Syllables" remains irrevocably a woman's story. The flavor and anguish which lace it and make it powerful come from the collision of Eastern and Western values. Tome steps outside her place as child bearer, housekeeper, and farmworker when she attempts to gain control and carve an independent artistic territory for herself, and she is smothered. Rosie identifies with her American background and culture. Ironically, even in Japanese class, she entertains her friend by mimicking a series of British and American movie stars. Rosie doesn't understand Tome, nor does she understand her own roots or the Japanese language and culture.

Both the Japanese and American cultures make demands which by themselves can create intense disequilibrium. In close juxtaposition, they seem to destroy the occupants or at best leave them in the middle of the woods (Hayashi). Perhaps a letter written by Yamamoto, which Koppleman quotes in her introduction to this story, throws additional light on the power of this tale; Yamamoto speaks of the pain she feels when she thinks of her mother, who could have used a more understanding daughter (162). Yamamoto goes on to say that "Seventeen Syllables" is her mother's story, even though the details are not true. Although the Japanese and American cultures do not fuse in this tale, art and the artist do, for "Seventeen Syllables" becomes the daughter's symbolic haiku for the mother—the "yes, yes" said finally, packed with all the intuitive meaning and understanding in Zen fashion.

SHIRLEY GEOK-LIN LIM

Japanese American Women's Life Stories: Maternality in Monica Sone's Nisei Daughter and Joy Kogawa's Obasan

Asian American writers and scholars are indebted to the editors of *Aiiieeeee! An Anthology of Asian-American Writers*, who in 1975 drafted an uncompromising attack on mainstream American literary criteria and in the process introduced a generation of readers to an ethnic literature that until then was relatively unknown or believed inconsequential. Enabling an understanding of the force and value of Asian American writing, Frank Chin, Jeffrey Paul Chan, Lawson Fusao Inada, and Shawn Hsu Wong countered the stereotype of Asian American docility with their own version of Asian American empowerment. In doing so, unfortunately, they moved from ethnic to gender stereotypes and situated their approach in an explicitly masculinist position.

> The white stereotype of the acceptable and unacceptable Asian is utterly without manhood. . . . At worst, the Asian-American is contemptible because he is womanly, effeminate, devoid of all the traditionally masculine qualities of originality, daring, physical courage and creativity. The mere fact that four, out of five American-born Chinese-American writers are women reinforces this aspect of the stereotype.

From *Feminist Studies*, Vol. 16, No. 2 (Summer 1990). © 1990 by Feminist Studies, Inc.

In arguing that American racial attitudes and relations emasculate Asian American men, relegating them to ostensibly female status, these critics fail to understand the American conjunction of racist and patriarchal attitudes; instead, they appear to direct their own race/gender animus especially against Asian American women writers.

The *Aiiieeeee!* critics offer an ideal of male Asian American writing defined as social history, possessing an original force beyond the reach of any tradition. John Okada's *No-No Boy* is their idealized textual type, a text they insist on receiving as "arrogantly self-begotten." Insisting on reading Okada's novel as an original invention, however, they are also implicitly rejecting any claim to a complexity of subjectivity constituted in domains other than the sociohistorical. To delegitimate the literary criteria that privileged white mainstream writing and marginalized ethnic literature, the *Aiiieeeee!* critics set up an alternate critical hegemony for Asian American writing based on masculinist and sociological evaluation. Because they indiscriminately reject any representation of duality in Asian American literature as "debilitating" and "phony," Asian American women's writing that exceeds the boundaries of the sociological to question a single and simple definition of ethnonational identity and to reconstitute racial and gender identity through the means of language is necessarily suspect.

Elaine Kim provides a coherent account of the aesthetics of male potency and fear of castration that fuels the argument in the *Aiiieeeee!* introduction. In her analysis of the various statements issued by Frank Chin and Jeffrey Paul Chan, she points out that "what seems to anger Chan and Chin the most is that 'white America is . . . securely indifferent about us as men' and that Chinese American men have become 'the white male's dream minority . . . patient, submissive, esthetic, passive, accommodating, essentially feminine in character,' a race without 'sinful manhood.'" According to Kim, Chin "views Chinese American history as a wholesale and systematic attempt to emasculate the Chinese American male."

Focusing on Asian American women's texts to define the history and traditions that these texts embody, later critics have implicitly denied the narrowly sociopolitical approach that reads Asian American texts as separate from other literatures and as "arrogantly self-begotten." Increasingly, critics such as Amy Ling, Leslie W. Rabine, and King-Kok Cheung encourage us to read Asian American writing as located in an intertextual web, their significance for us "mothered" and influenced by earlier and later companion pieces. My reading of two Japanese American women's books, I hope, will join in suggesting the inadequacies of the critical approach exhibited in *Aiiieeeee!*, which, in its emphasis on simple identities, single plots, and clear narrative lines, allows for an easy dismissal of Asian American women's texts, characterized as they are by multiple presences, ambivalent stories, and circular and fluid narratives. My feminist reading rests on a poetics, arguably a women's poetics, that values instead of disparages ambiguities and fluid boundaries in writing. The texts I will address are Monica Sone's *Nisei Daughter* (1953) and Joy Kogawa's *Obasan* (1981). *Nisei Daughter*, while it is constructed more linearly, displays thematic ironies and contradictions in narrator's stance that indicate ambivalences in point of view. Read together with *Obasan*, each text deepens and complicates the other, demonstrating the vitality of a Japanese American literary tradition that incorporates, intertextually, the thematics of internment, maternality, race, and gender.

In *Nisei Daughter* and *Obasan*, issues of race and gender intersect in self-consciously literary ways. Both show an interest in prose experimentalism; mixing genres; crossing the boundaries of prose and poetry; combining the work of memory and history, fact, reverie, and fiction; the discourse of myth and legend (both Eastern and Western), and the discourse of bureaucracy and law. *Nisei Daughter* is an autobiography of Kazuko Itoi, a second-generation Japanese American woman who struggles through the internal, familial, and racial conflicts of finding her identity. Kazuko Itoi, anglicized as the author Monica Sone, portrays the internment traumas of Japanese Americans after the outbreak of World War II and her "development" from childhood in her family, left behind in the internment camp of Minidoka, to her assimilation into a white American mainstream. Kogawa's book, *Obasan*, is the fictionalized life story of Naomi, separated from her mother at five when her mother visits Japan and is prevented by the outbreak of the Pacific War from returning to Canada. The novel traces her family's disintegration as they and other Japanese Canadians are exiled to the Canadian interior and recounts Naomi's persistent mystification at the numerous hardships and prejudices encountered as her relatives seek to protect her through their silent submission. Her mystification, Naomi learns later, derives from her Japanese American community's silent submission to Canadian racism. Although *Obasan* is a novel, it coincides with Kogawa's life story of internment in Canada on many points. In *Obasan*, especially, instabilities in the text correspond to the themes of instabilities of race and gender identification. Kogawa's novel deliberately rewrites a body of communal stories (the infamous history of Japanese Canadian wartime detention and nuclear holocaust in Nagasaki), reweaving these old fibers into new cloths.

The interest of Sone's and Kogawa's books for us lies not only or chiefly in their discourse as social history, especially as the blurring of boundaries between fact and fiction, history and myth, poetry and prose casts doubt on their identification with social history, but also in their insistent claims to a "writerly" status. Their "life stories" demand to be read within and against a tradition (history) of written texts as much as in a specific ethnopolitical history. Their achievement, the means by which they achieve their effects, their construction as texts, rest on their manifold inter-weavings of personal and family history, political and legal documents, myth, legend, talk-story and poetry. Their significance as social documentation cannot be separated from their significance as language.

These books are, of course, grounded in a shared sociopolitical and cultural history. Monica Sone's autobiography appeared in 1953 to positive reviews. Thirty years later, Kogawa's *Obasan* addressed in fiction historical materials similar to those that *Nisei Daughter* covered autobiographically. Similarly, Jeanne Wakatsuki Houston and James D. Houston have given a nonfiction account of Wakatsuki's experiences in the Japanese American internment camp in Manzanar; and in poetry, Janice Mirikitani has eloquently written of her family's internment at Tule Lake. These different works point to the paradox ruling much Japanese American autobiographical writing. Although the autobiographical impulse seeks to express a unique life, almost in contradiction these life stories repeat a common plot of race difference and conflict with white American hegemony. They therefore come to represent something other, both more communal and more abstract than the particular life.

The apparatus of allegory modifies the autobiographer's attempt at mimesis. Frederic Jameson's reading of Third World nationalist texts as alle-gorical can be carried to a reading of many minority texts in American liter-ature. To Jameson, Third World texts, "even those which are seemingly private and invested with a properly libidinal dynamic, necessarily project a political dimension in the form of a national allegory: the story of the private individual is always an allegory of the embattled situation of the public third-world culture and society." The same can be said of Asian American texts that inevitably "project a political dimension" in their inscription of embattled ethnic identity in a repressive and homogenizing society.

Moreover, read as women's texts, these books yield fresh and forceful interpretations of mother-daughter relations, in which the break/bond of generation is intensified by the break/bond of race. The relation of mother and daughter, of course, has been central to feminist cultural theory. The works of Nancy Chodorow, Dorothy Dinnerstein, Adrienne Rich, and others have led us to new understandings of human development. Chodorow

> identifies the fostering of mothering behavior in women and the asymmetrical female and male personalities as the keys to the reproduction of gender hierarchy. Through their primary rela-tionship with their mothers, girls develop the capacity to nurture

and the desire to become mothers; boys' nurturant capacities are curtailed, in exchange for gaining the ability to function in the impersonal world of public life.

Adrienne Rich has justly pointed to the "cathexis between mother and daughter—essential, distorted, misused—[as] the great unwritten story. . . . The materials are here for the deepest mutuality and the most painful estrangement." In works by Japanese American women, such as *Nisei Daughter* and *Obasan*, engenderd by, complicating and deepening the daughter's bond with and break from the maternal origin, the essential thematics of maternity is also the story of race. In these life stories, the Japanese mother is the figure not only of maternity but also of racial consciousness. The daughters' struggles to separate from their racial origin or to recover it, given the historical context of Japanese American internment, are therefore matters of political as well as psychological urgency. Thus, although such texts force masculinist Asian American critics to come to terms with the significance of women's experience and language in women's writing, they also ask feminist critics to expand their paradigms to include the problematics of race.

Nisei Daughter and *Obasan*, the first presented as autobiography, the second as fiction, are biographically and thematically writings of American daughters born of Asian parents. These two texts illustrate how an initial action—a move to assimilate—is followed by an equal and opposite reaction, a reclamation of the culture of origin. This dialectic, connected to the rejection and reclamation of the mother, in turn entails an attitude toward that American patriarchal system responsible for the internment of Japanese Americans during World War II. The signifying difference between *Nisei Daughter* and *Obasan* lies in the presence of the Japanese mother in the former and the absence of the Japanese mother in the latter. Paradoxically, where the 1953 narrative creates the mother's Japanese presence as a problematic which in the course of political events is repressed and erased, the 1981 narrative presents the Japanese mother's absence as the problematic and the recovery of her lost identity as the means to the daughter's recovery of psychic health. The daughter's quest for the lost mother echoes the "mourning for the mother-daughter relationship" which Cathy N. Davidson and E.M. Broner find in much contemporary women's fiction. Like other American women's texts, *Obasan* especially should be read as "restoring the image of our mothers" and "embracing . . . the maternal past." The reversal of thematics between the two books parallels their generational difference. Just as a too-active Japanese presence during the Pacific War period threatens a generation's attempt to assimilate into a majority white culture, so in a different, postwar generation, one in which political "integration" has been achieved, a lost racial origin may be used to account for and represent feelings of alienation, despair, and psychic deprivation.

In *Nisei Daughter*, the first-person narrator, the nisei (second-generation Japanese American) daughter, Kazuko Itoi, begins the story with the mother's instruction: "One day when I was a happy six-year-old, I made the shocking discovery that I had Japanese blood. I was a Japanese. Mother announced this fact of life to us in a quiet, deliberate manner one Sunday afternoon" (p. 3). The mother's "announcement" moves the daughter from "amoebic bliss," the stage of pre-fall existence, to uneasiness, then "shattering" anger. The knowledge of "difference" in race, "this sudden intrusion of blood into my affairs," is significantly a maternal matter; through the mother as agent, the daughter falls from the position where "life was sweet and reasonable" to one of division and psychological deformation.

> And now Mother was telling us we were Japanese. I had always thought I was a Yankee, because after all I had been born on Occidental and Main Street. . . . I didn't see how I could be a Yankee and Japanese at the same time. It was like being born with two heads. It sounded freakish and a lot of trouble. (p. 19)

Thus early in the book, the mother is presented as destroyer of an Edenic pre-racially corrupted childhood.

The trouble or puzzle of race is foregrounded in the mother's telling. Mrs. Itoi is the absolute pole of Japanese identity. She instructs her daughter on Japanese foods (pp. 72–73), customs (p. 80), and literature (pp. 117–18). "At the end of the quiet evening she would recite to us the tanka which she had created. . . . The fogbound night/ Ever deepening in somber silence/ Tinged with chilling sadness/ Could those be ships far off at sea/ Echoing and reechoing their deep foghorns?" The mother's poem, rendered in Japanese, translated by the daughter/narrator into English, images the issei's (first-generation Japanese American) homesickness and melancholy in the transience of "ships far off at sea" hidden in fog and night. It teaches the daughter an ancient sentiment of sad resignation: "On such evenings I felt suddenly old, wondering that I could like such a melancholy poem" (p. 118). And it is this maternal poetics, inscribing racial yearning or regression, which the daughter must learn to unlearn through the experience of political violence and racial war that constitutes the internment of Japanese Americans during the period of World War II.

Immediately following the description of the mother's poem, the narrator tells us, "Gradually I learned in many other ways the terrible curse that went with having Japanese blood" (p. 118). The mother's instruction on Japanese identity is an ambiguous good. Although it is framed as the primary theme of the daughter's childhood (stories to grow up on), the narrator persistently presents the instruction as "terrible" (p. 4) The knowledge of racial difference is an internal wound. The news of the Japanese bombing of Pearl Harbor repeats the primal pain of her first initiation into her Japanese identity: "An old wound opened up again, and I found myself shrinking inwardly from my Japanese blood, the blood of an enemy" (pp. 145–46).

The declaration of war brings to a head the tensions between Japanese racial origin and American identity. The mother, usually vivacious and voluble, is "limp," "collapsed," "dazed." The break is not only between Japan and the United States or between Americans and Japanese Americans but also within the Japanese American community, specifically between generations. To the question "Do you think we'll be considered Japanese or Americans? . . . a boy replied quietly, 'We'll be Japs, same as always. But our parents are enemy aliens now, you know'" (p. 146). The teenage daughter resents the war and her mother who represents, even for her, the Japanese alien. She quarrels with the mother's defense of Japan "Discussion of politics, especially Japan versus America, had become taboo in our family for it sent tempers skyrocketing. . . . During these arguments, we had eyed each other like strangers, parents against children" (p. 148). The mother's race becomes through the intervention of war, unambivalently alien; the mother can now be distanced, like "a stranger." In this way, the daughter, without any conscious decision or overt action, separates herself from the mother's presence.

Describing the degrading violence of camp life, the narrative elides the daughter's internally violent emotions. On hearing rifles intended to control rioters, "contrarily, I felt riotous emotion mounting in my breast" (p. 170). Surrounded by barbed wire and guarded towers, "a knot of anger tightened in my breast" (p. 177). She has "burning thoughts," "quiet hysteria" (p. 178). The family moves to Camp Minidoka in Idaho and suffers through dust storms, summer heat, prairie isolation, and privation.

But although the narrative of psychological and physical oppressions reverberates, a curiously muffled tone deadens the expression of this internal violence. The muting of rebellion, anger, and other socially unacceptable although psychologically understandable responses to racial oppression is most clearly marked in the passage on Reverend Thompson's preaching. A white Christian who had served as a missionary in Japan, "our minister kept on helping us build the foundation for a new outlook." With his instruction (the white, patriarchal, countermaternal instruction), "we had begun to read more slowly and conscientiously, as if we were finding new meanings and comfort in the passages in the Bible" (p 186). The Christian instruction is non-Japanese; it moves the narrator/daughter from the untenable position of racial conflict to acceptance of the majority "outlook" and so to her acceptance by the majority of white Americans.

What takes the place of the maternal figure and culture is not the daughter's discourse but the substitution of white American discourse with its separation of body and soul and insistence on individual faith and forgiveness, a substitution which is built on denial of political and material reality. "It dawned on me that we had not been physically mistreated. . . . I had been tense and angry all my life about prejudice, real and imaginary. . . . The time had come when it was more important to examine our own souls" (p. 186). Once Christian theology has transformed political, material reality to phantasms (denying physical imprisonment and racial prejudices which formed the experiences of Japanese Americans from 1942 to 1945 and affirming soul examination in their place), the narrator/daughter is able to erase the reality of the maternal presence, her Japanese blood, and transform her identity into a phantasm of American identity. Instead of portraying the humiliations and degradations of camp imprisonment (as Mine Okubo has done in her art and Wakatsuki in her nonfiction), the author/daughter concentrates on light social humor. With her story of a wedding tea party to illustrate the cultural divisions between issei and nisei women, the narrative slides swiftly past the compulsory drafting of young nisei men into a segregated combat unit, refusing to interrogate the disingenuous figment of patriotism offered them by the War Department: "We're interested in your future. The War Department is offering you a chance to volunteer and to distinguish yourselves as Japanese-Americans in the service of your country" (p. 200). (Those nisei who did not "volunteer" were incarcerated for refusing the draft.) The narrator turns away from the racial break between Japanese and white American (a radical and more dangerous examination of racial strife in which both sides were murderously and unforgivably engaged), to a less dangerous, a comic and trivialized inconsequence, the cultural misunderstanding about social rituals between first- and second-generation Japanese Americans. The killings and internments are erased in the social chitchat of the wedding tea party.

The middle section of the narrative traces the underlying text of loss of maternal identity, that is, the gradual abandonment of the Japanese discourse, in the figures of destruction of Japanese possessions, especially language possessions.

> I gathered together my well-worn Japanese language school-
> books which I had been saving over a period of ten years with the
> thought that they might come in handy when I wanted to teach
> Japanese to my own children. I threw them into the fire and

watched them flame and shrivel into black ashes. . . . Father piled
up his translated Japanese volumes of philosophy and religion
and carted them reluctantly to the basement. Mother had the
most to eliminate, with her scrapbooks of poems cut out from
newspapers and magazines, and her private collection of old
Japanese classic literature. (pp. 155–56).

Finally, even the mother's Bible printed in Japanese and the *Manyoshu*, a
Japanese classic collection of women's poems, are surrendered to the central
receiving stations. Although the mother argues, "there isn't one subversive
word in it," the American policy of destruction of Japanese writing rests on the
acknowledgment of the power invested in a different language to subvert
American identity, a knowledge which the six-year-old daughter had learned at
the beginning of the book. Instructively, it is the mother who protests against
the futile loss of these books and it is the mother who is associated with poetry,
the language of unrepressed consciousness. The mother's presence (her
"terrible" Japaneseness) is thus attenuated in the final third of the book.

Nisei Daughter is, by fact of its early appearance, a mother text;
however, it is unconscious of the deepest ironies in its narration of race
conflicts. The narrative constitutes a racial polarity between the Japanese and
the white American. The Japanese element is identified with a matriarchal
figure, the mother, the Japanese language and literature, the insider of the
family unit and Japanese community. The American element is identified
with the English language, which the mother misuses to the daughter's
shame (pp. 49–51), the outside society of school and playmates, the patriarchal law of discrimination and internment created by white politicians and
soldiers such as Attorney General Biddle and General DeWitt. The
narrator/daughter lives these conflicts in her life, seeing the destruction of
the mother's language possessions and the internment of her parents as a
punishment for their Japanese identity. Because of her nonalien status, she is
permitted finally to escape their imprisonment and to enter a college in the
Midwest. Her move figures the repression of one side of the polarity. As she
leaves Camp Minidoka to return to Wendell College, her mother in a devastating admission of defeat in her attempt to instruct her children into racial
pride and awareness, formally apologizes to her for her Japanese identity:
"We felt terribly bad about being your Japanese parents" (p. 236).

By this point, the autobiographical heroine has emerged from the
mother's language and instructional world into a white college and working
world. She has lived with the Richardsons and Mrs. Ashford, who offers her
an alternate maternal figure, a nurturant white mother who provides her
with "a wealth of enchanting memories which I could conjure up at the

thought of Wendell." When she is rejected by a sorority because of her Japanese origin, she excuses their action: "It took moral honesty to have come in the spirit which they did" (pp. 227–28). The narrator's ability to rationalize the white Americans' overt acts of discrimination—"national restrictions based on our membership"—(p. 227), like the mother's apology, demonstrates the utter defeat of the Japanese self, a defeat in which anger is repressed and submission to and guilty acceptance of the racial Other's point of view are total.

The reconciliation of Japanese and American in the book's conclusion evades recognition of the erasure of Japanese pride and identity. "I don't resent my Japanese blood anymore," the daughter reassures the mother. "It's really nice to be born into two cultures, like getting a real bargain in life, two for the price of one" (p. 236). The terror of discovery of racial difference with which the book opens, the humiliation and horror of internment, and the sociopolitical injustices bred out of racial difference are collapsed in the conclusion to the single weak adjective "nice." The psychological, economic, and cultural price the family has had to pay for being Japanese is distorted here to "a bargain . . . two for the price of one."

The narrative has consistently shown the exorbitant cost of twoness for one price, of a double identity in a repressive, racially homogenizing system. The daughter admits: "I used to think of the government as a paternal organization. When it failed me, I felt bitter and sullen. Now I know I'm just as responsible as the men in Washington for its actions. Somehow it all makes me feel much more at home in America." The daughter is able to give up her strangeness, to "feel at home," only by giving up the mother's discourse and adopting the discourse of the paternal organization. She is now in the same (patriarchal) system as "the men in Washington" and speaks in the same language of democratic and individual idealism. "Her [America's] ideas and ideals of democracy . . . her very existence depends on the faith and moral responsibilities of each individual" (p. 237). The book concludes with the narrator, "still with my Oriental eyes," although the eyes are now restricted to mere physical significance, "going back into [American] mainstream . . . with an entirely different outlook" (p. 238). The conclusion appears unequivocal: "The Japanese and the American parts of me were now blended into one." But the price of this oneness of vision, the outlook of the American mainstream, is the repression of that part of the narrator's identity represented by her Japanese mother. Ironically, but not intentionally so, the book ends with the lesson of one for the price of two: the mother's story of a different race is burned, confiscated, imprisoned, and finally engulfed in the mainstream.

Nisei Daughter is clearly an antecedent for *Obasan*, which begins with the narrative of the psychic costs of such repression of the maternal and racial figure. The epigraph from the Bible which begins the novel introduces the ironizing discourse which interrogates the course of submission and assimilation to white Christian ideology offered in *Nisei Daughter* as the political good: "To him that overcometh will I give to eat of the hidden manna and will give him a white stone and in the stone a new name written." Read in one way, the passage warns against Christian ideology. The overt message of eternal life (i.e., manna, new name) is also the covert message of death (white stone). Read another way, it appropriates Christian imagery to urge resistance and to prophesy the forging of a new identity. The epigraphic page picks up the thread of subversion in the biblical passage. The trope of silence, central to the text, elaborates itself in two forms of nonspeech: "There is a silence that cannot speak. There is a silence that will not speak." The silence that cannot speak, we learn later, belongs to Naomi's Japanese aunt, Obasan. But it is the maternal silence, the willed absence of speech associated with Naomi's absent mother, against which the daughter must struggle most. The first silence arises from powerlessness, the second, more willful, from denial. Contrasted to these disabling silences is that of "speaking dreams," "that amniotic deep" from which "the speech that frees comes forth." The first-person narrator who hears the speech of speaking dreams learns that, paradoxically, only by embracing "its absence" can she "attend its voice."

What is signified by the indeterminate "its" in the passage? Whose absence must be embraced? How is this absence related to the liberating speech coming from the "amniotic deep" (echoing Sone's image of "amoebic bliss" in her opening chapter, and, perhaps not coincidentally, Rich's term of "amniotic bliss" to describe the condition of mother-daughter bonding before birth)? The clue lies in "amniotic" and "absence." In the course of the novel we learn that the absent figure is the mother and that the silence of impotence and denial belongs to her and those Japanese Americans who for a generation kept the truth of the mother's death in the Nagasaki holocaust from her daughter. The epigraph introduces the major figures and configurations in the novel; the figure of despair ("There is no reply"), the figure of death ("the sealed vault with its cold icon"), and the figure of hope ("unless the stone bursts with telling, unless the seed flowers with speech"). The first-person narrator/daughter, Naomi, gives voice to the silence. In the tracing of that silence, in the unriddling of mystery of the mother's absent discourse, a discourse of absence, the narrator/protagonist is "telling" and transforming silence to speech, absence to presence. The untold story of Japanese Canadian despair is made hopeful in the telling.

Obasan begins where *Nisei Daughter* ends, with a Japanese Canadian daughter in search of a silenced, lost, and forgotten Japanese mother, and traces the daughter's reconstruction of this absent racial/maternal figure.

Countering the repressions of *Nisei Daughter*, *Obasan*, written three decades later, insists on the interrelations between the subject of the "I" and the language through which that subject is expressed and bases the thematics of recuperation of a lost mother in the thematics of the recuperative powers of language itself. In *Obasan*, the writing project is inseparable from the reconstruction of the maternal. The figure of the daughter is also the figure of the writer figuring her self. The images of writer, narrator, speaker, and protagonist collapse into a series of intimately related "I"s, all creating, as Janet Varner Gunn has said of the autobiographical genre, a trompe l'oeil effect of depth. *Obasan*, therefore, is both and more than a work of social realism. Using elements from her own life story as well as letters, diaries, and historical documents, Kogawa chose to write a fiction which impersonates the discourse of autobiography while at the same time she has masked the genre of autobiography through the liberating effects of poetic language. The integration of the thematics of the maternal with the text's structure is modernistic and totalizing. The subject of the novel can only be produced in the language of the novel, giving to the work an integrity of depth which distinguishes it from the earlier book.

The novel presents itself on one level as a mystery story, a historical and psychological riddle. Seeking to unravel the mystery of her mother's disappearance at the beginning of the Pacific War, Naomi must also unravel the mystery of the disappearance of a whole community of Japanese Canadians who uncomplainingly accepted the Government's Orders-in-Council to exile them from their West coast homes to the Canadian interior, the story of "the Issei and the Nisei and the Sansei, the Japanese Canadians. We disappear into the future undemanding as dew" (p. 112). The lost mother is also the figure for displacement of an entire people.

The first chapter opens on the scene of narrator/protagonist as mystified interrogator: "What is the matter, Uncle? . . . why do we come here (to the coulee) every year?" (p. 3). To Uncle Isamu, Naomi was too young (to be told) at eighteen, and too young still at thirty-six. With Uncle Isamu's death, Naomi returns to the house of her childhood, and through flashbacks and with the documents given to her by Aunt Emily finally proceeds to unriddle her family's story. "Some families grow on and on through the centuries, hardy and visible and procreative. Others disappear from the earth without a whimper" (p. 21). The central mystery of Naomi's family, prefiguring the deaths of her uncle, her father, her grandparents, even the childless conditions of her aunts Emily and Obasan, her brother Stephen and herself, is "Why did my mother not return? After all these years, I find myself wondering, but with the dullness of expecting no response" (p. 26).

Obasan comes from the obverse side, the maternal injunction against telling the story of race, which can therefore be figured only in the trope of silence. The mother/daughter relationship is constituted in silence, in the overflowing absence of the mother whose presence is acknowledged in the oppressive presence of silence as a central trope in the text. "'Please tell me about Mother,' I would say as a child to Obasan. I was consumed by the question. Devoured alive. But Obasan gave me no anwers" (p. 26). The subject/interrogator is herself "devoured"—destroyed by the question of her lost mother. The surrogate mother's inability to rescue the child from the "consuming" question prepares the reader for the discovery of the real mother's complicity in her daughter's mystifications, the Silent Mother whose final words were "Do not tell . . ." (p. 242).

Other critics have noted that silence forms a pervasive and powerful thematics in minority literature. The introduction to *Aiiieeeee!* argues that "one measure of white racism is the silence of the minority race and the amount of white energy necessary to maintain or increase that silence. . . . Silence has been a part of the price of the Chinese American's survival in a country that hated him" (p. 9). King-Kok Cheung points out that "silence runs even deeper in the work of minority women. . . . Some of these women are, moreover, thrice muted, on account of sexism, racism, and a 'tongue-lessness' that results from prohibition or language barriers" (p. 162). In *Obasan*, the minority thematics of silence (figured in Obasan, the Japanese bride who barely speaks English, and the mother who had returned to Japan, the mother country, to visit her mother, Naomi's grandmother) is countered by the logocentric energy figured in the opposing character of the Canadian-born Aunt Emily. Above all, it is successfully countered by the daughter's discourse, her persistent interrogative stance and attention to the "voice" which "comes forth from that amniotic deep." The fiction's structure parallels its plot, from amnesia and aphasia (Obasan), to logocentric documentation (Emily) to the centrality of the daughter's discourse, from silence to fact to poetry.

The two aunts typify two possibilities for racial response. Obasan, the Japanese aunt, brought over from Japan as a bride, Naomi's surrogate mother, speaks in fragments of English. But Naomi, the narrator, knows "the language of her grief is silence. She has learned it well, its idioms, its nuances. Over the years, silence within her small body has grown large and powerful" (p. 14). She is the figure of resisting silence: "The greater my urgency to know, the thicker her silences have always been. No prodding will elicit clues" (p. 45). She is also the figure of deliberately obfuscating silence, the silence whose obverse side of the protective shield is repression. Thus, when Stephen, Naomi's older brother, infected with tuberculosis, is shunned by the community, the puzzled Naomi asks, "Why was there no speaking?" To which Obasan replies, "There was nothing to speak of perhaps" (p. 164).

Ironically, Obasan "never discards anything." "There are some indescribable items in the dark recesses of the fridge that never see the light of day." It is because, like the putrified food, the hidden memories are so painful and horrible that she refuses questions. "If it is not seen, it does not horrify. What is past recall is past pain. Questions from all these papers, questions referring to turbulence in the past, are an unnecessary upheaval . . ." (p. 45). Unsurprisingly, therefore, to Obasan, "Everything" has become "forgetfulness" (p. 26).

In Obasan's house, Naomi is confronted with her own repressed identity:

> But we're trapped, Obasan and I, by our memories of the dead—
> all our dead—those who refuse to bury themselves. . . . When I
> least expect it, memory comes skittering out of the dark, spinning
> and netting the air, ready to snap me up and ensnare me in old
> and complex puzzles. . . . (p. 26).

Memory is figured as a giant predatory web and the human consciousness as a fearful thing which must negotiate its escape from the trap of memory. The narrative weaves Naomi's life story in a series of flashbacks whose constant theme is the tension between memory and forgetting. What saves memory from forgetting is speech. As Naomi tells the story, pushed on by Emily's insistence to remember, her story is also a meditation on the temptation of silences, on her education into silence and forgetting and her struggle against them.

Opposed to Obasan's passive, suffering silence, Aunt Emily raised in Canada, is the activist keeper of memories. Aunt Emily is a crusader. She gives Naomi the letters, diaries, records, memos and newspaper clippings which she has preserved for the last three decades for Naomi's "education" (p. 188). Where the Japanese maternal figure instructs in silence, the Canadian ancestress insists on the health-giving property of speech: "'You have to remember,' aunt Emily said. 'You are your history. If you cut it off you're an amputee. Don't deny the past. Remember everything. If you're bitter, be bitter. Cry it out! Scream! Denial is gangrene'" (p. 50). Aunt Emily appears to be the positivist occidental inscription to Obasan's negative oriental circumscription: "One lives in sound the other in stone. Obasan's language remains deeply underground but Aunt Emily, BA, MA, is a word warrior" (p. 32).

The narrator, however, does not privilege Aunt Emily as the affirmative answer to Obasan's negating silence. After all, through the decades of physical isolation, deprivation, and emotional hurt that the children experienced in the Canadian prairies, it is Obasan, rather than Emily, who has "mothered" them. Naomi ironically sees Aunt Emily's belief in documentation of fact as a limited and ineffectual mode: "Elsewhere, people like Aunt Emily clack away at their typewriters, spreading words like buckshot, aiming at the shadow in the sky. . . . But what good they do, I do not know. . . . They do not touch us where we are planted in Alberta" (pp. 188–89). Naomi mediates between the sociopolitical documentation figured in Aunt Emily's character and the reader's reading of these "nonfictional" texts, serving to ironize the sociopolitical references as well as paradoxically to multiply their effects. Against Aunt Emily's energetic indignation, Naomi is "curiously numb." Their interaction activates the dialogic quality of the fiction's sociopolitical materials. To Naomi, "People who talk about their victimization make me uncomfortable. It's as if they use their suffering as weapons or badges of some kind." To activist Aunt Emily, "A lot of academic talk just immobilizes the oppressed and maintains oppressors in their positions of power" (pp. 34–35). If Naomi is the question to Obasan's silence, Emily is the fact to Naomi's imagination. The opposition between Obasan and Emily is that of silence and fact, but the narrative does not rest on such dualisms. To heal herself, Naomi has to go beyond both modes of language, the language of recessive silence and of sociopolitical fact.

A third response to loss of origin (to racial forgetfulness and racial death brought on by political violence) is the Christian route of forgiveness (the path taken by Sone's protagonist). Unlike Sone's autobiography, however, *Obasan* carries a bitter critique of Christian discourse. The images offered in the use of biblical language are contextually "ironized" and depleted of their significance. In one instance, the narrative flashes back to a point in the internment experience when Naomi's family is broken up yet again and sent off on the government's orders to two different camps—her uncle, aunt, and the children to Kaslo, and her father to New Denver. The reason for the separation, and the separation itself, is not told to the uncomprehending Naomi/child who lives it as she has done all the previous upheavals in miserable un-understanding. The separation is marked by the prayers of the Anglican minister, Nakayama-sensei, who prays to "Almighty God, unto whom all hearts be open, all desires known and from whom no secrets are hid" (p. 175). The patriarchal God with his fantastic ability to "know" all is implicitly contrasted to the suffering Japanese Canadians whose confused fates are dictated by an incomprehensible and patently unfair government. The complicity between the Christian God and the Canadian government is strongly indicted here. To the children, the Christian service of consolation is undercut by the pathos of the accidental destruction of their mother's favorite "Silver Threads among the Gold" record. When the pastor tells the family, "'We will not abandon one another. We will meet again,'" his Christian consolation denies and underlines the reality of the family's disintegration. To Naomi, therefore, the familiar Christian rhetoric is only meaningless sound: "the meaning of the words is unknown" (p. 177).

Similarly, at the novel's climax when the riddle of the mother's disappearance is revealed, the narrator rejects the minister's consolations to listen to a more primary message. As the minister speaks of "Love," Naomi stands up "abruptly and leave[s] the room." When she returns, the minister says the Lord's Prayer and preaches the Christian doctrine of forgiveness. But Naomi is "not thinking of forgiveness." As the man's voice "grows . . . indistinct," the narrator is "listening and listening to the silent earth and the silent sky as I have done all my life" (p. 240). This listening to silent earth and sky ("as I have done all my life"), with the knowledge of her mother's death, is now transformed to a listening to the mother.

The following chapter (38) constructs a meditation on that Silent Mother's discourse. It is a powerfully moving, poetic passage which weaves the paradoxes of absence and presence, loss and recovery, to conclude in an emotional, internal reconciliation. The chapter begins with the figure of the mother, who remains voiceless. It charts the narrator's resentment of this martyred figure whose injunction against speech, intended to protect, had instead so wounded her children: "You pilot your powerful voicelessness over the ocean and across the mountain, straight as a missile to our hut. . . . You wish to protect us with lies, but the camouflage does not hide your cries" (p. 242).

The daughter's new knowledge of her mother's death enables her to imagine her mother's final sufferings and in imagination empowers her to possess her mother once again. "Young Mother at Nagasaki, am I not also there?" (p. 242). The adult Naomi, acknowledging the damage done by the mother's silence, describes the child/Naomi as suffering "a double wound. The child is forever unable to speak. The child forever fears to tell." But as an adult empowered with knowledge long kept secret from her and with enabling speech, the narrator/Naomi is able to "know" the mother's presence. "I am thinking that for a child there is no presence without flesh. But perhaps it is because I am no longer a child I can know your presence though you are not here" (p. 243). Naomi's knowing "presence though you are not here" is achieved through imagination, which is liberated through telling.

The imaginative apprehension of the lost mother can only be carried out by the adult daughter. The reclamation of racial origin can only occur in the realm of imagination. Through Naomi, the reader critiques the inadequacies of the Japanese-identified and Canadian-identified modes of discourse (Obasan's evasions and silences and Aunt Emily's memos and factual documentation), as well as the Christian rhetoric of patriarchal omni-science and submission. The novel dramatizes the emergence of the daughter's imagination/speech, the "voice" from "that amniotic deep," to reconcile contrary truths too painful and disjunctive to be borne otherwise, and so to find her own "lifelong song" (p. 246). What we hear finally is Naomi's own voice, freed at last through knowledge, coming from the breaking of silence, and leading to an internal reconciliation with the absent mother. Thus, the psychological drama thematizes the daughter's embracing of "absence" as the reconstruction of the maternal and racial figure. In rescuing/writing her maternal and racial past, the narrator/protagonist has rescued/written herself.

The novel is thus dense with dream language, for the work of memory is best expressed in the language of dreams. "The memories are dream images" (p. 112), the narrator/protagonist tells us at one point. The child's first separation from her mother, when she hides her experience of abuse by an elderly white neighbor from her, is imaged in "childhood dreams [when] the mountain yawns apart as the chasm spreads" (p. 65). Thus, also, in responding to Emily's urging to remember, "You are your history," the narrator finds in "the caverns of my mind . . . a collage of images—sombre paintings, a fireplace and a mantel clock with a heavy key like a small metal bird that fits in my palm" (p. 50). The initial movement toward recon-structing her lost childhood is imaged in the clock, recorder of time, and the key that fits in her palm like a bird, a winged access to time. Numerous dreams interrupt the narrative, suggesting that the experience of Japanese Canadian dislocation in the 1940s and 1950s, that forms the basic narrative action, shares the surrealistic and arbitrary nature of dreams.

Similarly, throughout the novel, the language of imagery and dream is balanced and edged by a sociopolitical horizon, provided by Emily's mate-rials and by the history of displacement on which the fiction is solidly based. Chapter twenty-two is an excellent example of dream discourse, the images produced, one can argue in Julia Kristeva's terms, when there is the eruption of the semiotic into the symbolic. If, as Kristeva argues, the semiotic is situ-ated in a preverbal locus when the child is still bound up in the mother's body, then dream images are the closest approximation to speech from "that amniotic deep" that the prologue apostrophizes. Naomi is in a hospital, recovering from a near-fatal drowning: "I am in a hospital. Father is in a hospital. A chicken is in a hospital. Father is a chicken is a dream that I am in a hospital . . ." (p. 150). The language, thick with images of death and inex-plicable connections, conveys Naomi's emotional misery and mystification. Naomi, already muted by events ("Can't read. Can't talk. What's the good of you?" someone asks her [p. 145]), has mostly questions in mind.

The daughter's quest/ion for her lost mother is also the political quest/ion that the novel explores. What happened to Japanese Canadians between 1941 and even after the Pacific War ended? The excerpt from the memorandum sent by the Co-Operative Committee on Japanese-Canadians on April 1946, a document providing a critical interpretation of Japanese Canadian internment, that concludes the novel, underlines the author's political intentions. Simultaneously, the text inscribes the narrative of the recuperation of the lost mother, which is also an interrogation of Japanese Canadian history, a narrative inseparable from a thematics of the recuperative powers of the imagination. If, for the daughter, "Gentle Mother, we were lost together in our silences. Our wordlessness was our mutual destruction" (p. 243), then the project of memory and writing is also the project of rescuing race history from "wordlessness" and of healing through poetic language itself the psychosocial wounds caused by the internment and dispersal of Japanese Canadian families under the Orders-in-Council.

In its emphasis on the mother's presence, constituted in her absence, *Obasan* continues *Nisei Daughter*'s reflections on the daughter/mother dyad. But where the (mother) text, *Nisei Daughter*, witnesses the erasure of the maternal/racial presence to allow the daughter to inhabit an ostensibly seamless, assimilative society, the following (daughter) text, *Obasan*, reinscribes the original presence. The daughter text recreates the Japanese mother, destroyed by a racist patriarchal system, which the elder Japanese American autobiography had hoped to leave behind.

With the discovery/recovery of the "Young Mother of Nagasaki," the narrative voice finally becomes an affirmative voice. In the poetic voice, the speaking subject celebrates the most personal of human bonds, and it is this childmother bond that then functions as the trope for the public bond of self and race. The presence of this poetic language in the novel reorders the other genres of writing (and memory) and gives to the expression of racial memory the power of the semiotic. As Kristeva uses the term, we see the semiotic working in *Obasan* in the way that "repressed consciousness"—all that is left out of Obasan's silences and Emily's documents—irrupts and disturbs the narrative. The semiotic is what the narrator appeals to in her reference to "speaking silence" in the prologue, silence that bears eloquent testimony and speech that recreates the experience of such silence. The novel encompasses and moves through the stages of muteness or aphasia (Obasan's character), logocentric documentation (Emily's character), and a speaking voice (the narrator's poetic voice). The fiction therefore enacts the movement of the daughter's marginal discourse into a position of centrality, placing the subjectivities of an Aunt Aya and Aunt Emily into question. The power of its message is also the power of its language, which shows this daughter's subjectivity in process.

Obasan reconfigures Japanese American literary traditions. Read as part of a body of Asian American women's writing, it announces the full emergence of a group of writers, doubly marginalized by race and gender but now in possession of its own themes and stylistics. As a distinctive corpus, Asian American women's writing goes back only to the early twentieth century with the life stories of elite Asian women living in the United States. But writers such as Maxine Hong Kingston, Joy Kogawa, Bharati Mukherjee, Hualing Nieh, Wendy Law-Yone, Cathy Song, Amy Tan, and others collectively are creating a body of literature that inscribes as central the experience of Asian American women in a society in which the Asian American is still the model, because invisible, minority.

ELAINE H. KIM

Carlos Bulosan: A Filipino American Community Portrait

Carlos Bulosan was born in a small village in the Philippine Islands in the same year as Younghill Kang. Like Kang, he sought entry into American life and, like him, was often frustrated and disappointed. It was Kang's writings, as a matter of fact, that encouraged Bulosan to produce his own books:

> . . . it was his indomitable courage that rekindled in me a fire of hope.
>
> Why could not I succeed as Younghill Kang had? He had come from a family of scholars and had gone to an American university—but is he not an Oriental like myself? Was there an Oriental without education who had become a writer in America? If there was one, maybe I could do it too!

But the similarities between the two men are not nearly as important as the differences. Kang was an aristocrat of sorts, certainly a man of letters. Bulosan was from a poor peasant family. While Kang writes of his native Korea as an individual rebelling against a land offering little opportunity to the free spirit he considered himself to be, Bulosan remains keenly aware of what feudal and colonial practices—sharecropping, land seizure, and exploitation of peasants by church and absentee landlordism—have done to

From *Asian American Literature: An Introduction to the Writings and Their Social Context.* © 1982 by Temple University.

his motherland. For Kang, the homeland is the "planet of death" from which he must flee to survive; for Bulosan, memories of the Islands never cease to offer inspiration for a continued struggle for a better future. Where Kang speaks chiefly for himself and the members of his elite, Bulosan consciously strives to give voice to thousands of agricultural and menial laborers of Asian America:

> What impelled me to write? The answer is—my grand dream of equality among men and freedom for all. To give literate voice to the voiceless one hundred thousand Filipinos in the United States, Hawaii, and Alaska. Above all and ultimately, to translate the desires and aspirations of the whole Filipino people in the Philippines and abroad in terms relevant to contemporary history.

Bulosan shares with Kang a "gigantic dream to know all America." But Kang's desire is to gain personal admission into the existing charmed circle, while Bulosan wants to contribute towards the fulfillment of America's promise of democracy and equality. Therefore, while Kang's narrator moves ever farther away from his own exiled compatriots, Bulosan's faith in the working man and in justice for the exploited as the key to American fulfillment turns him towards fellow Filipinos, since true democracy in America would have to mean acceptance of Filipinos into the pattern of American life.

> We must be united in the effort to make an America in which our people can find happiness. . . . We are all Americans that have toiled and suffered and known oppression and defeat, from the first Indian that offered peace in Manhattan to the last Filipino pea pickers. . . . America is in the hearts of men that died for freedom. . . . America is a prophecy of a new society of men. . . . America is also the nameless foreigner, the homeless refugee, the hungry boy begging for a job and the black body dangling on a tree. America is the illiterate immigrant who is ashamed that the world of books and intellectual opportunities is closed to him. . . . All of us, from the first Adams to the last Filipino, native born or alien, educated or illiterate—*we are America*!

There had been Filipino characters in the writings of Peter B. Kyne, Rupert Hughes, William Saroyan, and John Fante, although they were never as grotesquely omnipresent in American culture as Chinese and

Japanese caricatures had been. Bulosan believed that he would be best able to portray "Filipinos as human beings."

Bulosan became one of the best-known Filipinos in the Western world. A prolific writer, his published works include poetry, fiction, and essays. Within two years after his arrival in Seattle in 1930 at the age of sixteen, Bulosan had published several poems in poetry magazines. According to his brother Aurelio, as early as 1932 he was one of two Filipinos listed in *Who's Who*; the other was Carlos Romulo. By 1940, Bulosan had been published in journals such as *Poetry*, the *Lyric*, *Frontier* and *Midland*, the *Tramp*, and *Voices*. But it was during the war years that he attracted nationwide attention for his literary efforts: *Letter from America* (1942), *The Voice of Bataan* (1944), *Laughter of My Father* (1944; a collection of short stories first serialized in the *New Yorker*), *The Dark People* (1944), and *America Is in the Heart* (1946), the "autobiography" that has been considered his key work. Bulosan's book of stories about the Philippines, *Laughter of My Father*, was broadcast to the American armed forces around the world during the war in an attempt to encourage sympathy for American allies in the Pacific. His essay, "Freedom from Want," in the *Saturday Evening Post* (March 6, 1943), which had been inspired by President Franklin D. Roosevelt's January 1941 speech on the "Four Freedoms," was illustrated by Norman Rockwell and displayed in the examination room of the Federal Building in San Francisco as an example of an immigrant's faith in American democracy. *America Is in the Heart*, which emphasized the promise of democracy against fascism, was translated and sold in Sweden, Denmark, Italy, and Yugoslavia.

By 1947, Bulosan was recognized as one of the most prolific writers in America. His face appeared on covers of national magazines. *Look* hailed *America Is in the Heart* as one of the fifty most important American books ever published.

Bulosan's popularity waxed and waned with the political climate. Carey McWilliams notes that during the war, when Bulosan's reputation was at its apex, "this country was quite Philippine-conscious; the word 'Bataan' enjoyed a splendid resonance. . . . Most Americans seemed to be touched by the loyalty of the Filipinos who in turn, seemed to be grateful to us for helping them." But the final decade of Bulosan's life was a decline into poverty, alcohol, loneliness, and obscurity. Too frail and weak to work at strenuous labor, he had undergone eleven operations, some for lung lesions and others for leg cancers, before he died in 1956. One kneecap had been removed, and he walked with great difficulty. He drank heavily, especially with the white woman who lived with him for five years and had left him before he died. Finally, he collapsed in a Seattle street and apparently died of exposure.

According to Norman Jayo, Bulosan was filled with a sense of fore-boding and despair after the bombing of Hiroshima. He feared that the human race was entering a new, atomic, and nuclear era which he and his fellow travellers might be unable to "cope with." Another factor that contributed to his decline was a plagiarism charge brought against him late in 1946 by Guido D'Agostino, who accused Bulosan of copying his "The Dream of Angelo Zara" (*Story* magazine and *The Best American Short Stories of 1945*) and publishing it in the *New Yorker* under the title "The End of the War" (1944). Although the case was settled out of court and he was posthu-mously vindicated by the *New Yorker* editors, the publicity aroused by the case was extremely damaging to Bulosan, who subsequently had difficulty finding anyone to publish his writings. Also disheartening to him was the adverse criticism he was subject to from intellectuals in the Philippines, many of whom gloated over the plagiarism case, redbaited him during the cold war period, and delighted in pointing out the various inconsistencies in his auto-biography. They assailed him for exaggeration, pointing out discrepancies between representations in the book and the actual facts of his life.

Because of *America Is in the Heart*, for example, Bulosan is believed to have been a menial laborer who arrived in America illiterate and who educated himself in a convalescent hospital. This is only partially true. Bulosan has been described as "an outstanding child-man," artistic, sensitive, and driven by loneliness and an intense desire "to make others happy":

> A tiny person with a limp, with an exquisite face, almost facially beautiful, with gleaming teeth and lovely brown eyes, shy, generous, terribly poor, terribly exiled in California, adoring Caucasian women, sartorially exquisite, always laughing through a face that masked tragedy. A Filipino patriot, a touch of the melodramatic about him, given to telling wildly improbable stories about himself, disappearing from Southern California for months at a time, probably to work in a Seattle or Alaska cannery, showing up finally at my home with some touching gift, a book of poems, a box of Filipino candy. . . . If I were a good Christian, I think I might label him a saint, for he radiated kindness and gentleness.

The son of a small farmer in Central Luzon, Bulosan had almost completed secondary school in the Philippines before he accumulated enough money for the steerage passage to follow his brothers, Aurelio and Jose, who had left for America two years previously. Bulosan had already shown interest and ability in writing in high school, where he worked on the school literary journal. After he was admitted as a tuberculosis patient at Los Angeles County Hospital in 1936, he was befriended by two liberal young literary women, and, during the two years he spent convalescing, he read a book a day, he says, from among the various literature classics brought to him by Dorothy Babb. To this extent, he was self-educated.

Unlike the narrator of *America Is in the Heart*, Bulosan did not work for extended periods of time in the fields and canneries. From the beginning, his health was fragile, and one of his legs was two inches shorter than the other. Barred like other members of his race from all but the most menial labor and barred from that by his disability, Bulosan did undertake occasional work as a dishwasher or bakery employee, but he made his living largely from literary and union activities and was supported financially by friends and his brother Aurelio. When Bulosan met labor union leader Chris Mensalvas, who is represented in *America Is in the Heart* as Jose, and other Filipinos who were trying to organize Filipino cannery and packing-house workers during the Depression, Mensalvas encouraged Bulosan to write for the union papers. For a time, he edited a cannery workers' union publication. Bulosan helped found the UCAPAWA (United Cannery and Packing House Workers of America) between 1934 and 1938, but he was a writer rather than a cannery or packing-house worker. Mensalvas had arranged to have him hired as a UCAPAWA yearbook editor in 1952, and Bulosan lived on that income until he died four years later.

Bulosan addressed his writing to an American audience in an attempt to win better treatment for his compatriots: "[I]t has always been my desire to make [lots of people] cry anyway, and to make them feel the very depth of our sorrow and loneliness in America. I have always wanted to show them our capacities for love, our deep spiritual qualities, and our humanity." *America Is in the Heart* is in many ways part of that inclusive and characteristically Asian American genre of autobiography or personal history dedicated to the task of promoting cultural goodwill and understanding. Many Filipino writers felt that they should address an American readership, because of the unintelligibility of the forty-odd Filipino languages, because publishing facilities are thought to be better in America, and because many Filipino writers felt in the past that "the most effective way to put our nation on the cultural map of the world is to have excellent works of Filipino writers published in America . . . the cultural center of the world." Similar arguments held for the writing of personal histories. In most of Bulosan's short stories about Filipino American life there is a first-person narrator that could represent Bulosan himself, and though *America Is in the Heart* describes Filipino American life in California in a general way, it is presented as personal history so that its veracity and impact might be strengthened and so that it might have more market appeal. In fact, P. C. Morante recalls that Louis Adamic recommended to Bulosan that he write the book as an autobiography or personal history because it would sell best that way.

Most American critics and readers valued *America Is in the Heart* primarily as a personalized social document. Max Gissen classified the book with "the growing literature of protest coming from dark-skinned peoples all over the world." Another reviewer asserted that the book is important because it is "the kind of 'life history' document which provides the flesh for the bones of social theory"; that it is "life history" makes it credible. A third critic wrote that since the conditions described in the book are "so degrading" that they are "almost incredible," the reader is tempted to put down the book but for the compassion he feels for the narrator and his "touching determination to rise above the surrounding brutality." The presence of the narrator is critical: Bulosan is "an appealing little waif who could arouse the compassion of any good-hearted American" long enough to finish the book.

During his union organizing assignments, Bulosan witnessed, heard about, and in some cases experienced some of the events and incidents so vividly described in his "autobiography" and in his short stories. According to his brother Aurelio, Bulosan "used to mingle with the ordinary Filipinos, talk with them, and act like them. But they didn't know that Carlos was gathering materials from them. You see, when you write something about the people you have to be among them. You must feel every word you write." What seems quite clear is that Bulosan, like the narrator in "The Thief," viewed his life and his spirit as being essentially at one with the life and spirit of the compatriots who people his autobiography and his stories:

> He started to tell me about his life, and for the first time I began
> to understand him. I tried to piece the fragments together, and
> suddenly I discovered that I was also piecing the fragments of my
> life together. I was then beginning to write, and I felt like writing
> the complete story of his life.

Bulosan was primarily a fiction writer, and *America Is in the Heart* is both less and more than a personal history: it is a composite portrait of the Filipino American community, a social document from the point of view of a participant in that experience. According to Ruben R. Alcantra, all students of the Filipino experience in America should "start with the assumption that Carlos Bulosan's *America Is in the Heart* is a required text. In that concrete and sensitively written account of what it meant to be a Filipino in America before 1946, Bulosan set forth the primary themes in the Filipino-American experience." Another Filipino American scholar, Epifanio San Juan, Jr., asserts that the book "has become an identity-defining primer" for a million Filipinos in the United States. According to Carey McWilliams:

> One may doubt that Bulosan personally experienced each and every one of the manifold brutalities and indecencies so vividly described in this book. It can be fairly said . . . that some Filipino was indeed the victim of each of these or similar incidents. For this reason alone, *America Is in the Heart* is a social classic. It reflects the collective life of thousands of Filipino immigrants. . . . It is the first and best account in English of just what it was like to be a Filipino in California and its sister states in the period, say, from 1930 to 1941.

The saga of the Filipino American experience during the 1930s is governed by a profound compulsion to belong to the new land. It begins, in both *America Is in the Heart* and Bulosan's short stories, with an innocent youth, filled with bright hopes for the future. The youth is driven by poverty and desperation from his native land. Having heard about American democracy and equality, he is stunned when he finds himself excluded and victimized by American racism. As Bulosan had written in a letter:

> Western people are brought up to regard Orientals or colored peoples as inferior, but the mockery of it all is that Filipinos are taught to regard Americans as our equals. Adhering to American ideals, living American life, these are contributory to our feeling of equality. The terrible truth in America shatters the Filipinos' dream of fraternity.
>
> I was completely disillusioned when I came to know this American attitude. If I had not . . . studied about American institutions and racial equality in the Philippines I should never have minded so much the horrible impact of white chauvinism. I shall never forget what I have suffered in this country because of racial prejudice.
>
> Do you know what a Filipino feels in America? . . . He is the loneliest thing on earth. There is much to be appreciated all about him, beauty, wealth, power, grandeur. But is he part of these luxuries? He looks, poor man, through the fingers of his eyes. He is enchained, damnably, to his race, his heritage.

The newly arrived Filipino wants to become American, to participate in the beautiful country he has learned about in his homeland. In "My Education," Bulosan says his journey to America was a torturous search for roots in a new world:

> [I]n America I felt a vague desire to see what I had not seen in my country. I did not know how I would approach America. I only knew that here must be a common denominator which every immigrant or native American should look for in order to understand her, and be of service to her people.

The narrator of *America Is in the Heart* arrives in Seattle filled with hope. "Everything seemed familiar to me. . . . With a sudden surge of joy, I knew that I must find a home in this new land." Even after he and his companions have been cheated out of their money and suitcases and tricked into a season's cannery labor in Alaska, he clings to his dreams of America: "Surely the destitute and vicious people of Seattle were merely a small part of it. Where would I begin the pilgrimage, this search for a door into America? . . . I wanted to know Americans, and to be a part of their life. I wondered what I had in common with them."

The episodes described in *America Is in the Heart*, as well as in "I Would Remember" and other short stories, convey the fear, the poverty, and the decadence to which Filipino laborers in California had been condemned. The narrator of *America Is in the Heart* moves among the drunks and criminals, among the members of other exploited minorities— Blacks, American Indians, Mexicans, Koreans—witnessing murders, lynchings, assaults, and merciless violence, increasingly appalled by the degraded life he shares with them. His own brothers and friends become thieves and hustlers, and he himself drifts into petty crime, stealing bedsheets from transient hotels, cheating at cards, succumbing to the "planless, hopeless, directionless" life to which he and his compatriots have been condemned. He begins to live like a hunted animal, sleeping with a knife under his pillow, carrying a gun, watching in horror his own descent into despair and depravity:

> When I came face to face with brutality, I was afraid of what I would do to myself and to others. I was terribly afraid of myself, for it was the beast, the monster, the murderer of love and kindness that would raise its dark head to defy all that was good and beautiful in life.

Yet:

> As time went by I became as ruthless as the worst of them, and I
> became afraid that I would never feel like a human being again.
> Yet no matter what bestiality encompasses my life, I felt sure that
> somewhere, sometimes, I would break free. This faith kept me
> from completely succumbing to the degradation into which
> many of my countrymen had fallen.

Bulosan discerns the bitter distrust that has driven Filipinos together to hide
"cynically behind our mounting fears, hating the broad white universe at our
door," "narrowing . . . our life into an island, into a filthy segment of American society." And yet he discerns always, both in Filipinos and in other
Americans, "a seed of trust, that ached to grow to fruition." Filipinos were
both brutal and tender, cheating and betraying at one moment and risking
their lives for one another the next. America too was a paradox of kindness
and cruelty: Jose, whose feet had been amputated during his attempt to
escape the white railroad detectives, is well treated by the white hospital staff.
The narrator wonders why the police beat him brutally for no reason other
than the "crime of being Filipino," and again why a dying white girl helps
him escape death at the hands of anti-union goons: "I almost cried. What was
the matter with this land? Just a moment ago I was being beaten by white
men. But here was another white person, a woman, giving me food."

Bulosan was convinced that the social evils that plagued the Filipino in
America rose not out of man's nature but from the environmental factors that
had been created and could therefore be changed by human beings. The urge
for good, for the ideal, was lodged permanently in the human heart. The
America in his heart is the unrealized potential, the unfulfilled dream of a
democratic America, which could come into being through the labor of
Filipino immigrants and other Americans:

> [M]y faith in America . . . was something that had grown out of
> my defeats and successes, something shaped by my struggles for
> a place in this vast land . . . something that grew out of the sacri-
> fices and loneliness of my friends, of my brothers in America and
> my family in the Philippines—something that grew out of our
> desire to know America, and to become a part of her great tradi-
> tion, and to contribute something toward her final fulfillment.

It is often a white woman who symbolizes the America to which
Bulosan's Filipinos want to belong. In his letters, Bulosan reveals his fasci-
nation for the subject of the relationships between white women and
Filipino men:

> [A] Pinoy's feelings for a white woman, beautiful and necessary in
> many ways, but at the same time cruel and hard in a way that the
> primitive-minded Pinoy does not understand and refuses to
> understand. . . . There is really a need for a novel covering the ideal
> courtship and marriage of a Pinoy and an American white woman.

In "Silence," the unknown white woman becomes the Filipino protagonist's
reason for existing. Having lived alone for years, he had been writing in his
lonely room, working simply to "run away from the silence" all around him,
until one day he notices a white girl on the college lawn across the street
from his room. Every day from then on he watches her from his window, and
the sight of her makes it possible for him to go on living and working:

> [S]omething changed inside him. It was as if the void in his
> being had caved in and a flood of sunlight flowed warmly in its
> place. . . . Now the silence that had followed him everywhere
> was drowned by the riot of color in his room. She was alive in
> his room, in his mind and heart. She was the living music of his
> days and nights. . . . She was his own discovery and creation,
> and so long as she was in his mind the silences would be
> quieted.

In "The Romance of Magno Rubio," the tragicomic Filipino peapicker is in
love with a white woman he has seen only in a photograph:

> Magno Rubio, Filipino boy. Four-foot six inches tall, dark as a
> coconut. Head small on a body like a turtle. Magno Rubio.
> Picking peas on a California hillside for twenty-five cents an
> hour. Filipino boy. In love with a girl he had never seen. A girl
> twice his size sideward and upward.

Rubio "works like a carabao and lives like a dog," burrowing in the mud
"like a brown beetle" with other migrant workers. Even though the girl is
only interested in cheating him of some money, loving her makes him "a
human being again," gives him "somebody to work for," makes him feel
"clean in his soul."

The white woman is a dream, an ideal. She symbolizes the contradiction between what is brutal in America and what is kind and beautiful.
Concretely, the Filipino man's interest in white women did not stem merely
from sexual desire, powerful though that impulse might have been. Marrying
a white woman would free him from sexual oppression and emasculation,

give him the possibility of a stable family life and at least a partial entry into the mainstream of American life.

Bulosan struggles quite consciously against his tendency to idealize women. No one knows better than Bulosan that he cannot write realistically about women: "Throughout my life, from my farthest childhood until now, I was never really close enough to a woman to know what kind of animal she is. And this is why when writing, when talking, my thoughts of women are too idealized." In *America Is in the Heart*, Marian, the woman who rescues the narrator after his beating, is "the song of my dark hour," the one who proved to him that there was love and kindness in America. Mary, a girl who lived platonically with him and other Filipinos, has "milk-white skin" and "deep blue, frightened eyes"; her mere presence enraptures the men:

> She became the delicate object of our affections. She was an angel molded into purity by the cleanliness of our thoughts. When a stranger came into our household and looked at her longingly, I could see some of my companions doubling their fists. This platonic relationship among us was healthy and clean and in a way it gave me a new faith in myself.

Mary symbolizes not merely the good and pure, but also the unattainable. She simply disappears one day, a fleeting dream, probably unaware of the special meaning she had come to have for a lonely group of homeless men.

The combination of books and white women is particularly fascinating to the narrator of *America Is in the Heart*, dating back to a boyhood meeting with a kindly white librarian who seems to personify opportunity through education to the boy in the Philippines. Much later, when a young store clerk invites him to her apartment and shows him around, he is attracted by both her and her books: "I followed her slowly, drinking in her grace, the lovely way she moved her body. In the living room, piled along the wall, were books of many sizes and colors. Books! I was enchanted when I saw them. They drew me irresistibly to them." In *America*, the narrator is befriended by two sisters who give him books. There is a "disturbing sensuousness" about Alice Odell, and a kind of "maternal solicitude" about Eileen; in her, he finds again "the good of my youth": "I yearned for her and the world she represented. . . . She was undeniably the *America* I had wanted to find in those frantic days of fear and flight, in those acute hours of hunger and loneliness. This America was human, good, and real."

Besides white women, books and book knowledge hold out the abstract promise of equality for Bulosan. Like Kang, Bulosan's narrator dreams of belonging to the "domain of the universal intellectual discoveries of man."

While hospitalized, he reads Russian, Spanish, French, and American writers:

> [F]rom day to day I read, and reading widened my mental
> horizon, creating a spiritual kinship with other men who had
> pondered over the miseries of their countries. . . . I, too, reacted
> to my time. I promised myself that I would read ten thousand
> books when I got well. I plunged into books, boring through the
> earth's core, leveling all seas and oceans, swimming in the
> constellation.

American literature, he hopes, might give him access to American society:

> There was something definitely American, something positively
> vital in all of them [the American poets]. . . . I could follow the
> path of these poets, continue their tradition and [perhaps] I could
> arrive at a positive understanding of America. . . . I had been
> looking for this side of America; surely this was the real side of
> living America.

For a time, books provide Bulosan's narrator with a sense of belonging to America that he could not derive from any other source. He begins to wonder if there was "a happy situation in the world outside of books," and turns for a time to fables and fairy tales. Finally, he resists the temptation to try to escape from reality through books:

> Reading only made me live the acute pain of the past. When I
> came upon a scene that recalled my own experiences, I could not
> go on. But mostly I felt that other writers had lied about life, that
> they were afraid to depict it as it really was in their environment.

Bulosan finally concludes that it is "disastrous to know and live and work and struggle only with intellectuals." They are too often dreamers "incapable of working [a dynamic social idea] out to the end."

Carlos Bulosan hoped that he might contribute to the fulfillment of the American promise by integrating the Filipinos' struggle for freedom and equality in America with his writing, which would become a weapon in that struggle:

> I only want to expose what terror and ugliness I have seen, what
> shame and horror I have experienced, so that in my work,
> however limited in scope and penetration, others will find a

reason for a deeper grievance against social injustice and a higher dream of human perfection.

For the narrator of *America Is in the Heart*, writing is a kind of therapy for loneliness and a sense of futility. It lifts him above the limitations and ugliness of his narrow world, gives him a voice for his longing and sorrow, and puts him in touch with the currents of his time: "[W]hen I came home to our apartment, sitting alone in the midst of drab walls and ugly furniture, I felt like striking at my invisible foe. Then I began to write. . . . I had something to live for now, and to fight the world with."

It was socialist thought and the labor movement that finally made Bulosan feel he had become American. He is like the protagonist of "Be American": Consorcio arrives in America a native, innocent peasant boy from the Philippines, full of hope that he can become a "real American," only to slip into the wandering life of the itinerant Filipino menial worker. Consorcio becomes an American through his union organizing activities, by dedicating his quality for "our America":

> Socialist thinking was spreading among the workers, professionals, and intellectuals. . . . To most of us it was a revelation— and a new morning in America. Here was a collective faith dynamic enough to release the creative spirit that was long thwarted in America. My personal predicaments seemed to vanish and for the first time I could feel myself growing and becoming a living part of America.

Writing for the union magazine *New Tide*, participating in organizing activities among Filipino peapickers and cannery workers, made Bulosan feel that he was part of a vast and vital movement based on a common faith in the working man of every nationality. He felt the exhilaration of working for a cause that would become "part of history." The Filipino Communist movement on the West Coast gave Bulosan's narrator the "inspiration and courage to withstand the confusion and futility of my own life." Alone, he could never hope to "blast away the walls that imprisoned the American soul." Fighting alongside others who believed, as he did, that ideas had to be integrated with actions, he had found his own answer to nihilism, fear, and despair. Writing for the labor movement would be his weapon against injustice and his key to American life:

> I . . . became convinced that it was the duty of the artist to trace the origin of the disease that was festering American life. . . .

Labor demanded the active collaboration of writers. In the course of eight years, I had relived the whole course of American history. I drew inspiration from my active participation in the workers' movement. The most decisive move that the writer could make was to take his stand with the workers.

Through women, through art, through the labor movement, Carlos Bulosan sought an end to his lonely life as a social and psychological exile and a way to plant roots in American life. Finally Bulosan realizes that his search for roots in the new world end in loneliness because loneliness and rootlessness are part of a shared American identity: "It was a discovery of America and myself. . . . I began to recognize the forces that had driven many Americans to other countries and had made those who stayed at home homeless." As the years separate him from his homeland, he concludes that roots cannot be defined in terms of places or persons, but only in terms of ideals:

I knew, then, that I would be as rootless in the Philippines as I was in America, because these roots are not physical things but the quality of faith deeply felt and clearly understood and integrated in one's life. The roots I was looking for were not physical but intellectual and spiritual things. I was looking for a common faith to believe in and of which I could be a growing part.

As is characteristic of many immigrants, for many Filipinos the years of exclusion from participation in American life is strangely accompanied by a feeling of separation from a homeland to which they could no longer return. Nevertheless, Bulosan's memories of home grew more vivid with time, feeding his longing for freedom in America:

I seem to remember my world as a little boy in Binalonan vividly as if I were an artist. I think I could paint the whole town and village where I grew up. . . . I always write about that life beautifully, but when I take another background like the U.S., I become bitter and angry and cruel.

Bulosan's writing about the Philippines is shaped by the controlling vision of hindsight. Both *Laughter of My Father* and the first section of *America Is in the Heart*, which takes place in the islands, are evenly paced and written with almost pictorial clarity and vividness. The sections of *America Is in the Heart* that are set in this country suffer from a rapid, fluctuating pace that almost amounts to imbalance and undisciplined movement. It is also subject to disconcerting solemnity mixed with what Carey McWilliams has called "minor histrionics."

Bulosan himself was far from satisfied with the book. It had been poured out in haste, out of a sense of personal urgency and to satisfy impatient publishers:

> *America Is in the Heart* . . . is important in that it reveals, for the first time, our plight in America, and also in the islands. I could have written a great and wonderful book, but I worked too fast and the company was in a hurry to bring it out; so that what we have now is imperfect and fragmentary; but perhaps I will write a sequel someday.

Having been told by his doctors that he had not long to live, Bulosan says that he wrote six hundred pages of *America Is in the Heart* in twenty-eight days because he felt that he was "racing with death." This might explain the unevenness of the narrative. The humorlessness of this "undisciplined outpouring," he says, was deliberate. When *Laughter of My Father* was published two years earlier, critics had hailed Bulosan as the "manifestation of the pure Comic Spirit." Horrified, Bulosan replied that the book had been meant as a satirical indictment against an economic system that sealed off the possibility of development for the peasant and that he did not think his father's life, or the life of the other peasants of the Philippines, was funny in the slightest; on the contrary, the book had been written in tears. Anger at the thought of this misinterpretation of *Laughter of My Father* compelled Bulosan to write *America Is in the Heart* completely without humor:

> I made a little table in the backyard and started writing about my anger and how it grew inside me like a scimitar. But I found out that in writing about it, I was really writing my autobiography. "What a life," I said to myself. . . . "Now they will know that I am not a laughing man."

Although he had originally addressed his writing to an American audience on behalf of Filipinos in America, in the tradition of earlier Asian goodwill ambassador writers, towards the end of his life Bulosan turned his attention towards the Philippines and a Filipino audience. Perhaps he did so in part because he felt that he might be better understood by Filipinos. Even while American critics misinterpreted *Laughter of My Father*, Bulosan's belief that in the book "for the first time the Filipino people are depicted as human beings" was underscored by letters from Filipinos who said he had written "about them and their times": "I felt that I would be ineffectual if I did not return to my own people." When he died in 1956, Bulosan was working as a writer for the UCAPAWA in Seattle. He was working on a novel about Philippine national hero Jose Rizal, a work he considered his "gift and last will . . . to the Filipino people." Late in 1949, Bulosan mentioned wanting to write "a long novel covering thirty-five years of Philippine history" because "I owe it to the Filipino people."

Carlos Bulosan's writing is the "testament of one who longed to become part of America." At the same time, it is more than that: it is the chronicle of loneliness and compassion by a member of an oppressed and exploited minority on behalf of all the oppressed who might hope to contribute to "a better society and a more enlightened mankind." Younghill Kang and Carlos Bulosan share with the Asian goodwill ambassador writers a sustaining desire to win American acceptance. But unlike the Chinese sojourner intellectuals, Younghill Kang sought opportunities to set down roots in American life. Carlos Bulosan identified himself with the poor and disenfranchised of both Asia and America and dreamed fervently of a future world of social and racial equality where all men could be brothers.

QUI-PHIET TRAN

From Isolation to Integration: Vietnamese Americans in Tran Dieu Hang's Fiction

The paradox of modern mass media is its quickness in keeping its audience abreast of the latest event in the world and simultaneously its disposition to misinform them about that event. Reporters tend to fashion their coverage from a theme that they think might be of interest to the public, overlooking the real nature and meaning of the event being covered; they will also drop a subject they believe is worn out or no longer interests the audience.

The picture of Vietnamese refugees has received this kind of media treatment in the United States. Generally, the resettlement of Vietnamese in the new land has been presented as a success story. They enjoy a better life, their children excel in American schools, and they are no longer plagued by anxieties about the future as they were when they first arrived in America. To dramatize the smooth transition from their former society to their present one, the mass media portray these newest Americans beaming with happiness and pride as they celebrate major American holidays such as Thanksgiving and the Fourth of July. For Vietnamese immigrants, reporters like to tell us, America is not only the land of freedom and peace but the land of opportunities for those who were denied a future in their former countries.

To the casual observer this representation of Vietnamese Americans is nearly perfect. Resourceful, law-abiding, tenacious, and, most importantly, capable of adjusting quickly to American society, Vietnamese Americans are

From *Reading the Literatures of Asian America.* © 1992 by Temple University.

blessed with all the necessary qualities which enable them to join the melting pot with great ease. Surprisingly, this delineation of Vietnamese Americans matches the picture portrayed by the Vietnamese media. Stories about these newest Americans' successes in various areas appear on the front pages of major Vietnamese newspapers and magazines (many of which are bilingual) and on Vietnamese television. Vietnamese communities relish news about the opening of Little Saigon shopping center, the appointment of student X as Rhodes scholar, and the admission of valedictorian Y to Harvard University. These successes give Viemamese refugees a sense of great joy and pride and justify the cause of their voluntary exile in new land.

This idyllic portrayal of Vietnamese immigrants ironically finds no echo in Vietnamese American literature. For less than two decades since the arrival of the first wave of refugees in 1975, Vietnamese readers have witnessed a spectacular phenomenon that I call the flowering of exile Vietnamese literature. Written primarily in Vietnamese, this literature is the preoccupation of a great number of authors, many of whom are "boat people" and had never tried their hand at literature before. While the horrors of the refugees' journey to freedom—piracy, rape, starvation, death—are dominant themes in this literature, its main focus is the ordeal of being the newest Americans. After the nightmare of their sea voyage is past, Vietnamese refugees find themselves in another crucible: facing the uncertainties and difficulties of their life in America.

The problems of adjustment that confront the refugees find their fullest expression in Vietnamese emigre literature. Viewing themselves as exiles, Vietnamese writers see their haven in America as a "penal colony" where "one's body and soul are wearing away" with "mountains of grief and agony". They also react strongly to American civilization which they find too mechanical and hectic to allow one to enjoy "the quiet and leisure," the Tao of living of the East (Vo 67; Qui-Phiet Tran 104, 105). This view of the Vietnamese exile experience and American culture can be attributed to the refugees' frustrations about problems such as cultural differences, language barriers, and changes in their socioeconomic status as a result of their resettlement in the United States.

Because venting their bitterness about their American experience becomes a compelling need or perhaps a mode of salvation for many Vietnamese immigrants, writers have little difficulty in getting published. Though an official count of authors, their publications, and publishers is not available for lack of an adequate archival system, a quick survey of literary materials on display at a typical Vietnamese bookstore in an area with a large concentration of Vietnamese immigrants such as Orange County, California, will leave the researcher convinced about the boom in exile Vietnamese literature and publishing during these last sixteen years. Vietnamese experiences are richly documented in books, magazines, music, and art work. Authors are apprentices in creative writing or veterans in their fields. Publishers range from major firms to authors who print their own work expressly in order to alleviate their pain of exile.

The flowering of this literature is enhanced by a wide readership. Vietnamese immigrants turn to their literature for reasons similar to those for which their authors write: to recognize (and face) their problems, to understand how the stories of their ordeal are told and how their voices are rendered. They also turn to this literature for another important reason. Written in Vietnamese, it responds to the emotional needs of many Vietnamese who wish to relieve their nostalgia by seeking familiar images of their past in the process of reading.

These preliminary remarks suggest that to see the true picture of Vietnamese immigrants, we should, as Jacques Lacan might advise, turn away from the idea that the conscious "autonomous" ego is the center of the human psyche. The mass media's view of the Vietnamese American as an objective, strong, and healthy ego capable of synthesis, integration, and adaptability to realistic norms is, according to Lacan's theory, an illusion because the human subject is neither unified nor unifiable (Ragland-Sullivan 120). To understand the complexity of Vietnamese Americans' psyches, we should therefore turn to their literature. Again Lacan's teaching about the role for literature in unraveling the repressed unconscious, the reservoir of signifiers and language of the real, is useful. When studying Vietnamese Americans we take up their literature because literature, in Lacan's view, is not only "unthinkable without repression" but equated with the language of the unconscious—the language of indestructible desire, dreams, and madness. "But one has only to listen to poetry . . . for a polyphony to be heard, for it to become clear that all discourse is aligned along the several staves of a score," Lacan explains (Bowie 203). Vietnamese American literature, in depicting the refugees' aspirations as well as their outrage, anguish, and insanity, is what we should concern ourselves with in our study of the Vietnamese experience in the United States.

This representation of the Vietnamese American psyche is bound up with the identity of the speaking subject. A quick glance at the bulk of publications by Vietnamese American writers reveals this interesting fact: women write more extensively and offer a different rendering of the Vietnamese American experience than men. Men concentrate on their past ordeal at home and in refugee camps; women present problems of adjustment to the new society. Men speak about their exile and missed opportunities with anger; women speak about their destiny with anguished resignation. Men see their quest for happiness as a dead end, women see the quest as a meaningful and rewarding experience. Men, probably because they are still bitter about the United States "betrayal" of South Vietnam in 1975, are angry with America and refuse to draw any significance from their American experience, whereas women view the whole story at worst as a karmic debt and at best as a dear price the refugees have to pay for their freedom.

An important representative of contemporary Vietnamese women writers who have explored the above problems is Tran Dieu Hang. Her two major collections of short stories, *Vu dieu cua loai cong* (*The Peacock Dance*) and *Mua dat la* (*The Rain Falls on the Strange Land*) deal with the complexity of the refugee consciousness and unconscious, the adverse circumstances Vietnamese Americans face and the death instinct they try to repress, their hopes and expectations as well as their despair and fear. The following essay examines these issues in Tran Dieu Hang's writing.

≈≈≈≈≈≈≈≈≈

The Vietnamese exodus to the United States in 1975 had no parallel in Vietnam's history. It happened so suddenly that most evacuees had little or no time to prepare themselves for their permanent departure. Not only did many leave Vietnam empty-handed, but also they had no knowledge of the language, customs, and culture of the country to which they were fleeing. No sooner did they get over the panic of their escape than they found themselves wrestling with a new life for which they were totally unprepared. In their moments of greatest depression many Vietnamese had second thoughts about their American experience. They questioned the purpose of their expatriation (which they came to regard as a brutal uprooting from their native land); they lost interest in their struggle to integrate into American society; they gave themselves up to despair or escaped to their idyllic past. America, which they had thought was a haven, turned out to be a penal colony in the minds of these exiles.

The problems that confront Vietnamese immigrants assume a special meaning and perhaps more tragic dimensions in Tran Dieu Hang's fiction because most of her protagonists are women. Victims of circumstances harsher than male refugees', they are both objects of men's desire and targets for cultural, sexist, and racist discrimination. Unlike male refugees who are able to channel their outrage against injustices into violent acts, women are condemned to bear their indignities in secrecy, silenced many times over by deeply rooted cultural inhibitions, male oppression, language barriers, and menaces of damnation from the dominant host culture.

The protagonist of "Bong toi, que nguoi" ("Darkness, Strange Land") epitomizes the educated Vietnamese female immigrant's condition. Chan, a former student from the University of Saigon now toiling in a sweatshop to support herself and her family, finds herself in "an anguished state of self-defense" because of the repeated advances made to her by her Vietnamese and American coworkers and the hostile attitude of her female colleagues (*Vu dieu 75*). Chan's condition as a young female refugee—an object of male seduction and female hatred compounded by her overweening pride in her Asian heritage, her indignation over her tribulations, and her educational background—plunges her into a stubborn silence and causes her to turn down her American friend's marriage proposal. Chan's utter estrangement and loneliness mark the gloomy aspects of her, and other Vietnamese women's, integration into American society and are suggested by her bidding farewell to Tim as darkness pervades the landscape.

One of the reasons Chan cites to decline Tim's offer is her concern about the oppression of her native culture by her suitor's. Clearly, her conditions preclude a future with Tim and what he represents. She wants her future husband to be able to appreciate things Vietnamese that are endearing to her; she wants her future children to be able to "sing Vietnamese songs that her mother had taught her" (90). Unlike her American friend who thinks that "language is just a means of communicating immediate ideas and feeling" and is not connected at all with memories, Chan argues in defense of her native tongue that language is a vital link between the past and future of a people and to suppress language is to sever that link, their mode of survival. Chan's dilemma as a transplanted Vietnamese American is unresolved, nonetheless. While apparently succeeding in preserving her identity by escaping into her past and cutting off her contact with the host culture, she imposes silence on herself, deprives herself of the power of language as well as of the opportunity for self-expression, and exacerbates her condition of exile.

Chan's condition results from her choice not to participate in the mainstream of American life. By contrast, most of Tran Dieu Hang's other characters are caught up in their dilemma of integration. Representing mostly the larger group of refugees known as the "boat people" who came to America to seek freedom and a better future, these characters express for the refugees a fervent desire to integrate into American society. Their dream of becoming Americans, however, is thwarted by practical realities such as language problems and racism. This drama of Vietnamese acculturation is aggravated by the subversion or even destruction of Vietnamese traditional values, which have morally sustained many Vietnamese immigrants in their exile, by the formidable force of American culture. The family, the foundation of Vietnamese culture and society, disintegrates under the onslaughts of American material civilization. Ideal values such as loyal friendship and matrimony, filial piety, and reverence for old age are rejected by many Vietnamese Americans in favor of individualism and materialism. As always, women, rather than men, fall victims to these cruel circumstances.

Two stories, "Mua dat la" ("The Rain Falls on the Strange Land") and "Roi ngay van moi" ("There Will Come New Days"), dramatize the difficulties of integrating into American society. The narrator of the former story, a young refugee reunited with a mother who married an American, feels rejected by her new American family because of her language problems. Muted by her repressed outrage over her handicap, her siblings' hostility, cultural dissimilarities, and particularly her mother's remarriage while her father languishes in a reeducation camp in Vietnam (a grave violation of the Confucian ethical code for Asian women), she stays out of the mainstream like "a dumb, insignificant shadow," viewing her being in "Mr. John's" family as superfluous, "a scion grafted on to an alien stock" (*Mua* 43). Her alienation increases when she finds American life threatening. Seeing the vortex of a freeway interchange packed with traffic, the menace of American life, she is led to think of "a colossal monster whose lightest breath can crush me to death" (40).

While in "The Rain Falls on the Strange Land" America is seen as an imminent threat, in "There Will Come New Days" it turns into a destructive power. Wishing to dissolve quickly into American culture by choosing to live with an American family, Thoi, a peasant from the Mekong Delta, is horrified to find her dream smashed. Taking advantage of her vulnerability, her sponsor rapes her despite her tearful pleas in broken English and then he attempts to buy her silence. Her successful escape from her offender's home and her determination to learn English suggest her realization that speech is a weapon to resist male oppression and to fight for recognition in American society.

While articulateness is thought by some of Tran Dieu Hang's characters as a possible way to fight sexist and racist oppression, it proves useless when coping with their tragic condition as refugees and women. Victimization is not merely associated with male brutality and female muteness but also stems from the tension between Asian and Western cultures, and particularly from the encroachment of American materialism on Vietnamese moral and spiritual values. Jealousy alone, therefore, cannot be blamed for the death of a young beautiful woman gunned down by her husband in "Can chung cu so 7" ("Apartment 7"). Trapped in the clash between the traditional culture to which he clings and the new culture to which she is drawn, both characters fall victim to, and are silenced by, the force of circumstances, one behind bars and the other in the grave. Similarly, the victimization of the woman does not merely result from male brutality in "Cho tam" ("Temporary Asylum"). Not only is the protagonist jilted by her husband and sexually abused by her lover, but also she is alienated by the new society which condemns her and her little child to a quest for a temporary asylum which they can never find. The final scene of the story suggests a Kafkaesque quest in a wasteland completely despoiled of humanity: "The road in front of us is vast and endless, and our footsteps are the solitary sounds in the cold winter morning when the town is half-awake" (*Mua* 89). In their utter despondency Vietnamese women blame American mechanical life for their condition. "Have you wondered," the protagonist of "Ngay thang qua doi" ("The Onrush of Time") ponders, "why there are so many vehicles rushing on the highway and yet you can't find a companion for yourself? And why does twilight often make you feel that you never come to the end of your journey?" (*Vu dieu* 155).

The quest for an ideal, however illusory, as a way to cope with victimization is behavior common to many of Tran Dieu Hang's characters. Their search for happiness, however, is doomed to failure. In "Mot chut bien chieu" ("The Seas of Evening") a thirty-year-old woman and a middle-aged man, despite their attempt to converge with each other, are "destined to return to their loneliness . . . like the two trains heading off in in opposite directions" (*Mua* 105). Missed opportunities, lost time, and advanced age are some of the main causes of Vietnamese adults' estrangement not only from American society but also from their native community. Though at times these solitary souls manage to come together, they end up torturing each other because of their incompatibilities. "There is something wrong, something disjointed," comments the narrator of "Bua tiec" ("The Feast") on the union of a young couple with nothing in common (*Mua* 19). The union is "wrong" because in their eagerness to come together to help each other wrestle with the difficulties of life the two characters do not see love as most essential to matrimonial happiness.

The trauma of family discord caused by "mismatching" is depicted at length in "Ben ngoai khung cue" ("Outside the Window"). Nga's incompatibility with her husband, a materialist, flippant, and hypocritical man, plunges her into a series of fantasies (or flashbacks?) about an idyllic love. Her last fantasy becomes a death-wish at the story's end when her husband shows no sign of caring for her after her labor. The story illustrates a dilemma faced by many adult refugees. While loneliness brings them together, their union estranges and victimizes them. Still, their incompatible characters compel them to search again for an illusory, impractical mode of salvation, alienating them even more from reality.

The victimization of Vietnamese adults by adverse circumstances, is, though brutal, not entirely tragic. Dreaming away sorrowful reality or searching for an unattainable ideal, they are not completely deprived of hope for a better future. The condition of elderly refugees, in contrast, is desperate. Threatened by prospects of damnation in the new land because they are ill-equipped to deal with reality and rejected by the Americanized young generation, old Vietnamese escape into their past, go insane, or resort to self-destruction. Though Tran Dieu Hang's fiction does not exclusively dramatize this last recourse, it does portray the sad consequences of the elders' uprooting from their native land and their maladaptation to American life. In "The Feast" a group of old artists seeks to voice through music the repressed sorrow of exile—their only means of survival—and succeeds somewhat in evoking momentarily a happy past. Yet, the elderly characters' brief joy is tainted with anguish over their present condition. Instead of hymns, they choose to sing doleful dirges. For these old people, seeking salvation in the past is futile because songs from their past can give them only a brief respite from reality. After the concert, the parents of the protagonist have to make the painful decision, because of their daughter-in-law's disrespect, to move out of the house of the son with whom they were just reunited. Very soon they will have to lead a solitary life and face a reality that quells their creative voice, their only way of holding on to their past and identity.

The themes of the shock of reality and, particularly, the tragic consequences of the old Vietnamese refugees' quest for the past are treated at length in "Chuyen xe ve lang Dai Tu" ("The Trip to Dai Tu Village"). Instead of sustaining them like a life force, the past victimizes and destroys them. The grandmother in the story suffers a schizophrenic split. Completely losing hold of the real world (she is no longer aware of her body's biological functions), she paradoxically recalls the most minute details of her distant past, which in her mind is transformed into a permanent present. Her continual conversation with her absent son (who is pining in a reeducation camp in Vietnam) and with her fictional friends during her imaginary trip back to her native village in North Vietnam are reminiscent of Proust's observation of people who can talk to physical objects as if they possessed an animate life. Freud attributes the power of this sort of memory to the unconscious, whose process he sees as timeless because it is not altered by the passage of time. Bergson speaks of pure memory which, because it hovers far above the plane of experience out of touch with reality, is able to keep our entire past life intact. The narrator of Tran Dieu Hang's story provides yet another interesting interpretation of this perception phenomenon. The grandmother has little recollection of the recent past and is completely cut off from the present because her memory, like a roll of film nearing its last exposure, can no longer store current information. The last time she saw her son, her last memory-trace (to use a Freudian trope), remains nevertheless indelible in her damaged memory because it is associated with her fear for his safety, which in time becomes a permanent delirious obsession and plunges her into schizophrenia.

The general picture of Vietnamese Americans depicted thus far in Tran Dieu Hang is that of outcasts, misfits, and recluses—unfit for American society. This picture also applies to a group of Vietnamese often neglected by other writers: the adolescents. For many Vietnamese and Americans these youngsters are adjusting too well to American society to pose any problem detrimental to their future in this country. By contrast, Tran Dieu Hang portrays a gloomy picture of these young Vietnamese Americans. Electrified by the new macho culture and at the same time suffering from his inferiority complex, Binh in "Cuoc choi" ("The Game") joins a gang to test out his newly learned "Godfather theory": survival of the fittest. The meaning of the story, according to the narrator, is crystal clear: in his quest for salvation, Binh "chose a violent, tragic end destined for wild plants that seek to grow too fast, not caring about the consequences of their reckless course of action" (*Mua* 63). The story's hero typifies a predicament faced by many Vietnamese American adolescents. Too young and too rebellious to be held back by their roots, they dissolve too fast into America's destructive subculture. Binh's final cry, as well as that of many Vietnamese adolescent refugees who suffer from a destiny like his, a destiny that forces them into early maturity, also confirms the emptiness of life. "His cry," says the narrator, "disappeared into silence, nothingness. It was the cry of the kids who already lost their innocence, though not yet fully grown" (63). It is the cry that disturbs the narrator, the young hero's mentor, who wonders who should be held responsible for his young friend's folly—fate or his lack of care for the teenager's education.

≈≈≈≈≈≈≈

An analysis of a selection of Tran Dieu Hang's stories suggests that Vietnamese immigrants have traveled many roads in search of different meanings. Some have cut short their journeys or dropped out, but others stay on to fulfill their arduous destinies. Who remains in this second group and what enables them to endure? This question is answered in many of Tran Dieu Hang's stories and particularly in her trilogy, "Nguoi em vuon ngoai" ("The Young Cousin"), "Giac mo cua co" ("The Dream of Grass") and "Roi ngay van moi" ("There Will Come New Days"). In general, characters in these stories are able to withstand their catastrophic times and avoid the despair of suicide because they are equipped with a rural background, rooted in their native soil, armed with a strong belief in their traditional values, or capable of dreaming harsh reality away.

Conceived in the same vein as "The Game" but obviously purported to counteract the baneful effects of American culture, "The Young Cousin" advocates returning to the Vietnamese past. Interestingly, the past, no longer viewed as an abstract ideal representing unfulfilled dreams, is now equated with a concrete life force, "a property so simple and yet so solid like the earth" to which the protagonist "usually return[s] in imagination when I feel I have lost my identity, when I am alienated, weak, and cowardly in this strange world" (129-30). Empowered with the past, the fountainhead of protection, security, and love, the protagonist feels undaunted, like "a traveler who has eaten a hearty meal before making a long trip" (130). He feels sorry for his cousin who is deprived of such an important heritage because she left home at a very tender age. Lured by a culture too permissive, this young cousin commits the most vicious acts imaginable, short of destroying herself. Having no weapon with which to fight harsh circumstances, she is a lost soul in the new country.

The association of the past with the earth suggests that the past is bound up in *place* and derives its redemptive power from it. According to Eudora Welty, place transcends the human world, because, instead of being hostile to the latter, it "heals the hurt, soothes the outrage, fills the terrible vacuum" (131). More important, both art and feelings, as Welty puts it, are tied to the native soil from which they spring (118). Welty's remarks about the role of place in fiction explains Tran Dieu Hang's preoccupation with her native land as a mode of salvation in her trilogy. It abounds with homely and simple images such as "our garden-grown fruits," "our farm-raised shrimps," "ricefield mud," "reflections of coconut trees on a tranquil rivulet." The exception to Welty's theory of place is that Tran Dieu Hang's characters, lacking a physical locality due to their exile in a strange land, are not able, as Welty might observe, to "put out roots, wherever birth, chance, fate or our traveling selves set us down" (Welty 132–33). Unlike American and European writers whose nomadic destiny Welty seems to have in mind, Vietnamese authors, because of their reluctance to accept their "second homes," have to compensate for their loss by dreaming about their native soil. "The Dream of Grass" illustrates this quest for salvation. Though becoming full-fledged Americans, the protagonist and his narrator do not give up their search for an idealistic vision—"rowing on a moonlit night when the country is at peace and listening to the vast river echo our voice reciting poetry" (*Vu dieu* 133). Though place is an illusory ideal for Vietnamese immigrants, it is inseparably bound up with their destiny. Pursuing this quest—dreaming of going home—is not only their mode of behavior but, as the narrator exclaims at the end of the story, a means for keeping them sound and safe "till our last breath" (136).

The glorification of the native soil finds its fullest and perhaps clearest expression in "There Will Come New Days." Native locality provides moral and spiritual values and principles that have contributed to the victory of the Vietnamese people over countless adversities in their nation's tormented history: endurance, fortitude, and faith. Thoi, the most unfortunate victim of the force of circumstances and yet the most heroic protagonist in Tran Dieu Hang's fiction, embodies such principles and values. Brutally violated by pirates in her sea voyage, ravished and gagged by her sponsor in America, handicapped by the language barrier, she nevertheless turns her outrage and death instinct into her determination to fight for a better future. Her resolve to study English and to enroll in a vocational training program indicates her realization that speech and action are the only way for a refugee woman to transcend her condition. Her moral strength comes from her faith in the redemptive power of suffering and endurance and from her conviction about the dear price she has to pay for her freedom. This strong belief, the source of her fortitude, has been nurtured, as her narrrator puts it, by her family's and her native country's traditional values and particularly her rural upbringing (*Vu dieu* 195). Her cultural values explain both her formidable will power and, paradoxically, her "innocent, care-free manners as if she never bothered to know that she had in hand that mighty weapon" (195). By creating this unique character in whom is crystallized the best of Vietnam's cultural heritage and by significantly titling her story to point optimistically to the future, Tran Dieu Hang demonstrates that the truest Vietnamese, to borrow Welty's apt metaphor, "put out roots whenever . . . fate set[s] down" (Welty 132–33) and achieve their dreams by apotheosizing their native values.

"The Dream of Grass," "The Cousin," and "There Will Come New Days" suggest that Vietnamese immigrants have come full circle in their American experience. No longer isolating themselves in their enclaves, these stories demonstrate their desire and ability to integrate into the mainstream, as their ultimate goal. Yet, for these people integration does not spell cooptation or monologic dominance by the host culture. Rather, by merging with the mainstream without repressing their nostalgic dreams, native heritage, and distinctive voices, they can assert their identity and participate as Americans in the enrichment of their new country's pluralistic culture. Tran Dieu Hang's vision recalls Ihab Hassan's "critical pluralism" which calls for "pragmatic constituencies of knowledge that would share values, traditions, expectancies, goals" to "bring back the reign of wonder into our lives"

(Hassan 182). In this apocalyptic age, as the world is giving up its "total-izing principle" (169) and opening to dissenting views and consciousnesses, one can only hope, as Hassan might say, that the Vietnamese voice will be heeded in the polyphonic postmodern discourse.

RUTH Y. HSIAO

Facing the Incurable: Patriarchy in Eat a Bowl of Tea

Chinese American writers have all had to reckon with patriarchal tradition. Their attitudes range from agreeing with the value of this tradition to designing its collapse with a subversive plot. The earliest questioning of patriarchy exists in nineteenth-century Cantonese folk rhymes, which came into circulation when Chinese laborers immigrated to California. A female speaker challenges, "How can we tolerate the confines of those dated moral conventions" when education has brought equality? Another female speaker declares, "We don't submit ourselves to oppression. . . . What's there to fear?" (*Songs of Gold Mountain* 220–21). The first Eurasian writer to publish in the United States, Edith Eaton, used a subtler means of subverting patriarchal tyranny; her character Mrs. Spring Fragrance couches put-downs of her husband and his fellow male chauvinists in irony (Amy Ling 411–19). These occasional expressions of feminism in Chinese American writings were the exception rather than the rule. Most writings resemble a group of stories in the short-lived New York Chinatown literary magazine, *The Bud* (1947–48), which depicts women as no more than "appendages to men" with little complexity and no inner needs (Sau-ling Wong 71–13).

By the late 1940s, as a result of China's role as an American ally in World War II, the United States lifted some of its anti-Chinese immigration laws to admit Chinese women. Not accidentally, these events coincided with

From *Reading the Literatures of Asian America.* © 1992 by Temple University.

the publication of the two autobiographies, *Father and Glorious Descendant* (1943) by Pardee Lowe and *Fifth Chinese Daughter* (1945) by Jade Snow Wong. Both offspring of stern Confucian fathers, these authors extolled patriarchal precepts; but their defiant behavior, such as Wong's going to college against her father's wish and Lowe's marrying a Caucasian wife, constitutes unintended criticism of their autocratic fathers. Appropriate for their time, they erred on the side of applauding the patriarchal but much-maligned Chinese emigrants, who had come to be associated with opium, coolies, and tong wars. But as hostility lessened toward the Chinese, veiled criticism of patriarchy gave way to more open warfare between generations.

In comparison to these two autobiographies published before the civil rights era of the sixties, Louis Chu's only novel, *Eat a Bowl of Tea* (1961), reveals the uneasy truce between American-born children and their patriarchal elders. The emerging antipatriarchal tradition barely started by Chu's predecessors becomes prominent. The novel depicts male characters subjected to humiliations no healthy patriarchal society would have allowed. When transplanted to America, patriarchy itself became a victim. Discriminatory laws deprived the men of respectability and blighted their lives. Yet, when more liberal laws brought Chinese women to Chinatown, their presence created havoc, which the tragicomic novel uses to great advantage. The novel treats women as an intrusive nuisance that throws the male dominant community out of kilter, but not for long. Not only does the novel restore the ruffled, old-order social hierarchy, but it also suggests the birth of a new age patriarchy.

To be sure, Chu shows the negative effects of an autocratic upbringing. Chu's characters bear the unmistakable marks of patriarchy's sons and daughters: they are dependent, limited, and unfulfilled. At the end of the novel, however, rejuvenation and potency return to the beleaguered young couple Ben Loy and Mei Oi when they move away from the collective control of New York in paternalistic Chinatown and begin a new breed of Chinese Americans.

In the introduction, Jeffrey Chan credits Chu with locating the source of Chinese American vitality:

> It is no coincidence that Chu sends Ben Loy and Mei Oi to San Francisco for Ben Loy to reclaim his virility, his paternity, and his wife. His return to San Francisco to make himself anew is not the response of a sojourner. He is a Chinese-American remaking a covenant with Gum Sahn, what the first generation called America, the Golden Mountain. He returns to the city where Chinese-America first began. (5)

Ben Loy reclaims in one swoop "his virility, his paternity, and his wife." (Patriarchy reigns *again*.) Ben Loy is cured of the enervating effects of patriarchy and racism that rob him of manhood, but can we purge Chinese American writings of patriarchal views? I think not. A bowl of herbal tea restores Ben Loy's virility only to install him as the new-generation patriarch. If *Eat a Bowl of Tea* is an attempt to purge the patriarchal tradition in literature, it has failed.

Because of his depiction of the twin evils—patriarchy and racism, Chu is widely acclaimed by Asian American writers and critics. His novel has had two revivals, a reissue in 1979 and a film version in 1989. This continued interest also has much to do with his achievement as a herald of the new Asian American sensibility, a sensibility supposedly free of such anachronisms as patriarchy. Since his novel plays a pivotal role in the evolution of the Asian American sensibility, we should first place the novel in its historical context.

By the late 1950s, demographic changes brought on by more liberal immigration laws resulted in the conditions depicted in Chu's novel. The War Bride Act of 1945 finally allowed more Chinese women to enter the United States. This act changed the previously male dominant so-called bachelor society of Chinatown. Set in 1947, *Eat a Bowl of Tea* shows the authoritarian father reduced to a pathetic parody, while the newly arrived women flaunt shocking freedoms. Mei Oi, Ben Loy's wife, even violates the cardinal female virtue of chastity and marital fidelity. Ideologically advanced, Ben Loy accepts her "love child" as his own and thus damages the Confucian image of patrilineal purity. This un-Chinese ending marks patriarchy's first serious fall into disrepute in Chinese American fiction.

The fall begins with the decline of family after decades of male emigration and harsh realities in the new land. Compared to Lowe and Wong's paeans to family life, Chu's fictionalized "family," headed by Wong Wah Gay and barely held together by Ben Loy and Mei Oi, becomes a mockery of Chinese family. Men are reduced to "paper sons," "bachelor fathers," and absent husbands. The circle of Wah Gay's foul-mouthed cronies who meet at lunch counters and basement gambling halls takes the place of family. These "bachelors" cannot return to China because of inertia, lack of money, and immigration restrictions. Their wives, amply represented by the capable and energetic Lau Shee (Ben Loy's mother and Wah Gay's wife), bring up the children in the ancestral village. The "rice cookers," as they are referred to by their "*gimshunhock*" (gold-mountain sojourner) husbands, take on domineering aspects as the husbands' self-esteem diminishes. Left to Wah Gay and Lee Gong, without their wives' goading, their children would not find suitable parentally approved matches. Wah Gay remains a subordinate, accountable to his wife in China, who has been separated from him for over two decades.

The fathers' foibles lend an un-Confucian sensibility to the novel. Chu legitimized this sensibility: he wrote in a salty vernacular, describing the pleasures of the flesh and evoking the raw, harsh life of waiters, barbers, cooks, gamblers, and hangers-on. Consequently Chu became something of a trailblazer in his portrayal of emotionally damaged sons and daughters locked in battles of independence with their fathers or with the tradition that gives the fathers power. Since then, overtly or subversively, the literature has repeatedly attacked the Confucian fathers. Chu's iconoclastic treatment of Chinatown fathers emboldened later writers to express what has now come to be accepted as the Chinese American sensibility. During the postsixties flowering of Asian American literature in general, antipatriarchal and anti-Confucian attitudes colored most of the writings. Indeed Chinatown, the symbol of Chinese America, is now regarded as a culture unto itself, rather than the inauthentic imitation of two mother cultures, forever split by a hyphen. This prevailing sentiment has become so strong in the last decade, in fact, that in writing, the hyphen in "Chinese-American" has disappeared. Chinatown is its own source of language and expression—and these are good enough for high art.

After the consciousness-raising 1960s, many critics and writers held up Chu's book as a model of a realistic portrayal of Chinatown. The current crop of Asian American writers who abandon their characters to alienation, raw anger, patricidal obsessions, self-contempt, and marginality follow in the same tradition as *Eat a Bowl of Tea*. Ben Loy, the emasculated and frustrated son, has many literary descendants in the stories and plays by Asian Americans, as can also be said of Mei Oi, the threatening Chinese female characterized by male writers.

This new sensibility came first from Chu's intimate knowledge of the ossified Chinese traditions that had survived and flourished in America's Chinatown. Chu shows that while customs changed in China's villages, ethnic culture remained entrenched in the insulated ghetto of cosmopolitan New York City. Ben Loy and Mei Oi's wedding, emblematic of Chinatown's anachronism, is celebrated twice—in the "new generation" style back in Sunwei village and then at a banquet given in New York's Chinatown. The village wedding arranged by the couple's mothers combines East and West: a Christian minister officiates on a day picked by an astrologer. The church wedding reflects the Westernization China was going through and the inroads missionaries had made into the hamlets and villages. In Sunwei, without the *gimshun* fathers, the bride and groom occupy the center of attention and receive their benediction. But in Chinatown, U.S.A., which is cut off from mainstream American society, the banquet—more a stag party than a nuptial feast—is untouched by American custom. Chu describes in detail the customs that the oldtime "bachelors" still cling to. The bride and groom's presence is incidental. In keeping with the feudalistic social network of family associations, Wang Chuck Ting, as president and elder statesman, takes over as host and introduces the officers of the organizations. The banquet serves Wah Gay's need to curry their favor rather than celebrating the marriage of his son and daughter-in-law, Ben Loy and Mei Oi.

By depicting the old and new ways, Chu echoes the silencing of women and the young in earlier writings. Jade Snow Wong notes that at the Fourth Older Sister's wedding "hardly anyone talked to the bride; they all talked to the parents," and the bride "was merely a sort of decorative, noneating, nondrinking, nonspeaking accessory to the wedding celebration" (144). In Pardee Lowe's autobiography, as the contrite elder son that he is, he never once mentions his Caucasian wife by name but only as one who adds "luster to the family honor" and is "one of the models for Chinatown's feminine etiquette, a preserver of its ancient traditions of social intercourse" (237). In spite of their implicit criticism of patriarchy, Wong and Lowe acquiesced in its practices. Chu, however, does not allow the bride to be forgotten, and his pivots on Mei Oi's affair with Ah Song. It is a tale of the bride's revenge. Ben Loy becomes a cuckold, and their marital crisis sends the community reeling.

In New York, patriarchy can no longer exert moral influence over the entire community; it contains its own undoing. Among the invited guests at the feast is Mei Oi's seducer, Ah Song, who first sees her there. Although the watchful eyes of the Chinatown fathers follow Ah Song, a notorious wife stealer, he is an outsider with no powerful family associations to kowtow to or to lean on, and he confesses to Mei Oi that he rather enjoys "this bachelor life." He is free to cause trouble. As one scholar of labor and political history points out, the internal structure of village and family associations "was not as functional as it seemed. Its organizational model, after all, was the feudal China of the Ch'ing Dynasty, whose self-sufficient rural economy was scarcely comparable to the urban industrialized setting of New York's China-town. The traditional associations were run on strict hierarchical lines; they demanded unquestioning obedience and total control" (Kwong 41). New York's Chinatown has many competing tongs and family associations, plus all kinds of unaffiliated drifters. Thus control cannot be "total." Ah Song sets off a chain of events that humiliate, infuriate, and fragment the family and the community.

Finally, Chu's antipatriarchal portrayal resides in the two fathers' char-acters. Wah Gay and Lee Gong, gambling partners and now inlaws through Ben Loy and Mei Oi's marriage, are mere shadows of the Confucian father.

Wah Gay, proprietor of the gambling shop Money Come, knows all too painfully that his life is far from exemplary and sends Ben Loy to work in a restaurant in Connecticut to keep him out of "harm's way." Lee Gong has been an absent father and has never set eyes on his daughter until the day she arrives in New York as Ben Loy's bride. The pregnant Mei Oi longs to confide in her father about her illicit affair, but they have no father-daughter bond and she gets neither solace nor guidance. In Chinatown, children disgrace their parents as often as fathers fail their children.

Chu places the blame for male inadequacy, however, squarely on the social and historical conditions of the Chinese emigrants in America. Circumstances excuse these failed fathers' and husbands' lack of ambition. They cling to the only tradition they know, which is reflected in Wah Gay's view of Ben Loy's impending marriage:

> He ventured to think that, after the marriage, Ben Loy would work that much harder because he would have a family to support. Instead of having to keep track of his son himself, he would have a daughter-in-law to take over the responsibility. A year or so after the wedding, a grandson, perhaps. Or a grand-daughter? A boy first, Our Chinese people always like boys. But what if . . ." (46)

Children exist to propagate future generations, with the daughters-in-law as accessories to the whole process. Patriarchal loyalty also dictates that the fathers do everything they can to protect the reputation of the family association, which in turn protects their livelihood They do not care about the suffering of their offspring—Ben Loy and Mei Oi. In fact throughout the family crisis Wah Gay and Lee Gong behave as the wronged party. In a community supposedly dedicated to mutual aid, Ben Loy and Mei Oi stand alone in their crisis. Without the social and family network of a normal community, they have nowhere to turn for advice and solace.

Patriarchy is unyielding and unforgiving in its characteristic sternness. The wrongdoer Ah Song has his ear sliced off in one melodramatic stroke by Wah Gay and is banished. Even the aging fathers, Wah Gay and Lee Gong, must pull up stakes and go elsewhere to rid the community of any trace of shame. Because Chu has made the implacable patriarchy the emotional center of his novel, Wong Chuck Ting's mediation of the incident takes over the plot. In the tense negotiations between Wah Gay and the Wang Family Association (headed by Chuck Ting), the young couple nearly disappears from the plot. In fact there are two plots, with the plot having Ben Loy and Mei Oi as its focus subordinate to the main plot: how Chinatown fathers maintain order. New York's Chinatown remains strangled by the feudalism that has held sway in China for centuries and rules it even now. However benevolent, Chuck Ting and his lieutenants exert their power and influence. They intrude into Chinatown's private lives. The intricate power structure of family associations and tongs still rules supreme in the insulated Chinatown. Its grip is relentless, its judgment swift, and its power unyielding. Under this system, the ruling patriarchs mete out rewards and punishments. Ben Loy and Mei Oi, and even their fathers, live at the mercy of the collective decisions.

In the limited world of Chinatown, failure begets failure. The impoverished old-fashioned males cannot provide the authoritarian guidance a son like Ben Loy is conditioned to need. Coming to New York at the age of seventeen, Ben Loy is a cultural orphan, ill-equipped to handle his new life. His parents dictate what work he should do and when and whom he should marry. Filial obedience makes him passive and dull. The freedom he has stolen—whoring behind his father's back—robs him finally of his manhood. As a character, Ben Loy seems totally acted upon by the social forces Chu describes.

Ben Loy's limitations are further aggravated by the community's sense of proprietorship over all its sons. He is not only his father's son but also a son of Chinatown. The community's gossip places further strain on the couple's childless state. As the whispered rumor of Mei Oi's affair spreads, Ben Loy sinks deeper into inaction and becomes more susceptible to his elders' maneuverings. Although he moves to San Francisco, the source and cradle of Chinese America, and comes into his own, the cure for his impotence comes appropriately from a bowl of medicinal tea. He finds renewal outside himself. The perfunctory happy ending only underscores the extent of Ben Loy's impotence. Louis Chu's art may be ahead of his time, but he could not conceive of any inner change in the sons of patriarchy.

Unlike the rags-to-riches prototype in many immigrant memoirs, Chu's Ben Loy languishes in indecision and ineptitude. In this respect Ben Loy has many literary descendants in the stories and plays of the next decade. He is reincarnated in Frank Chin's Johnny in "Food for All His Dead" and Tam in *Chickencoop Chinaman* and in Jeffrey Chan's Bill Wong in "Chinese in Haifa." Conditioned by Chinese tradition and the standards of the masculine image in American culture, these Chinese sons and husbands prove defenseless and impotent, mastered by rather than mastering their fate. These schlemiels seem to wallow in their self-emasculation, with no hope of measuring up to either the patriarchal Chinese image of authority or the American model of masculinity. The fathers, dead or alive, remain in control. The frustrated and passive sons rail against what their fathers represent, yet they cannot break out of the confines of tradition. Failed dreams, unfulfilling marriages and relationships, and what they see as a cultural conspiracy to rob them of power plague their lives. By the same token the male authors yearn for the potency the once-powerful patriarchy would have conferred on them.

Chu's greatest achievement lies in his exploitation of the complications created by women who are not prostitutes in the "bachelor society" of Chinatown. The presence of women brings out patriarchy's most ruthless character—its misogyny—manifested in the language and attitudes of the bachelor community. The otherwise enfeebled male community joins in a swelling chorus of "Nowadays women are not to be trusted" echoed by "*Gim Peng Moy*," the Cantonese opera the bachelors listen to in the barber's chair. Despite their own loose morals, the men demand purity and fidelity of their wives and daughters. This double standard is ingrained in the culture. But the feudal code is a thing of the past. Given the education that women now receive and the male-female imbalance in Chinatown, women have freedoms that the bachelors cannot stem. On one level, *Eat a Bowl of Tea* satirizes the "bachelor society's" hollow show of authority.

But Chu's achievement is limited by his depiction of Mei Oi. It shows his ambivalence toward the heroine he both liberates from and imprisons in traditional ideas of womanhood. Although he gives Mei Oi the role of discrediting and humiliating patriarchy, he does not entirely transcend his male view of women. To be sure, he acknowledges the independence of the "new woman" as represented by the middle-school graduate Mei Oi. This educated "school girl" can shake up the rickety patriarchy. Mei Oi has a mind of her own and has already chosen a path for herself: "She knew she wouldn't marry a farmer. A farmer's wife worked from dawn till dusk out in the fields. . . . Marry a school teacher? Not Mei Oi. There was this common observation. Unless you're poor you would not be teaching" (66). Yet for all the benefits of a middle school education, Mei Oi must stay home and be economically dependent. Bored and childless, the listless Mei Oi wants to find work outside. Ben Loy turns down her request—but not before he consults his father. Ben Loy says he wants to preserve family dignity, but he really fears that Mei Oi may meet other men. By an ironic twist of fate, Ben Loy's worst fear materializes right in his own house, which is where Mei Oi meets Ah Song. Here as elsewhere Chu's treatment of this pivotal event is ambiguous. He metes out freedoms to Mei Oi with one hand and takes them back with the other.

Not only is Mei Oi's freedom limited, but her character gets scant development. The briefly introduced school-girl image of Mei Oi undergoes a drastic change with her crossing the Pacific. Mei Oi turns into a dangerous seductress overnight—with little preparation by Chu. Abruptly, the innocent village girl discards her loose two-piece suits in favor of clinging gowns. For the Chinatown banquet she wears a "snugly" fitted satin gown, which is appropriately red for a wedding but also portends Mei Oi's subsequent behavior as bordering on that of a scarlet woman. In fact she rather relishes her affair with Ah Song: "The great pleasures she got from her indiscretions were worth the risk" (124). While Ben Loy is haunted by his past dalliance with prostitutes, no qualms bother Mei Oi. Confronted by Ben Loy she counterattacks: "'What kind of a husband have you been?'" she declares; "'I didn't do anything wrong . . . but it turns out that I've married an old man . . . an old man who's too old to make love to me'" (145). Here again ambivalence governs Chu's attitude toward Mei Oi's sexuality. Her aggressive role makes Ben Loy all the more a victim of social forces over which he has no control. The author builds up our sympathy for Ben Loy as Mei Oi steps up her pursuit of extramarital gratification. Like the unfaithful wife in *Gim Peng Moy*, Mei Oi has the destructive potential to bring about her husband's downfall—and her destructiveness erodes Ben Loy's self-esteem.

In effect, Mei Oi personifies the proverbial temptress, both to be desired and feared. Male artists and writers have often put their female subjects in such paradoxical light, and Chu is no exception. Chu's narrative, perhaps unconsciously, reinforces this connection for us. The early morning call of the prostitute in the opening scene invites us to link the white prostitute with the bride who is lying in Ben Loy's arms. The juxtaposition of the two women is meant to show the source of Ben Loy's guilt and its symptom, impotence. But the two women have even more in common than suggested by this opening image: both are dependent on the economically independent man as well as being objects of his sexual desire (though Ben Loy's is in temporary suspension). The prostitute sells her body just as Mei Oi marries a *gimsunhock* for his money and the chance to come to America. Even if this parallel is not intended by the author, Mei Oi has limited autonomy as a character and is manipulated by father, husband, father-in-law, seducer and, finally, the novelist—to achieve his narrative ends.

At best, Chu's Mei Oi calls up a sensual Suzy Wong, easily lured by attention and gifts. Vain and frivolous, the eighteen-year-old cannot handle the temptation of adultery: "Mei Oi's affair with Ah Song was the sort of thing that a country girl would never dream could happen to her. Once it happened it was not within the easy-going personality of Mei Oi to halt it" (103). Her beauty, as seen by Ben Loy and expressed in hackneyed Chinese terms, further casts her as a cardboard character: "Her eyebrows were like the crescent of the new moon. Her full lips, forming a small mouth, were cherry-red. Her nose . . . perfect as a distant star" (50). The telling scene of

Mei Oi admiring herself in the mirror underscores her lack of an inner dimension: "Mel Oi turned to face the mirror again. She inspected the collar. She spun around and glanced at the curves reflected in the mirror. She tugged at the lower half of the dress and wiggled a little bit" (82). In this gesture she conforms with the male image of women: all exterior and no inner dimension. As the proverbial China doll and Suzy Wong combined, she displays no perceptible change or growth. She has no self-understanding and is solely propelled by vanity. For a fuller portrait of Asian American woman we have to wait for later writers—women writers—to reveal the struggle and confusion that crossing cultural boundaries could generate in the female psyche. *Eat a Bowl of Tea* adopts both the Western and the Chinese patriarchal caricatures of Asian women.

For all his ambiguous and stereotypical treatment of Mei Oi, however, Chu provides us with an alternative to the "rice cookers." Even Eng Shee, Mei Oi's rival and the 1950 facsimile of an old-time "rice cooker," does so little cooking that her husband brings home food from the restaurant. Such "new women" freely express their sexuality, as Mei Oi does by flirting with her husband's friend while carrying on an affair with another man. She does not tolerate a sexless marriage as a traditional wife would. But Chu's portrait of a liberated woman stops here. As a character, Mei Oi merely occupies the other side of the same coin as the shrewish "rice cooker," reinforcing the double-vision image of women in male eyes.

Female characters created by male writers that have come after Mei Oi are also subservient to their male counterparts; the female characters serve as foils for the flawed and ineffective husbands, sons, and fathers, who are casualties in a racist and stifling society. The authors are not interested in developing the women and granting them dimensions of their own. Rather than their sympathy for the plight of women, what is significant is these authors' criticism of a process that robs the men of their accustomed authority and manhood. In their eyes, women fare better in America. For all their criticism of patriarchy, the male writers perpetuate the patriarchy-centered world, in which the woman is a polemical tool to reinforce the emasculation of Asian males.

The lack of inner dimension in Chu's characters, male and female, is not necessarily a function of artistic failure but a result of the limited individual power such characters would have in Chinatown, and by extension in the larger American society. Several times, the plot teeters melodramatically on such flimsy devices as Wah Gay's knife or bowls of herbal tea. Chu cannot tell us much more about these characters who are limited by the limiting world that forms them. Moreover, Chu is himself a son of patriarchy, the source of his vision and understanding. The refurbishing of this tattered tradition was not within his capability.

Thus *Eat a Bowl of Tea* serves as a culmination of the early attempts to debunk patriarchy as a viable social structure in Asian America. On a scale and with a complexity not found in earlier works, Louis Chu uses patriarchy as the villain of his tragicomic story. That his story should survive as one of the influential texts in the post-civil rights decades indicates the lively interest Asian American writers still have in the patriarchal tradition. The same forces that stymied a marriage on the rocky soil of forced "bachelor-hood" also hampered Chu from seeing a woman beyond her exterior and her mechanical role in the plot. Just as the community is not freed from the patriarchal vise, so Chu's handling of Mei Oi and other female characters is still dictated by male images of women. Whether a ghost or a living tyrant, the ubiquitous figure of the patriarch still stalks Asian American literature even as it concocts endless cures to ward off patriarchy's ill effects. But patriarchy remains incurable in *Eat a Bowl of Tea*.

OSCAR V. CAMPOMANES

Filipinos in the United States and Their Literature of Exile

Is there a "Filipino American" literature? Current and inclusive notions of Asian American literature assume the existence of this substratum without really delineating its contours. There is no sustained discussion of how "Filipino American" literature, if shaped as such a substructure, problematizes some of the claims of Asian American literature as a constitutive paradigm. Although developed unevenly as a category and distinctive body of writing, "Asian American", literature now commands a significant presence in the American academy and the movement to revise the national literary canon. The imperative, then, is to test the descriptive and explanatory powers of this general paradigm in light of its as yet undetermined but nominally acknowledged tributary formation of "Filipino American" writing. To leave this area unmapped is to create exclusion, internal hierarchy, and misrepresentation in the supposedly heterogeneous field of Asian American cultural production.

The informal but long-standing directive to align "Filipino American" literature with the Chinese and Japanese American mainstream of Asian American literature has had its own consequences. When asked to construct "a literary background of Filipino-American works" for a founding Asian American anthology, the writers Oscar Penaranda, Serafin Syquia, and Sam Tagatac declared: "We cannot write any literary background because there

From *Reading the Literatures of Asian America.* © 1992 by Temple University.

isn't any. No history. No published literature. No nothing" (49). Their statement proved not only to be quite precipitate but also uncritical of the
limiting assumptions foisted on their prose by the anthologists. Already
implicit in this view was their disconnection from the exilic literature created
by N.V.M. Gonzalez and Bienvenido Santos or, in more recent times, by
Ninotchka Rosca and Linda Ty-Casper. Perhaps, rather than the veracity of
its claim, what remains compelling is how this declaration expresses the
incommensurable sense of nonbeing that stalks many Filipinos in the United
States and many Americans of Filipino descent.

WITHOUT NAMES: WHO ARE WE?

Indeed, one cannot discuss the (non)existence of "Filipino American" literature without interrogating the more decisive issues of self and peoplehood,
of invisibility. This combined problematic certainly shapes the available
expressions. For example, the Bay Area Filipino American Writers titled
their first collection of poetry after Jeff Tagami's historically textured piece,
"Without Names" (in Ancheta et al.). "Who are we? / What are we?" (230)
asks public historian Fred Cordova in his picture book and oral history on
Filipino Americans. In a 1989 essay, the journalist Cielo Fuentebella point-
edly observes that even with the group nearing the one-million mark, "our
numbers don't add up to visibility in business, media and the cultural field.
And all these at a time in history that is being dubbed as the Asian/Pacific
Century" (17).

From these various expressions, one detects some hesitance to claim the
name "Filipino American" unproblematically. The term "Filipino American"
itself seems inadequate, if oxymoronic. "The Filipino American cannot be
defined without elucidating what the problematic relationship is between the
two terms which dictates the conditions of possibility for each—the addition
of the hyphen which spells a relation of subordination and domination" (San
Juan, "Boundaries" 125). There is some recognition, in other words, of the
irreducible specificity of the Filipino predicament in the United States and,
corollarily, of the literary and cultural expressions that it has generated.
Although one finds many self-identified Filipino Americans and Filipino
American works (the preferred term is "Pilipino American"), their relationship
to this provisional term seems to be ambivalent and indeterminate, shored up
only by its roots in 1960s ethnic identity politics. Hence, I choose the formulation "Filipinos in the United States" for this discussion while also tactically
deploying the conditional but meaningful category "Filipino American."

The task of my essay is to characterize the available writings by

Filipinos in the United States and Filipino Americans in light of community formation and Philippine-American (neo)colonial relations. I seek to describe a literary tradition of Filipino exilic writing and an exilic sensibility that informs both the identity politics and the cultural production of this "community-in-the-making" (San Juan, "Filipano Artist" 36).

As does any preliminary account, this essay has several limitations. Because of the urgency of the task and space considerations, the survey of some of the available writings is only suggestive, if incomplete, and the arguments of propositions (along with the bases) for constituting them as a tradition are abbreviated. That the writings and the history of the group codify their own theoretical claims is a question to which I pay the most attention, for "each literary tradition, at least implicitly, contains within it an argument for how it can be read" (Gates xix–xx). I concentrate on the older writers whose works have reached a certain consolidation and then suggest some beginning orientations with which to steer future readings of the work of the younger writers who are in several stages of emergence.

Motifs of departure, nostalgia, incompletion, rootlessness, leave taking, and dispossession recur with force in most writing produced by Filipinos in the United States and by Filipino Americans, with the Philippines as either the original or terminal reference point. Rather than the United States as the locus of claims or "the promised land" that Werner Sollors argues is the typological trope of "ethnic" American writing (40–50), the Filipino case represents a reverse telos, an opposite movement. It is on this basis that I argue for a literature of exile and emergence rather than a literature of immigration and settlement whereby life in the United States serves as the space for displacement, suspension, and perspective. Exile becomes a necessary, if inescapable, state for Filipinos in the United States—at once susceptible to the vagaries of the (neo)colonial U.S.-Philippine relationship and redeemable only by its radical restructuring.

The intergenerational experience will certainly dim this literary/ historical connection to the Philippines for many Filipino Americans. But the signifiers "Filipino" and "Philippines" evoke colonialist meanings and cultural redactions which possess inordinate power to shape the fates of the writers and of Filipino peoples everywhere. These considerations overdetermine their dominant sense of nonbelonging in the United States, the Philippines, and other places. The word "overdetermine" adequately describes the complex of historical inscriptions, developments, processes, interventions, and accidents in which their present predicament is embedded.

For Filipinos in the United States and their history of community formation, it is not enough to examine immigration policies (symptomatic of a U.S.-centric approach to which most sociologists/historians are prone) that by themselves fail to account for the diversity of immigration patterns. "The historical, economic, and political relationships between the United States and the country of origin, as well as the social and economic conditions in the source country, have to be examined to explain the major differences in immigration streams" (Carino and Fawcett 305). Robert Blauner's point that the stems of any Asian American group should roughly equal the status of its country of origin in relation to the United States bears remembering (Takaki, *Race and Ethnicity* 159). Conceptually useful for the Philippine case, both of these views also expand American immigration, ethnic, and cultural studies beyond their parochial purviews of American nation building, acculturation, and settlement.

INVISIBILITY AND (NON)IDENTITY: THE ROOTS IN HISTORY

Among the various Asian countries of origin, the Philippines holds the sole distinction of being drawn into a truly colonial and neocolonial relation with the United States, and for this reason it has been absorbed almost totally into the vacuum of American innocence. It was the founding moment of colonialism, "a primal loss suffered through the Filipino-American War (1899–1902) and the resistance ordeal of the revolutionary forces of the First Philippine Republic up to 1911 that opened the way for the large-scale transport of cheap Filipino labor to Hawaii and California [and inaugurated] this long, tortuous exodus from the periphery to the metropolis" (San Juan, "Boundaries" 117). Hence, while rooted in the earlier period of Spanish rule, the spectre of "invisibility" for Filipinos is specific to the immediate and long-term consequences of American colonialism.

The invisibility of the Philippines became a necessary historiographical phenomenon because the annexation of the Philippines proved to be constitutionally and culturally problematic for American political and civil society around the turn of the century and thereafter. (A consequent case in point was the anomalous status of migrant workers and students for much of the formal colonial period when they were considered American "nationals" but without the basic rights of "citizens.") To understand the absence of the Philippines in American history, one faces the immense task of charting the intense ideological contestation that developed in the United States around the Philippine question at the point of colonial conquest, and the active rewriting of American historical records from then on that articulated and rearticulated the verities of "American exceptionalism." As Amy Kaplan suggestively notes, "The invisibility of the Philippines in American history has everything to do with the invisibility of American imperialism to itself."

Discursively, the unbroken continuity of this historic amnesia concerning the Philippines has had real invidious effects. Note the repetitious and unreflective use of the modifier "forgotten" to describe, even renew, this curse of invisibility which may be said to have been bestowed on the Philippines as soon as the bloody war of conquest and resistance began to require stringent official/military censorship in the United States around 1900. No one has bothered to ask some of the more unsettling questions: Who is doing the forgetting? What is being forgotten? How much has been forgotten? Why the need to continue forgetting?

Contemporary examples abound. An essay by the American historian Peter Stanley bears the title "The Forgotten Philippines, 1790–1946" and sticks out in a retrospective survey of American-East Asian studies, a field which has always revolved around China and Japan (May and Thomson 291–316). Quoted in Russell Roth's journalistic account of the long and costly Filipino-American War, one writer admits that "our movement into the Philippines is one of the least understood phases of our history, one of those obscure episodes swept under the rug, and forgotten" (1981). In a truthful exemplification of the workings of hegemony, a chapter of Takaki's *Strangers from a Different Shore* is devoted to "The Forgotten Filipinos" (314–54), and one Filipino American documentary work itself, *Filipinos: Forgotten Asian Americans*, finds the term as unproblematic and adequate (Cordova 1983).

GENEALOGIES OF EXILE AND THE IMAGINED COMMUNITY

So it is that "in the Philippine experience, History has provided its own despotism" (Gonzalez, *Kalutang* 32). It is in the various forms and manifestations of this despotism that one can locate the productive conditions of possibility for Filipino writing and the making of Filipino identities. For something as specific as Filipino writing in the United States, the banishment of the Philippines and Filipinos from history, the global disperal of Filipinos, the migrant realities of Pinoy workers and urban expatriates, and "the alienation of the English-speaking intellectuals from workers and peasants speaking the vernacular" (San Juan, *Ruptures* 25) must constitute the set of tangled contexts. They amount to a common orientation of the experiences, writings, and identity politics toward a "national mythos," following the creation of a "Filipino diaspora . . . the scattering of a people, not yet a fully matured nation, to the ends of the earth, across the planet" by the colonial moment (Brennan, "Cosmopolitans" 4; San Juan, "Homeland" 40).

Through a coordination of the expressive tendencies and impulses of

Filipino and Filipino American writers in the United States, a "literature of exile and emergence" can be constructed from the normally separated realms of the old and new countries. I see the obsessive search for identity that marks Philippine literature in the colonial language (and in the vernacular, which is not possible to cover here), and the identity politics articulated by first- and second-generation Filipino American writers (after the social and ethnic movements of the 1960s and 1970s) as specific streams with certain points of confluence.

In recognizing the intimate connection between Filipino nation building and the problematics of Filipino American community formation and, hence, the radical contingency of both processes, the seeming scarcity of "published literature" (sometimes attributed to the smallness of the Filipino American second generation) ceases to be a problem. That "we still don't have anyone resembling Maxine Hong Kingston for the Filipino immigrant community here" begins to make sense and points us to the many writers who write about the situation in the Philippines and the Filipino American writers who may be U.S. grounded yet articulate this same ancestral focus. The orientation toward the Philippines prevents prevailing notions of Asian American literature from reducing Filipino writing in the United States to just another variant of the immigrant epic, even if this in itself must be seen as an everpresent and partial possibility as time passes and Philippine-American relations change.

In what follows, I examine some expressions of exile and gestures toward return—either explicit or latent—that typify the available writings. How do they characteristically respond to, or even embody, the experience of exile and indeterminacy and the question of redemptive return? Put another way, what are the intersections between historical experience and literary history, between subjection and subject positions? I organize my review around several interrelated issues: exilic experience and perspective, exilic identity and language, and exilic sensibility and attitude toward history and place, all of which account for the forms of indeterminacy and visionary resolutions in the writings.

The writers may be clustered into three "cohorts" that need not necessarily coincide with the migration and immigration patterns or cycles documented by historians and sociologists (see, for example, Carino and Fawcett 305–25; and Pido). There is the pioneering generation consisting of Bienvenido Santos, N.V.M. Gonzalez, José García Villa, and Carlos Bulosan for the period of the 1930s to the 1950s; a settled generation that matures and emerges by the 1960s who, after Penaranda, Tagatac, and Syquia, may be called the "Flips"; and the politically expatriated generation of Epifanio San Juan, Linda Ty-Casper, Ninotchka Rosca, and Michelle Skinner from the

1970s to the present. These writers whom I have specifically mentioned must be taken as demarcating, rather than definitive, figures for each group.

This periodization has obvious limits. Bulosan died in 1956 and Villa ceased to write nearly three decades ago, while Santos and Gonzalez continue to be prolific and have exhibited significant shifts in their perspectives and writings after extended residence in the United States as professors. Bulosan, with the intervention of U.S. cultural workers, has earned some critical attention and student readership in ethnic studies courses, yet to be matched in the cases of Santos and Gonzalez, whose exilic writing did not fit with the immigrant ethos. Villa has languished in self-selected obscurity even as Sollors recently and curiously recuperated him as an "ethnic modernist" (253–54). My concern here is much more in comparison than in contemporaneity, since these writers' works are uneven in quality, their developments divergent in pattern, and their influence diffuse in reception. By "comparison" I mean their styles of coping with the experiential reality of exile given their initial and subsequent ties with, or alienation from, each other—and their relevant self-definition and development of certain forms of writing on this basis.

I also make the Flips assume a kind of corporate existence, although this is suggested itself by their self-designation as "Bay Area Filipino American Writers" and their networks that are rooted in the ethnic movements of the late 1960s and 1970s. Of these writers (mostly poets), I find a few who exhibit tendencies to outgrow the agonized temporizings associated with that historic juncture, namely Jeff Tagami, Virginia Cerrenio, and Jaime Jacinto. What concerns me here is their search for kinship with their predecessors in the pioneering generation and their symbolic appropriations of Philippine history and identities from the perspective of a second, or consciously American, generation (hence, "Pilipino American").

Not all those who may belong to the "politically expatriated" were literally so, by the yardstick of martial law politics and the sensibility of nationalism that grew out of the social and political turmoil of the late 1960s and the subsequent period of authoritarian rule in the homeland. It is the peculiar elaboration of the theme of exile from a more troubling historical moment and its consequent suspension of Filipinos within a more ideologically and politically bounded sphere that distinguish the actions and predicament of this group. San Juan shifted to Philippine and Third World literary and historical studies from traditional literary scholarship and creative writing in the conjuncture between his initial residence in the United States as an academic, and the politicizing movements in the United States and the Philippines in the early 1970s. Skinner came to the United States with the sensibility of her martial law generation back home but did not exactly flee from political persecution as Rosca did. And yet again, their relationships of affinity and alienation as a group, and with the other two, may be divined in what they have written and how they have defined themselves.

My groupings are not chronological but synchronic, concerned with what Benedict Anderson has called "the deep horizontal comradeship" that enables profoundly dispersed populations to imagine peoplehood and community, to overcome historically disabling differences, and to occupy new spaces of historical, literary, and cultural possibility (15–16). Writers can find a home in the relevant pattern or cohort of affinity specific to their own origins in any of these three historical moments of colonial generation, ethnic identity politics, and political expatriation. The groupings need not be rigid, since certain movements between them are possible, within defensible bounds, and depending to some extent on the stronger sentiment of the writer or reader.

EXILE AND RETURN: LITERARY AND EXPERIENTIAL PARALLELS

In looking at the plurality of Filipino experiences, positions, and writings in the United States as a generalized condition of exile, I refer to the ensemble of its many relations, degrees, and forms, and not to its easy reduction to a single thematic. One cannot succumb to the homogenizing assertion that "immigration is the opposite of expatriation" (Mukherjee 28) or the tendency to construe the West as only a base for "cosmopolitan exiles" and not a place "where unknown men and women have spent years of miserable loneliness" (Said 359). The need is to "map territories of experience beyond those mapped by the literature of exile itself" (Said 358) and, if I might add, the areas of exile and writing overlap.

Sam Solberg notes that "if there is one indisputable fact about Filipino-American writing nurtured on American shores that sets it apart from other Asian American writings, it is that it is inextricably linked with indigenous Filipino writing in English" (50). He adds that Carlos Bulosan, José García Villa, Bienvenido Santos, and N.V.M. Gonzalez did not find the distinction between writing in the Philippines and the United States meaningful. Yet, also, their common experiences of migration to the United States and the vicissitudes of their careers in this setting consigned them to the same state of indeterminacy and limbo of invisibility as their less noted kinfolk.

Bharati Mukherjee posits that "exiles come wrapped in a cloak of mystery and world-weariness [and in] refusing to play the game of immigration, they certify to the world, and especially to their hosts, the purity of their pain and their moral superiority to the world around them" (28). Aside from making exile sound like a choice, this view fails to consider that there is nothing to romanticize about this condition even if it might sometimes generate romantic visions of one's origins. "Exile is a grim fate and its recourses equally grim" (Seidel x). Although exile gives birth to varieties of nationalist sentiment, even imagined communities and unlikely kinships among peoples with enduring differences, "these are no more than efforts to overcome the crippling sorrow of estrangement . . . the loss of something left behind forever" (Said 357).

Just as it has been for similarly situated peoples, the exilic experience for Filipinos and Filipino Americans has engendered such "enormously constructive pressures" (Gurr 9) as self-recovery and the critical distance from a putative homeland whose outlines are sharpened from the perspective of their new or "other" home in the metropolis. More, for Filipinos as "colonial exiles," the "search for identity and the construction of a vision of home amount to the same thing" (Gurr 11). In turn, this "identity" (now in the sense of specular experiences and visions), condenses itself in the institution of creative genealogies, mythic reinterpretations of colonial history, and reevaluations of the linguistic and cultural losses caused by colonialism. These may be seen as notations of redemptive return to a "home" in the imagination, with specific inflections for Filipinos and Filipino Americans.

When Bienvenido Santos declares that "in a special sense I, too, am an oldtimer" ("Pilipino Old Timers" 89) and a Flip poet like Jeff Tagami (1987) memorializes these migrant workers (also called Pinoys or Manongs) in his work, there is already this particular reciprocity of self-representations among unlikely "allies." Distances are being bridged here among generational locations, social classes, and particular experiences, from the pioneering experiences and enduring ties to the native territory of such workers in the Pacific Coast states as the privileged point of origin. Documentary works have described the exilic conditions of these Pinoys in paradigmatic terms because of the complexity of their displacements: "Between themselves and their homeland, between themselves and their children who have known only America, and between themselves and recent arrivals whose Philippines is in some ways, drastically different from their own" (Santos, *Apples* xiv).

Santos's claim of affinity with the "survivors of those who immigrated in the 1920s or even earlier, through the 1940s" ("Pilipino Old Timers" 89) may seem ill-considered because of the large wedge in class, migratory pattern, and education between this former "pensionado" or colonial government scholar and resident writer of a Kansas university and the faceless, nameless "Manongs." Carlos Bulosan—valorized as the supreme chronicler of the Pinoy story and claimed as an immigrant writer even while moved to state once that "I think I am forever an exile" (*Falling Light* 198)— particularly lamented this great divide. Regarding the pensionados of his time (and the ruling/middling classes they helped form in the Philippines) with suspicion and contempt, Bulosan foregrounded his shared peasant origins with the oldtimers in his identity as a writer. Among many expressions of affiliation with them are his controversial letter to a friend concerning his critique of Filipino writers in English and their "contrary feelings" for him (*Falling Light* 228) and his narrator Allos's discovery of the estranging and demarcating stance of this social class in regard to the Philippine peasantry in *America Is in the Heart* (1946), in the humiliating encounter between the narrator's mother and a middle-class girl (37–38).

This great wedge partly originated in the institution of education as a form of social hierarchy in the Philippines during the colonial period (the pensionados were sent to the United States to train in government and cultural administration) and threatened Bulosan's own close kinship with the migrant workers as his writing career took off in the 1930s and 1940s. He obviated this successfully with a symbolic return to their ranks and their lives in his writing and by articulating a Pinoy critique of upper/middle-class conceit: "There is no need for Filipino writers to feel that . . . they are educated because they went to colleges, nor should they think that I am ignorant because I lack formal education" (*Falling Light* 228). If Bulosan's "return" to the oldtimers is warranted by an original class affinity, this makes Santos's gesture from the other side toward this group striking.

The sense of indeterminacy conveyed by Santos in his many stories and essays, and in interviews, resonates with the Pinoy's suspension in eternal time and alien place, "deracinated and tortured by the long wait to go home" (Gurr 18). Like Bulosan, he has codified this linkage in his work, as in the symbolic kinship between the Michigan farmworker Celestino Fabia and "the first class Filipino" in the moving story "A Scent of Apples" (*Apples* 21–29). Especially revealing is Santos's juxtaposition in an essay of his fictional transfiguration of the oldtimers's characters and lives with their documentation in oral and social history to illustrate his point—when asked "to explain the difference between the old timer as character in fiction and in real life"—"that there is nothing to explain because there is no difference" ("Pilipino Old Timers" 91).

These heroes with all their little triumphs and tragic losses as exiles but "survivors" populate Santos's tightly crafted stories, endowing his identity as a writer and his writing with a pointed specificity. One detects the origin of Santos's notion of the struggling exilic writer as a "straggler"—doomed into irrelevance and hermitage for writing in English—in the condition of the migrant worker as a "survivor [who] lives through years of hiding [and waits] until a miracle of change happens in the homeland and in this, our other home" ("Personal Saga" 404, 399, 405). That the construction of kinship and identity among Filipinos is fraught with difficulty and paradox is also in the foreground of much of the writing, but especially as emblematized in Santos's "The Day the Dancers Came." While Santos finds common cause with his Pinoy subjects, he also confronts the tensions of this affiliation on the level of symbolism.

Like "Scent of Apples," this story concerns the re-encounter of the Pinoy with the other-self, a representative of one's time-bound vision of home, in visitors from the islands. "Identity," as in similitude, in mutual recognition as Filipinos, is sought by the oldtimer Fil in the young members of a dance troupe from the Philippines who stop by Chicago for a visiting performance. But just as the middle-class girl reduces Allos's mother to humiliation in Bulosan's *America Is in the Heart*, the visiting dancers reduce Fil to an "ugly Filipino" (Santos, *Apples* 116), subtly spurning his attempts to communicate with them and his offer to entertain them in his humble abode (an eventuality foreseen by his fellow oldtimer and roommate Tony, who is dying of cancer). There is none of the natural affinity that develops between Fabia and the visiting lecturer in "Scent of Apples," only the edge of class hierarchy and generational or experiential difference. While making his overtures to the dancers in the Chicago hotel lobby where they milled after the performance, "All the things he had been trying to hide now showed: the age in his face, his horny hands. . . . Fil wanted to leave, but he seemed caught up in the tangle of moving bodies that merged and broke in a fluid strangle hold. Everybody was talking, mostly in English" (120).

The frequent impossibility of "identity" (as similitude) between Filipinos expatriated by colonialism, placed in different social/historical rungs, and separated by transoceanic timelines, is figured by this story in specular instances. Focused on the predicament of Fil, these compounded mirrorings of the other-self reflect the many dimensions of Filipino exilic identity and perspective. A memory that Fil associates with one of his many jobs—as "a menial in a hospital [where] he took charge . . . of bottles on a shelf, each shelf, each bottle containing a stage of the human embryo in preservatives, from the lizard-like fetus of a few days, through the newly-born infant with its position unchanged, cold, and cowering and afraid"—is of "nightmares through the years of himself inside a bottle" (114). This reflection of himself in these aborted, disowned, and arrested lives, mediated by the figure of the "bottle" that both exhibits and encloses them, is a powerful statement on the utter disconnection of the oldtimer from the flow of time and from a Philippines whose birthing as a nation itself has been aborted by American colonialism. (Perhaps it is significant that his name is "Fil," almost "Filipino," but attenuated into an American nickname).

The relationship between Fil and Tony also takes this form of allegorical doubling. When Fil castigates Tony in one of their playful spats: "You don't care for nothing but your pain, your imaginary pain," Tony retorts: "You're the imagining fellow. I got the real thing." Tony's skin not only "whitens" from the terminal ailment that is inexplicably but slowly consuming him, but he also feels "a pain in his insides, like dull scissors scraping his intestines" (115). Yet, if Tony's pain is indeed excruciatingly physical, it only seems to be the correlative for Fil's pain which, in a sense, is more real. For after being denied his last few memories of home by the dancers's disavowal, the pain that guts him is similar but more keen: "Was it his looks that kept them away? The thought was a sharpness inside him" (121); and then again, in recounting their rebuff to Tony, "The memory, distinctly recalled, was a rock on his breast. He gasped for breath." (124)

The identity between Fil and Tony (they are both oldtimers wrapped in pain and warped in time) stands for the singular problem of constructing Filipino American identity in light of colonialism. The doubling of colonizer and colonized, its conflictedness, is signified in Fil's specular but contrastive relationship with Tony, even as this is also kinship forged by their history of shared banishment. Tony stands for one's translation into a colonial: "All over Tony's body, a gradual peeling was taking place. . . . His face looked as if it was healing from severe burns. . . . 'I'm becoming a white man,' Tony had said once" (114). Note also that Tony is figured as looking young. "Gosh, I wish I had your looks, even with those white spots," Fil says to him (116)— Fil, who feels and looks old and ugly in the company of the *young* dancers. Where Tony "was the better speaker of the two in English," Fil displayed "greater mastery" in the dialect (117), although Fil's prepared speeches for inviting the dancers "stumbled and broke on his lips into a jumble of incoherence" in their presence (120). If Tony is his other-self, a desired ideal of being, then even turning to him for identity is unsuccessful as the reader knows that Tony will die to signify Fil's own rebirth.

As the dancers board their bus for the next destination and Fil imagines or sees them waving their hands and smiling toward him, Fil raises his hand to wave back. But wary of misrecognition one more time, he turns to check behind him but finds "no one there except his own reflection in the glass door, a double exposure of himself and a giant plant with its thorny branches around him like arms in a loving embrace" (122). Here, the reader is being alerted to the strength of an identity that is reflected in and by the constituted self, the spectral but appropriate figure being a "a giant plant with its thorny branches.

In vowing to commit the performance and memory of the dancers to a tape recording in what he calls "my magic sound mirror" (he loses the "record" by accidentally pushing the eraser near the end, symbolizing the fragility of his "memories" of home), Fil wonders if the magic sound mirror could also keep "a record of silence because it was to him the richest sound?" (117). This implicit recognition of himself as the supreme record, the actual referent of his identity, is brought to the fore at the conclusion of the story when he exclaims: "Tony! Tony! . . . I've lost them all." The last glimpse the reader has is of Fil "biting his lips . . . turn[ing] towards the window, startled by the first light of dawn. He hadn't realized till then that the long night was over" (128). Looking through the bottle at "frozen time" early in the story, Fil looks through a window at "time unfolding" by the end. Fil is somehow restored to history, to the sufficiency of his silence and resilience.

The interposition of "English" in the story (Tony speaks better English, he is turning into a "white" man; the dancers talk mostly in English, they are all beautiful) as the radical mode of difference for and among "Fils" (Filipinos) implies the organizing relation between exilic identity and language. Recall the symptomatic link or parallelism in Solberg's argument between the exile experienced by Filipino writers of English in the Philippines and that expressed by the "writing nurtured on American shores"—or between literary and experiential exile, generally. But this historically interesting nexus, this "inextricable link," is usually disarticulated in universalizing formulations like "the human condition" or the "alienation of the soul" (Gonzalez, *Kalutang* 64–65). Language has a historical specificity in relation to the development of "indigenous writing," "writing nurtured on American shores," and the migratory movements of writers and laborers to/in the United States that these careless oversimplifications flatten out. The result has been to compound these literatures and experiences imperceptibly or to explain them away in terms of the inescapable alienations that afflict the dislocated, as if there were nothing more to say about their historic concurrence or recurrence.

As Santos's work suggests, writing in English, the colonizer's language, and migrating to the United States, the colonizing country, are analogous and fundamentally imbricated processes, or are parallel while related forms of cultural translation and historical exile. Carlos Bulosan's consummate piece "The Story of a Letter" starkly embodies such relationships in aesthetic form and supplies another paradigm for beholding these various writings and experiences together. In this allegory of the epic of migration and expatriation, the narrator is a peasant son who finds himself heading for the United States with the migratory waves of workers in the late colonial period, partly as a consequence of a letter to his father written in English—a language alien in history and social class to his father and his people—by the narrator's brother Berto who had migrated earlier. Simply, the letter remains unread until the narrator himself has gone through the linguistic, cultural, and historical translation necessary for him to decode the letter for his father and himself. The letter reads: "Dear father . . . America is a great country. Tall buildings. Wide good land. The people walking. But I feel sad. I am writing to you this hour of my sentimental. Your son.—Berto" (*Bulosan Reader* 44). It is an attempt by an exiled son to bridge the distance between him and his origins in truncated language that aptly mirrors Berto's and his family's truncated lives.

The narrator's voyage is propelled by various developments (climaxed by the loss of the family's small landholding), and prefigured by the father's plea to the narrator "to learn English so that [he] would be able to read [the letter] to him" (41). After landing in the United States and being whirled into the vortex of displacement, labor exploitation, and fragmentation of Pinoy life, he accrues the experience needed to make sense of the letter and develops some mastery of the language that it speaks. In this process of personal translation (experientially and symbolically), he sustains a series of losses, for one always risks losing the original matter substantially in the historic passage from one experiential/cultural realm to another. The father dies before the narrator reaches the point of linguistic and historical competence and therefore before he can read his son's translation; the narrator himself experiences the deep-seated removal from origin and the past that acquiring such a competence entails; and he is only able to glimpse (not to reunite with) Berto in the United States.

With the letter returned to him after a series of disconnected deliveries, the narrator muses: "It was now ten years since my brother had written the letter to Father. It was eighteen years since he had run away from home. . . . I bent down and read the letter—the letter that had driven me away from the village and had sent me half way around the world. . . . I held the letter in my hand and, suddenly, I started to laugh—choking with tears at the mystery and wonder of it all" (44). Being able to decode the simple message of the letter (couched in his brother's fractured English) endows him with an expansive consciousness, agency, renewed memory, and the sign of redemptive return to his moorings.

The story of the letter then can be read allegorically, whereby one's search for self or identity is enabled and simultaneously codified in the transpacific voyage to the United States, condensed here primarily in the demarcating and analogic role ascribed to "English." But particular stress must be placed on the symbolic weight of language in the story and in cultural history itself. By viewing English as a material and symbolic mode of alienation and transformation, one can account for the inextricable link as well as the great wedge among various classes, generations, and experiences of Filipino peoples. In surveying the thematic landscape of contemporary writing, David Quemada concludes that the recurrent themes of rootlessness indicate "a spiritual dislocation which is nurtured by the act of writing in a foreign language" (428). "Spiritual" here suggests that one's translation and transformation *through* the colonial language is fundamental and all-encompassing.

Albert Memmi refers to this phenomenon as "colonial bilingualism," describing it also as a "linguistic drama" because it is the struggle between the colonizer's and colonized's cultures in and through the linguistic sphere (108). The "possession of two languages" means immersion in "two psychical and cultural realms" that, because "symbolized and conveyed in the two tongues" of the colonizer and colonized, generates an irremediably conflicted and complicated condition for the colonial subject. Memmi qualifies that most of the colonized are spared this condition since their native tongue is not given the same level of circulation and status in the colony itself (108). This can be extended to mean that not every Filipino can be allowed through the gates of immigration or his/her impossible dream of statehood for the Philippines. Yet, English becomes a mechanism of social hierarchy and thinking that ensnares the colonial/neocolonial natives or immigrants/citizens into the same circuit of exilic suspension while also segmenting them from each other in class or experiential terms.

In his many creative and scholarly works, N.V.M. Gonzalez has dwelt extensively on the linguistic alienation of Filipino English writers from their people and what he calls its "national and historical dimension" ("Drumming" 423). He specifies the period "when English was adopted as a national language" in the Philippines as the inaugural moment for the complicated American reconstruction of the Filipino, recalling Frantz Fanon's metaphor of consequent "changes in the flesh, even in the composition of the body fluids" of the colonized (*Kalutang* 32, 34). Quoting the writer Wilfrido Nolledo, Gonzalez avers that with the "receiving" (the term he uses to reckon with the American imposition) of English, the Filipino writer was converted into a "domestic exile, an expatriate who has not left his homeland" ("Drumming" 418–19). Yet this also locates the writer at a particular remove from his subject since, as Raymond Williams argues, "To be a writer in English is already to be socially specified" (193).

For Gonzalez, writing in English about the *kaingineros*, the peasant folk of Mindoro and the other islands of his imagination, "separated each actuality from me at every moment of composition. . . . Rendered in an alien tongue, that life attained the distinction of a translation even before it had been made into a representation of reality through form. . . . The English language thus had the effect of continually presenting that life as non-actual, even as it had affirmed the insecurity of its making" (*Kalutang* 40–41). Like Santos, however, Gonzalez shortcircuits these multiple determinations of linguistic/cultural exile and seeks identity with and in the "poor folk going from clearing to clearing, island to island, working in the saltwater sweat of their brows for whatever the earth will yield" (Guzman 111). Consequently, his writing has been critiqued for creating a literary brand of nativism and ethnography about a "bygone rural Philippines . . . no longer mapped by American anthropologists . . . but by insurgents (San Juan, *Ruptures* 31). But like Santos, Gonzalez has also reflected upon the contradictions of his identity claims and codified several important categories of the exilic sensibility.

From *Seven Hills Away* (1947) to his most recent writings, Gonzalez has lyrically valorized the people of the "backwoods, barrio, and town," graphing their lifeways and folk culture in styles, rhythms, and forms of storytelling that express a pointed fidelity to this point of origin. Like Santos in his oldtimers, Gonzalez mirrors his exilic condition in the patterns of migration, dispersal, and selfhood of these people who populate the past that he remembers: "Although they might become city folk, I seem to see them at their best against the background to which they eventually return" (*Kalutang* 66). In a parallel vein, Gonzalez re-turns to this life and place by the power of a language that renders his gesture always already imaginative. A very early piece, "Far Horizons" (Mindoro 23–26), harbors the beginnings of Gonzalez's model and vision of exile. As in his other stories that feature the sea, voyaging/sailing, and the island-hopping lifestyle of his past as metaphors for exilic distances, departures, and arrivals, this piece involves characters who find themselves ineluctably separated from their habitat by seafaring as a way of life.

Juancho, the surviving crew member of a sailboat sunk off Marinduque island recalls that among the casualties is Gorio, a sailor from a remote barrio in Mindoro. Juancho surmises that the news of Gorio's death will not have reached his village at all, and this worries him until he meets a fellow sailor, Bastian, who turns out to be Gorio's brother. Bastian finds himself making an unintended homecoming after so long, but as a bearer of sorrowful news for his mother and kinfolk. When the sailboat (suggestively called *Pag-asa* or "hope") bound for southern Mindoro comes to lie at anchor off the coast leading to his village, Bastian convinces Ka Martin, the *piloto*, to let him ashore for one night to make this important visit.

What sets off this story is a classic scene in exilic writing: the actual and transient return and the first glimpse of home after an absence of many years. When Bastian sees the first familiar landmarks of home, "A strange feeling swept over him. There came some kind of itching in the soles of his feet and his heart began to throb wildly as though trying to get out of his mouth. . . . Then it occurred to him that it was some seven or eight years since he had left home" (*Mindoro* 24). Yet mindful of the tragic news that he brings with him and the grief it may cause his mother, Bastian reflects: "Perhaps it would be better to tell her nothing at all. Should she learn of his brother's death, it might prove difficult for him to go to sea again. And how he loved the sea although it might claim him too" (24). Bastian loses his nerve and, at the call of Ka Martin's horn, stealthily heads out to sea. He entrusts the news of his brother's death to the boatman who ferries the villagers across the river and trusts him to spread it after he, Bastian, is gone. The mother, Aling Betud, receives the news of the death of one son and the sudden departure of another with a curious response. It occurs to her that "it must have been Bastian himself who had died and what had come was his ghost" (26).

In this act of substitution, Aling Betud nurses her "hope" for her other son's apparition and return, and she irritatedly responds to the villagers's disbelief: "We shall know all, we shall know all. For my other son Gorio will come—and we shall ask him, and he will tell us" (26). In this instance of "identity" (as similitude), the dream of return as formed from the site of departure reflects back the idea of exile's loss and gain—signified here in the dialectic between sorrow and hope, when the mother represents to herself the incalculable transience yet worth of her sons' "imagined" and imaginable returns.

Indeed, "the sea might claim him too," and it is the idea of home-coming as ever deferred for the pleasure and curse of voyaging (miming the ever-deferred nature of representation of loss and gain in language) that Gonzalez suggests here. Still, for Gonzalez, it is place as the locus of rooted-ness, the islands from which sailboats and sailors flee and to which they return, and the clearings between which peasant folk shuttle, that supply the coordinates and the orientations for these movements.

In many stories, including "Children of the Ash-Covered Loam," "Seven Hills Away," and "Hunger in Barok" (*Mindoro* 49–61, 32–42, 27–31), Gonzalez also foregrounds the tensions of Philippine social relationships, the difficulties of mutuality and kinship. He maps this historical geography by paraphrasing John Kenneth Galbraith's description of India as not a country but a continent: "Understanding the Philippines begins in the realization that it is one nation made up of three countries. . . . Manila is the capital of the first country of the city. The second country—the Barrio—has a capital known by many names: Aplaya, Bondok, Wawa, whatever. . . . the third country—the Mountain—by its very nature needs no capital or center, although it shares with the Barrio a calculated distance from the city" (*Kalutang* 29). Whether concerned with the calibrated frictions between the citified and the folk or the benign feudal paternalism of landlords over their tenants and its illusion of reciprocity, Gonzalez recognizes the problems of constructing a unitary notion of national identity.

The movements of the folk are defined by the location of gain and loss in the oppositional relationship between places of power and disenfranchisement: "We of the Barrio—for it is to that country that I belong . . . trudged in the direction of the country of the City" (*Kalutang* 32). By figuring his expatriation as always already determined by the uneven development of the colonized homeland, Gonzalez restores a dimension of internal conflict that gets lost in the accustomed antinomy between colony and metropole. His memorialization of "the country of the Barrio" (a particular re-vision of the Philippines) constitutes what Said calls a "cartographic impulse," since "for the native, the history of his or her colonial servitude is inaugurated by the loss to an outsider of the local place, whose concrete geographical identity must thereafter be searched for and somehow restored" (Eagleton et al. 77). Yet the dispossession creates a rhetoric of placelessness, nostalgia, and wandering, and in Gonzalez's case, one drawn from the "local place," the *kaingin*: "It is enough that solid ground, whether illusory or real, lies under our feet, and that not too far away is the next clearing, and the next, and the next" (*Kalutang* 74).

These pioneering writers have constructed literary analogues of the national mythos that are not without their dangers. The mythic tropes of native and native territory in Gonzalez's work, like the sense of suspension endemic to the oldtimers of Santos's or Bulosan's uneven idealization of peasant folk, stop short of becoming "demagogic assertions about a native past, history, or actuality that seems to stand free of the colonizer and worldly time itself" (Eagleton et al. 82). What these gestures sketch is a "new territoriality" that recovers or repossesses the colonized land imaginatively, and from which, in turn, the countercolonial "search for authenticity, for a more congenial national origin than provided by colonial history, for a new pantheon of heroes, myths and religions" should emerge (Eagleton et al. 79).

It is to the younger and more recent writers that one must turn for an extension of these suggestive tendencies in the exilic identities and writings of the pioneering writers. Recent writers (nearly all women) are turning their own exilic condition into a powerful stance, an engagement with the reality of invisibility that is doubled by the absence of the appropriation of woman as a metaphorical presence in the historical antecedents and models of the pioneers. (Here I have in mind Bulosan's dualized representations of women characters or even, specifically, the gendering of the homeland as female in Santos's "Scent of Apples," among countless instances.) The Flip poets are writing from an alienation that is double-sided as they address their own historical absence in the United States and remain implicated in the historic invisibility of the nation that permanently identifies them.

With a set of concerns and questions determined by their own historical conjunctures and different from the pioneers, recent writers view "history [as] the rubbish heap in which lie hidden the materials from which self-knowledge can come" (Gurr 10). This is a disposition that the Flips share with politically expatriated writers because their politics of emergence builds from a dialectic between past and present, not "a past sealed off from the vigorously altering effects of contemporary events" (Brennan 17). For example, although the oldtimers continue to serve as figures of origin for many Flip poets, there is a re-search into their social history for a stronger genealogical link. It is an attempt to "turn over the rubbish heap of history by studying the past and in that way fixing a sense of identity" (Gurr 10). This is an impulse codified in Virginia Cerennio's "you lovely people": "ay manong / your old brown hands / hold life, many lives / within each crack / a story" (Bruchac 11). History is inscribed in, is an imprint on, the appropriated Pinoy body: "and it is in his hands / cracked and raw / that never heal. / Shotgunned stomach. One-kidney Franky. / One hot day he revealed / that stomach to me, slowly raising / his T-shirt, and proclaimed it the map of California" (Tagami 13).

The probing of history for Flip poets also takes the form of social analysis, but of the conditions in a country as alien to them as they are to it. Perhaps this critical distance is what allows Jaime Jacinto to dramatize, in measured tones of grief and tension, the enduring inequities of Philippine life as sanctioned by the Church and the semifeudal order, and as symbolized by the burial of a peasant woman's little daughter: "As the blonde Spanish priest / anoints you, touching your / lips and feet with oil, / your mother wonders if ever there was enough to eat or / if only she had given in / to the landlord's whispers, / that extra fistful of rice / might have fattened the hollow / in your cheeks" (Ancheta et al. 48–49).

Nearly all the emergent writers are women, and this amplitude of women's writing is a development observable for other emergent literatures in the United States and the postcolonial world. Compared to the two other groups, it is the women or Filipina writers who recognize that "the relationship to the inherited past and its cultural legacy has been rendered problematic by the violent interference of colonial and imperial history' (Harlow 19). As Filipino historical crises are intensified by the authoritarian rule of Ferdinand Marcos and its aftermath, history and its countermythic writing become their own forms and visions of return, identity building, and self-recovery.

Linda Ty-Casper returned to early colonial Philippine history and

showed the way for this group with *The Peninsulars* (1964). The novel has
been critiqued for its "ill-advised" revisions of some historical documents but
also commended for setting "certain precedents that are bound to subsequent efforts" (Galdon 202). In fact, Ty-Casper went on to handle Philippine
historical subjects more boldly, seeking to make material out of the moral
atrophy and political intrigues that mark the period of authoritarian rule by
Marcos (see, for example, *Wings of Stone*, 1986; *Fortress in the Plaza*, 1985).
One can profit from examining the intertextuality between Ty-Casper's and
Ninotchka Rosca's ventures, specifically as borne out by Rosca's historical
novel *State of War* (1988). This novel alerts the reader to Rosca's indebted-
ness to Ty-Casper's pioneering efforts, establishing certain genealogical links
between both writers on the narrative level.

In *The Three-Cornered Sun* (1979), Ty-Casper turns to the Philippine
Revolution of 1896 against Spain, creating a somewhat indecisive picture
of national identity through the members of the Viardo family, whose individual traits are unevenly endowed with allegorical weight. As N.V.M.
Gonzalez notes, the call is for "a depiction of private lives that would
encompass Philippine experience within living memory," and as Rosca
herself qualifies, "The problem is how to tell a story that was not anybody's
story yet was everybody's story" (Gonzalez, "Filipino and the Novel" 962;
Mestrovic 90). In *State of War*, Rosca re-visions the whole stretch of colonial history in the context of the period of Marcos's dictatorship through a
mélange of dreamy sequences, historical vignettes, and hyperrealized characters and events. She balances allegory with personal history in the triadic
relationship of her main characters, Anna Villaverde, Adrian Banyaga, and
Eliza Hansen, whose genealogies and symbolic stories intertwine in a series
of historical wars and developments that are symbolized by a 24-hour
period of festivity and political conspiracies. The interrelated carnivalesque
of merrymaking and political conflict is emphasized by narrative pattern
and design, as supremely exemplified by the three-part structure of the
novel ("Acts," "Numbers," "Revelations . . .").

An obvious footnote to the triangulated characteristic of Ty-Casper's
Awaiting Trespass as "a small book of hours about those waiting for their
lives to begin . . . a book of numbers about those who stand up to be
counted . . . a book of revelations about what tyranny forces people to
become; and what, by resisting, they can insist on being" (author's preface,
n.p.), Rosca's organizing stratagem also directs the reader to incremental
and interreferential layers internal to the work of either author. In Rosca's
case, for example, Eliza and Anna (along with Colonel Amor, incarnated as
the Loved One in *State of War*, symbol of the authoritarian and military
reign of terror) first make their appearance as character sketches in the

piece "Earthquake Weather" (see *Monsoon Collection* 129).

This movement continues outward as Michelle Skinner packs her extremely short stories in *Balikbayan: A Filipino Homecoming* (1988) with powerful allusion and subtexts concerning the life under dictatorial rule as it was subtended by American neocolonial support for Marcos; or as Cecilia Manguerra-Brainard compresses into a story ("The Black Man in the Forest," in *Woman with Horns* 21–25) the many historical ramifications of the Filipino-American war, which had concerned Ty-Casper in *Ten Thousand Seeds* (1987).

Experientially, these writers create from the same sense of expatriation from the past and their history that stems quite immediately from the founding moment of American colonization and the cultural translocation through the master's language. But the distance is not crippling, as they invert its anthropological commonplaces from their perspective as colonized natives or immigrants/citizens who regard from the outside that is also the country of the colonizer the whole spectacle of their transhistorical movements and displacements. Return for them is redefining and rewriting "history" from the perspective of banishment: "Physical departure from the scene of one's personal history provides a break in time and separates the present from the past. History then becomes what preceded departure" (Gurr 10–11).

For these writers, the pioneers serve as stark examples and models. Either one is disabled and "waits for miracles to happen"—as Santos seems to express when recalling how his writing teacher Philip Roth excised his desired ending image for a short story, that, significantly enough, of "floating in a shoreless sea" (Fernandez and Alegre 245)—or one is enabled, moving on, as the narrator in Bulosan's story does, to tell the "story" (history) of the "letter" (one's transcription or codification of the self-in-history) through the language and experience of one's subjection.

CHUNG-HEI YUN

Beyond "Clay Walls": Korean American Literature

Asian American literature is a child born of uprootedness and transplantation. The pain of dislocation is followed by nostalgia for the lost home, for in many instances there is no more "homeland" one can return to (*The Woman Warrior* 125). This nostalgia often haunts the psyche and imagination of the exiled like a hungry ghost that refuses to be appeased (*The Woman Warrior* 19).

The Puritan exodus from England and subsequent entry into America is one example of the journey-quest for the Holy Grail/the New Canaan. Woven into this teleological matrix is a spiritual struggle and a typology consonant with Western metaphysical dualism. The Puritans' journey was not an ordinary sea voyage; it was a spiritual pilgrimage through the sea of faith to fulfill Providence as God's instrument in the unfolding of the grand design and telos of human destiny. Taming the wilderness, therefore, became an external counterpart of the Holy War: conquest of the wilderness and wild men was a struggle between good and evil, the ultimate triumph of "The City of God" over "The City of Man."

Unlike Puritan Americans, the impetus for the Asian exodus-emigration is rooted mainly in economic, political, and social reality. Although Asians also came on a quest for "a New Canaan full of milk and honey," it is a Canaan that exists within an earthly kingdom without Moses. An earthly

From *Reading the Literatures of Asian America.* © 1992 by Temple University.

"manna" embodied in money, education, and success lured and beckoned Asian immigrants to the "Gold Mountain" with a vision of streets cobbled with "gold nuggets" (*China Men* 41).

Often economic necessity is accompanied by political conditions in the nation that spurred emigration. Such was the case for the Korean immigrants depicted in the four works by three Korean American authors that this chapter examines: Younghill Kang's *The Grass Roof* (1931) and *East Goes West* (1937), Theresa Hak Kyung Cha's *Dictée* (1982), and Ronyoung Kim's *Clay Walls* (1986). All three authors share the same dark tragedy of the Korean past, which they narrate from various angles of vision

The centrifugal force shaping the Korean American literary imagination is generated from the loss of homeland through Japanese annexation, the mutilation of the land when it was divided into North and South Korea following the liberation from Japan after World War II, the Korean War, and the post-1965 exodus.

Although *The Grass Roof* is about Kang's early experience in Korea under the "grass roof" recollected in nostalgia, it serves as a necessary psychological bridge to *East Goes West*, the record of his experience in America and Canada as a displaced person. Not long after the Japanese annexed Korea, Chung-Pa Han, the narrator-author of the novel-autobiography, departs for America in quest of "New Knowledge." Han recalls his first encounter with the West: "I thought them [the Arabic numerals, 1, 2, 3, etc.] beautiful, fascinating and a little bit black magic. This was my first taste of the Western learning" (31). Han enlarges his knowledge of the West through Japanese translations of works by various Western authors, including Shakespeare, Shelley, Coleridge, Arnold, Schopenhauer, Goethe, Poe, and Whitman. Ideas from these authors largely shape the contours of Han's vision of the West. For him, "Shakespeare and Michael Angelo [*sic*] . . . were heroes" (258).

Han perceives that enlightened Western ideology and its scientific advancements are externally manifest in the political strength of Japan, for "Japan has conquered Korea by Western Science. We [Koreans] must regain our freedom by a superior knowledge of that Science" (185). Park Soo-San, Han's history teacher, asserts that Korea must emulate Japan and master the entire learning of the West. Thus, Han's odyssey begins with his journey to Japan, his first great leap. He makes this leap first by cutting off his topknot (sang-too), the traditional hairstyle for Korean men, "something like a baptism" (186) before he "takes the solitary pilgrimage" (235). For Han, the act is "a symbol . . . of breaking away from the bondage of tradition, [his] oath, that [he] had set [himself] toward Western learning and all the West had to give and to teach" (186).

Though Japan serves as a bridge to the West, his sojourn in Japan is a brief one. Restless and disenchanted, Han returns to Korea with an altered perspective on his village and his own people: "My people now seemed the foreign element m their own country, still in top knots and white clothes wandering around in the market place with perplexed expression, faces wrinkled and ghost-like with worry, wondering what was to happen tomorrow!" (299). With his altered vision, he can no longer see his village Song-Dune-Chi (the Village of the Pine Trees) nestled in "the Valley of Utopia" with its "delicious taste of the first frost" and the brilliance of chrysanthemums nodding in the breeze, sending forth their "pungent aroma under the grass roof" (17). Instead, he sees "the round shaggy roofs clustered close to the ground on the wide floor of the valley, [he] had an illusion that every soul in [his] childhood village was dead, swept away by a plague, and that the spot was abandoned" (306). This bleak landscape aptly corresponds to the oppressive political reality of Korea under Japanese colonialism. Yet the passion of the March 1, 1919 uprising, the Korean "Declaration of Independence," fails to touch or inspire Han. The only action he takes is that of flight to Manchuria and then, once more, return, thus ending his second abortive odyssey.

Han's passionate and desperate yearning for Western civilization in all its glory and grandeur is not without conflict. Western civilization, as manifested in its arts, its achievements in the practical spheres of life, politics, and war, is ultimately the external embodiment of a weltanschauung shaped by Judeo-Christian ideology. To comprehend the West, then, one must comprehend Christianity. Han observed that Mr. Park "had become a liberal Christian, wishing to turn his back on the past, and his face toward the future, he made me see that the road of a scholar's future prominence lay toward America like the shortest distance between two points . . . in a straight line" (186). Again, Han resolves to flee from Korea, and he approaches Mr. Parker, an American missionary, only to be rejected with the words, "We only take care of Christians! We don't take care of heathens" (226). Mr. Parker adds that he does not think it a good idea for Koreans to come to America, although it is the native home of missionaries, for there they will forget all the good that they learned from missionaries while in Korea (227).

The disparity between Western ideology and its practice is succinctly articulated in light of the existing social and political reality:

> The War . . . So the West didn't act what they said! They were just as bad as the East,—or worse, for the East didn't send out missionaries, saying "Our Christianity has the superior righteousness. You are heathen and your sages are no good. Why don't you follow our example?" . . . [Japan] became more powerful than China, since she learned rapidly from the West

whatever the West had to teach in the way of skillful homicide. Then Japan tested that art out on China and defeated her in 1894. (259)

Han sees the ultimate contradiction in the disparity between an increased quality of life and decreased humanity, for "the West . . . makes life better, because it reduces death, and adds to the refinements of life by inventions and mechanical improvements. But now they were killing in wholesale business the life that was saved. It seemed to [him] that the refinement was all in warfare, not in high superiority of mind, or in scholarship" (261). Nevertheless, with these conflicting attitudes towards the West still unresolved, Han crosses the Pacific.

On his voyage to America, Han encounters a young girl who reminds him of another girl whose fleeting form he had seen at the station on his way to Seoul from Japan. The girl in the past voyage had seemed to balance "in her two hands the Eastern and Western world" (276). Recollecting the vision of the girl from the past, Han says of the girl before him:

> She seems isolated like myself, a woman with no nationality. Is she of West or East? Is she a Chinese or a Japanese? Is she European or American? Now she alone touches the chord to which my heart dances, because of how she stands and looks into the night. Her eyes are on the far off stars. And from the milky way they move to look at me. . . . Is it possible that the Princess Immortality is in the same boat going with me to America? (377)

As the embodiment of his desire and dream, the girl is transformed into his Princess Immortality, perhaps the Faustean *Ewigweibliche* befitting his Faustean dream/quest.

The Grass Roof, then, as Elaine Kim remarks in her illuminating account of the work, "is a justification of Han's departure from Korea" (34). The validity of this justification is yet to be substantiated in Kang's next work, *East Goes West*. In the beginning of this second book, Han clearly states why he left Korea and what the book is going to be about:

> I cried for the food for my growth and there seemed no food. And I felt I was looking on death, the death of an ancient planet, a spiritual planet that had been my father's home. . . . In loathing of death, I hurtled forward, out into space, out toward a foreign body . . . and a younger culture drew me by natural gravity. I entered a new life like one born again. Here I wandered on soil

as strange as Mars, seeking roots, roots for an exile's soul. . . . It was here in America for me to find. But where? This book is the record of my early search, and the arch of my projectile toward the goal. (4–5)

The strength of the dreams spun in Korea is to be tested through Han's experiences in America. In New York, Han understands for the first time the fear of "the pavement famine, with plenty all around but in the end not even grass to chew" (32). He also comes to a painful realization of "how far [his] little grass-roofed, hillwrapped village [is removed] from this gigantic rebellion which was New York!" (6). From his solitary, dingy hotel room, Han ventures out to have a glimpse of Harlem, the "Other Kingdom" (19) within the kingdom of exile, where the inhabitants are leading "the plaintive, alluring sadness of life's farthest exile . . . a dimmer, vaster captivity than the Babylonian one" (20). Han identifies himself with these "exiles" in the "Other Kingdom" and, in turn, is identified with them by white American society. Han is told by Mr. Allen, who interviews him for a job at the YMCA, that the vacancy is not to be filled by a "Negro" or an "Oriental."

His first job as a houseboy confirms and further intensifies this initial rejection. When his books fall out of his suitcase, the lady of the house, seeing the dingy Oriental covers of some secondhand books he had bought in Japan, exclaims, "I hope they have no germs" (62). The visible difference —race and color—that signifies separateness and alienation in white American consciousness seems like a vermin invested with the power to contaminate white society.

Han's experience at Maritime College in Canada reinforces his isolation and loneliness in a converse manner. With the exception of the hostile Leslie Robin, one of Han's classmates, everyone is generous and overly kind toward the "poor and humiliated protégé of the right honorable British Canadian theologues [sic]" (112). For Han, "there was always special favor, special kindliness, special protection . . . the white man's-burden attitude toward dark colonies" (126). Han summarizes this experience in the following brooding reflection: "Why then did I feel myself so lonely and sad, small, lowly, and unappreciated? Why, in short, did I long once more . . . for escape? The magnificent journey to America, the avid desire for Western knowledge, had it come to this?" (112).

Han's experiences as a displaced person are interwoven with various portraits of other Korean exiles in New York, all of whom crossed the ocean hoping to realize their separate dreams. George Jum becomes a hedonist who has denounced Confucius, Christ, and Buddha, and found life's meaning only in women's arms, for "life lies with woman, not with the classics or the ancestors" (44). The Westernized and Christianized Dr. Ko, in spite of his belief that he is an earnest Christian, is not able to eradicate his Confucian root: "He had simply changed the letter of his faith" (49). Mr. Pyun learns American pragmatism, efficiency, and the Protestant work ethic fast and becomes a good businessman who can be held up as a model for an Oriental success story. He enjoys food, works hard, and enjoys his night life (57).

Han describes Pak, who accompanies Han to his first job as a houseboy, as a "typical Korean" who is "an exile only in body, not in soul, as if Western civilization had rolled over him as water over a rock" (58). A typical model Korean is a nationalist, a good Christian, a hard worker, and a supporter of all organizations working for Korea's revolutionary cause. Often the immigrant's tenacious hold on his cultural heritage, pride, and identity, juxtaposed against his lurking desire to be rid of the grip of nostalgia, creates resistance and ambivalence. These tantalizing paradoxes and double binds fill the immigrant's imagination, as has been expressed in many Asian American literary works.

Fulchoon Chang's dreams and ambitions are representative of the mental state of contemporary Korean American students. "Chang was studying to be an engineer—and unlike Guru, the Hindoo, overcame all theosophical [sic] temptations—he stuck to engineering" (248). Often stifling the whispers of their desires and resisting "temptations," many young immigrants today pursue medicine, engineering, business management, or computer science in hope of translating their dreams into reality in the most efficient, practical, and expedient way. The Muse must be banished; otherwise, she is likely to lead them to despair and nihilism, as we are to see in the fate of To Wan Kim in Greenwich Village.

It is, however, with this Greenwich Village romantic aesthete Kim that Han finds an intellectual and spiritual kinship, as Han discovers in him the mirror wherein are reflected his own dreams, ideals, frustrations, and despair. In a utilitarian civilization where aesthetes are not appreciated, Kim feels that his "life is like the useless tree. [He tries] to plant [his] tree in the land of nonexistence" (233). Unable to transplant his tender roots in the hard concrete pavement of the New World, yet also unable to retransplant them in his native soil, Kim's "roots" slowly wither.

The first formidable task that all immigrants undertake is to "enter into the economic life of Americans" (277). Kim is aware of the socioeconomic reality that Korean immigrants confront in the New World, where "the only goal for a man is money and power. But money and power in New York are not for men of my race. Even if we succeeded, we would not be admired for that, but only hated and feared" (231).

To Kim's lamentation on the state of the arts in America, Han responds: "We do not come to the West for poetry . . . but for man's new way of mastering Nature" (177). In America, the destination of their quest, the urgency of existential choices persists: the old or the new, the "homeland" or the land one stands on, muse or gold? In this ethical battleground, inexorable conditions relentlessly drive one to choose. To the idealistic Kim, who "came to the West to find a new beauty, a new life" (178) only to discover the great void around him, Han remarks: "But tell me, what now is to be our fate? Being unable to go back to that previous existence, being unable to label ourselves in this New World . . . becoming lost within another lost world?" (178).

One ray of light enters the gloom of Kim's exile—his relationship with Helen, a white American girl from a proper New England family. With Helen, Kim no longer feels a lonely exile and is "always happy . . . as with Nature" (240). Although this episode intimates hope, hope that one human heart could emancipate another heart in exile, the flickering light is soon extinguished by the end of their relationship, leaving Kim in darkness and despair. Kim chooses to make Greenwich Village his grave and becomes an exile both in life and death. Lamenting Kim's suicide, Han reflects:

> The greatest loss . . . was himself [Kim], his brain which bore in its fine involutions our ancient characters deeply and simply incised, familiar to me. And over their classic economy, their primitive chaste elegance, was scrawled the West's handwriting, the incoherent labyrinth. . . . To me—to me almost alone—a priceless and awful parchment was in him destroyed. (395)

Han's search in the New World concludes on an inconclusive note. Yunkoo, his childhood friend under "the grass roof," appears in his dream. As Yunkoo is pointing Han toward a never-never-land, things begin tumbling out of Han's pockets: money, contracts, and business letters. He desperately clutches on "to the key to his . . . American car" (401). He dreams that the cellar is attacked and on fire, but he awakes "like the phoenix out of a burst of flames" (401). Also in this dream journey to the grass-roofed village of his childhood, appears Trip, an American girl he met in New York. Han returns to New York and calls Trip early in the morning, for "he had to be saved quickly from going quite empty like Kim. It was real emergency" (401). Perhaps, in Trip, Han is determined to see a fragmented embodiment of the Princess Immortality. With a suggestion of rebirth and the forging of a new identity through community bonds, one chapter in Han's odyssey ends. Its conclusion, I believe, inaugurates his quest for the village without the "grass roof," life "here and now" in

America with "the *key* (italics mine) to his American car" (401).

The struggle to nurture and cultivate transplanted roots so that they can survive is the focus of Ronyoung Kim's *Clay Walls*. As with Kang's *Han*, the increasingly oppressive political reality of Korea after it is annexed by Japan in 1910 is the moving force that drives Chun and Haesu to emigrate. The novel depicts their life in Los Angeles during the mid-twentieth century. Realistic descriptions of their struggle and of life within the Korean "enclave," their initiation into an alien mode of life and culture, their innocence and ignorance, their knowledge gained through experience—these constitute the substance of this novel. It begins with the saga of the first-generation Korean immigrants and ends with the emergence of the second generation. Like "the grass roof," the image of the "clay walls" that surround the thatched-roof houses elicits in many Koreans both nostalgic and ambivalent responses.

The antipodal forces and values manifest themselves in two opposing attitudes toward life, as figured in the characters of Haesu and her husband, Chun. The tentacles of the old tradition encircle both Haesu and Chun, at times threatening to choke their precariously rooted existence. The tradition-clad social hierarchy binds Haesu, causing her to quit her job as a maid and curse her employer Mrs. Randolph as a *sangnyun* (a woman of the lowest class). Haesu feels humiliated at having to clean toilet bowls, for she is from a *yangban* (aristocratic) family in Korea, and no yangban would stoop to clean a toilet, a menial task tended to only by the sangnyun. Deeply conscious of the traditional social rank reserved for the scholar class, Haesu never reconciles herself to her arranged marriage to a mere farmer. For Chun, "just a farmer's son," "any work is good enough" and is "just a job" (10), but for Haesu, Chun's work is a most demeaning and humiliating one. Haesu resorts to reviling him: "How you can remain mute while someone orders you to come here, go there, do this, do that . . . like you were some trained animal. They call you a houseboy. A twenty-five year old man being called 'boy'" (10). Constantly measuring their status as defined by their having to perform menial tasks for a living against traditional values, Haesu perceives her life in America to be utterly meaningless. Haesu repeats the question to herself and to Chun: "What are we doing here? As soon as we make enough money, we are going back to Korea. We don't belong here. Just tell me, what are we doing here?" (10).

Haesu soon discovers that walls, whether of stone or clay, circumscribe the fragile world of the displaced. Many apartments are restricted and not for Orientals; their house has to be bought by Charles Bancroft, an American citizen. Harold, their eldest son born in America, is barred from entering Edward Military Academy because the founders of the Academy desire to accept only white Anglo-Saxon Protestants.

Haesu goes back to Korea with her children, intending never to return, but once in Korea, she realizes that her homeland under Japanese colonialism has ceased to be a home. She feels trapped, for every time she thinks she has a way out, she is up against a stone wall. Feeling "out of sorts in her homeland, homesick in Korea without being homesick for America" (125) and suffering exile in their own homeland, the family decides to return to America, although they are fully aware of the all-too-familiar "walls" that await them there.

After moving to their first home, Chun wants to "put up a fence or a wall of some kind," for he was used "to having a clay wall around [his] house" (28) in Korea. Haesu rejects this suggestion, preferring an open space, and exclaims: "If they can see us, we can see them. No one can hide anything." (28). The Janus-faced wall stands for protection and the security of tradition for Chun, but for Haesu, it represents enervating and paralyzing constraint. Clay walls, like her heritage, are an anachronism in America. These "clay walls" of tradition, indeed, have long confined and sequestered Korean women:

> The higher the woman's rank, the more she was sequestered, and hers was of the upper class. Her country had fought for its own seclusion, struggling against the penetration of eastern invaders and western ideology. A futile struggle, she thought. Korean walls were made of clay, crumbling under repeated blows, leaving nothing as it was before. Chun had wanted a wall around their house in L.A. She remembered and she had ridiculed him. (103)

Chun's desire to cling to the crumbling and ineffectual "clay walls" also determines his attitude toward life. He believes that to "not contend" is the highest level of human behavior and that if one wants "muddy water to become clean" (163), one has to lie still. When he realizes that he has been cheated on his wholesale produce contract with the government, Chun, to control his rage, recalls his father's Taoist injunction: "Breathe in deep and empty your thoughts. Give play to your feelings and everything will fall into place" (135). Against this quietism Haesu rebels and asks him to "abandon the tenets of his ancestors" (163) in defiance of the ineffectual clay walls of the past.

In the struggle of the displaced, the "clay walls" that Chun refuses to relinquish fail to protect him. Drifting from one place to another in search of work and exhausted from his futile wandering, he dies in a hospital room in Reno, Nevada—an exile and homeless even in death. Left with three children, Haesu grapples with the hard economic reality. Bending over a piece of cloth, squinting her eyes to embroider handkerchiefs, for which she is paid by the piece, Haesu carries the burden of living. Yet, Haesu, together with innumerable displaced people, survives triumphantly. Her children will further cultivate the roots of this heroism, the legacy of the displaced.

In a gesture that seems to symbolize her last effort to cling to the land that she had left and, at the same time, her refusal to embrace the new land as her home, Haesu had bought a piece of land in Qwaksan, North Korea, a place to which she can no longer return: for "the South Korean government says the KPR is a communist group. We can't get into North Korea either. . . . My land in Qwaksan is gone" (300). At the novel's conclusion, the daughter Faye has a sudden flash of revelation:

> The land was Momma's only holding in her homeland and it had been taken away from her; her only holding in the world. Suddenly, I felt as if I had been stamped with stupidity. That was what I was supposed to understand. She had clung onto Qwaksan as long as she could. (300)

Human desire and the belief that a piece of land would make one's home a homeland turn out to be another human folly and illusion. Letting go of a corner of the remote land to which she has clung not only emancipates Haesu from crippling nostalgia but also impels her to accept the alien land as "my country."

When Faye, Haesu's daughter, meets Daniel Lee, a student at Yale who wants to be a medical doctor, she tells him that she loves to read; she wants to see "how other people live," yet she hasn't "found a book written about the people she knows" (297). Dan responds: "That would be another form of isolation. . . . Unless one becomes part of that 'other world'" (297). Dan's response to Faye's desire to know how "other people" live through books attests to the conflicts he has experienced as a Korean American, the conflicts he acknowledges to Haesu: "Most of my life has not been spent with my 'father's people' but with the other people of this country. I live among one group of people while my commitments are to another. WASP assumptions require that I be one thing and my ancestry demands another" (297). Dan's resolution of this conflict is shown by the choice he makes: "We do live in the United States. You and I do speak English to one another. I do wear the uniform of this country. We are part of this society. Segments of it may not be completely accessible to everyone, but we who live here have something in common." (297-98). Beyond a piece of land and beyond the dichotomy of "others" and "we," Dan perceives that the true meaning of home and homeland is found in the commonality of human experiences.

The novel ends with the arrival of a special delivery letter from Daniel. The unopened letter seems full of promises to Faye. The vision of a daughter marrying a medical doctor—the unequivocal hope of many immigrant parents—is perhaps too pat. Yet, this land is theirs, Dan's and Faye's, to mold, shape, and cherish. Faye, together with all children of the displaced, not only must chart and shape the path of her destiny but also cultivate the path in this new land, freed from sequestration by "clay walls."

Before Dan's departure from Los Angeles, Faye has asked him about New Haven. "White Anglo-Saxon Protestant," Dan replies. "Oh, like Beverly Hills?" she asks, to which he responds, "No, not at all. It's conservative with a Puritan tradition. Morality denuded of imagination. Beverly Hills, on the other hand, strikes me as being based on imagination denuded of morality" (296). One can only hope that a world will emerge from their dreams where aesthetic and ethical visions are harmoniously wedded and realized, where "morality" is adorned by "imagination" and imagination is illumined by morality.

Although its publication precedes Kim's *Clay Walls* (1986), Theresa Hak Kyung Cha's *Dictée* (1982) can be read as the last coda for the "exiles in the kingdom." Cha's vision goes beyond the boundary of historical time and space, blending her aesthetic and religious visions and placing the remembered tragic history of Korea in a mythical context.

The title, *Dictée*, with its connotations and intentional ambiguities, defines that indefinable and ineffable realm of memory. The "dictée" of *Dictée* assumes both an active agent who transcribes the tales told by her mother as well as a passive agent serving as the repository and the vessel for that memory, which in turn is being remembered and shaped by the dictée finally manifesting itself in the pages of *Dictée*.

The very act of dictating through the process of remembering, the process manipulated by the dictée, emerges in the palpable form of the book, *Dictée*, which defies categorization. It encompasses multiple avenues of human communications: language/signs; visual media (pictures of Yu Kwan Soon, Cha's mother, Joan of Arc, Chinese ideograms, and ruins); and semiotic devices (rearrangement and manipulation of the words; juxtaposition of English, French, Korean, and Chinese). The term *dictée* in French also signifies "inspired." The basic structure of the work, which is divided into nine sections "dictated" by the nine Muses, respectively, gives cogency to this inspiration. The dictée's act of remembering by re-membering the dismembered fragments of memory scattered onto the void of the past and the attempt to create an ordered form out of the chaos are to be taken as an act inspired by the Muses.

The dedicatory lines by Sappho placed like an epitaph on the "tomb of the naked and [displaced]" (20), denote an act of resurrecting the "dead dust" from memories: from the mere smear of signs are born "living words" that are "more naked than flesh, stronger than bone, more resilient than sinew, sensitive than nerve." Recording of the past, thus, begins with the birth pang of words, which resemble "bared noise, groan, bits torn from words" (3). Moreover,

> it [speech] murmurs inside. . . . Inside is the pain of speech the pain to say. Larger still. Greater than is the pain not to say. To not say. . . . It festers inside. The wound, liquid, dust. Must break. Must void. (3)

This symbolic act of releasing the speech/words imprisoned within a cold, silent marble is superimposed with the images of Holy Communion, evoking a mystic religious experience (13).

The tragic history of Korea is recollected in a pensive and melancholic prelude to her destiny as well as to the plight of the displaced:

> *From A Far* / What Nationality / or what kindred and relation
> what blood relation / what blood ties of blood / what ancestry /
> what race generation / what house clan tribe stock strain
> what lineage extraction
> what breed sect gender denomination caste
> what stray *ejection misplaced*
> *Tertium Quid neither one thing nor the other*
> *Tombe des nues de naturalized*
> what *transplant to dispel upon.* (20, italics mine)

On the abortive revolution of March 1, 1919, and the martyrdom of a young revolutionary, Yu Kwan Soon, Cha concludes with the following lines: "The decapitated forms. . . . The present form face to face reveals the missing, the absent. Would-be-said remnant, memory. But the remnant is the whole. The memory is entire. The longing in the face of the lost" (38). Cha continues to "re-member" by retelling her mother's story as told to her. The painful memory of the time when her mother and all Koreans became "tongueless" and nameless, when her mother was forced to denounce her mother tongue and even to change her name, blends into the Catholic Mass. The tragic strain of one nation dissolves into the chorus of humanity carried by the "ebb and tide of echo" (47) toward the "Antiphonal hymn" (46).

Memories of Korea's liberation from Japan in 1945 and those of the Korean War of 1950 fuse and blend together beyond historical time as if

Korea's destiny "is fixed on the perpetual motion of search. Fixed in its perpetual exile" (81). This "perpetual motion of search" manifests itself in the section "Erato" (love poetry), where human love and marriage are juxtaposed with the heavenly love represented by Christ as the Bridegroom. Though "only through a glass darkly," this dusky shadow of the Divine Love in and through human love (erato) is all that our darkened vision can "see" here and now, yet it is not without an intimation of the miracle of transubstantiation. Erato's song ascends and blends into the ecstasy of the heavenly song of martyrdom (117).

However, this vision of flight from time and space is not long sustained, and it inevitably returns "to the very memory" (131) of the past in time, whose "stain attaches itself and darkens on the pale formless sheet, a hole increasing its size larger and larger until it assimilates the boundaries and becomes itself formless. All memory. Occupies the entire" (131). To restore memory, one must return to this formlessness; hence the following invocation: "Let the one who is mother Restore memory . . . one who is daughter restore spring with her each appearance from beneath the earth" (133). The mythic figures of Demeter, Persephone, and Pluto are suggested here. The timeless myth finds its counterparts in time through the figures of the Mother, the Daughter, and the Limbo of Memory. The returning emergence of Persephone ushering in the spring of "re-membering" and the rebirth of nature become analogous to the dictée / daughter's act of recording the past through the words, restoring words which had been mere signs and "dead words" "buried in Time's memory" (133) "from beneath the earth."

This rebirth in the eternal cycle of birth/death heralds the celebration and affirmation of life in and through the creative act: "She says to herself if she were able to write she could continue to live. Says to herself if she would write without ceasing. To herself if by writing she could abolish real time. She would live. If she could display it before her and become its voyeur" (141). To write (create through re-membering), then, is to live; to live, to write. In the timebound reality where there is "only the onslaught of time" (140) obliterating the future, memory and past are all and "entire" (131), a continuum along infinitesimal points of time. Recording what has been re-membered out of the dismembered past becomes a monument chiseled from the stone of oblivion, a monument to the "simulated pasts resurrected in memoriam" (150).

The child exhausted and burdened with the "dead words" of the past is restored and healed by the water given by a woman who drew it from the fountain, so that she can continue her journey toward the flickering "small candle" (170) in spite of the "entering dusk" (170). This vision is followed by an image of a child imploring her mother: "Lift me up mom to the window"

(179). To be able to see the vista of the future as well as the present through the window of time, Cha, like the child, has to be lifted up by the arms of her mother who links her to the past, by her mother's memories, which, told to Cha, the dictée re-members.

Without the past, without the dismembered history to be remembered, the child of the present cannot redeem future or past. In retelling as a dictée/diseuse, the child born of exile is able to speak the words. The very act of retelling and re-membering the past emancipates her from the prison of stony and immobile silence.

All three authors bear the wounds of the past. Kang's works reflect the early Korean immigrants' dreams, a quest-journey accompanied by disillusionment and despair yet not without hope that the immigrant can accept the world he chooses, in spite of the grip of nostalgia. Kim's work depicts the struggle of one Korean immigrant family in Los Angeles. It is also a realistic picture of the Korean community there, an arena for praxis where they realize or fail to realize their dreams, and where, as Lim has phrased it, they can "assay the gold."

The vision offered by Cha's work places the tragic fate of Korea within the concentric circles of human drama and in the luminous light of eternal myth as well as the mystery of religious transfiguration. *Dictée* suggests that a child born in exile with a tragic history can be redeemed only in and through the wounds of the past. Herein lies the profound paradoxical truth of the law of compensation and evaluation: out of dark tragedy, the light of Sacred Poesy; through the agony of dismemberment, the joy and ecstasy of creation through re-membering; through the "Babylonian exile," the shore of "Siloam." Amidst the landscape circumscribed by time and space, the ruins of the past inexorably loom, yet within it one "remains dismembered with the belief that magnolia blooms white even on seemingly dead branches and one must wait" (155) with hope and, Cha would add, with faith.

This intimation of the possibility of transcendence through mystical vision in no way obliterates the immanence of time or "abolish[es] real time" (141). The ruins of the past relentlessly intrude upon the present like the indelible marks chiseled on the wall of the mine in Kyushu, Japan, by a young Korean performing forced labor, a cry that, in the very beginning of the book *Dictée*, invites the reader to participate in the act of re-membering: "I want my mother; I am hungry; I want to go home" (cited in Korean and translated by Yun). In the fugue of *Dictée*, we hear this human "peal to the sky" (179) with its primordial desire and longing for "home" counterposed by the "Antiphonal hymn" that comes after "the Misere" (47).

The Korean American literature discussed in this essay illustrates the life of the displaced in the chiaroscuro of hope and despair, dream and disillusionment, the ideal and the real, life balanced between the weight of the past and that of the present. Each author offers his/her own resolution: Kang, through his effort to inaugurate a quest for his "new life"; Kim, through the children born in exile who would become pioneers in shaping their own destiny; and Cha, through her aesthetic and religious visions that enable her to transcend the tragic past, transforming it into a creative act of re-membering

INDERPAL GREWAL

Reading and Writing the South Asian Diaspora: Feminism and Nationalism in North America

On the back cover of Bharati Mukherjee's novel, *Jasmine*, the blurb from the Baltimore Sun reads "Poignant . . . Heartrending . . . The story of the transformation of an Indian village girl, whose grandmother wants to marry her off at 11, into an American woman who finally thinks for herself."

To this reviewer of *Jasmine*, South Asian women are an exploited and oppressed category that serves to construct by contrast the free and independent "American woman". Within this comparison which has its origins in European colonial discourses, India is a uniformly oppressive place for women. In contrast, the U.S. becomes the land of hope, freedom and independence for women. The problem of such a formulation is that it enables the erasure, or the deliberate forgetting, of women's exploitation and oppression in the U.S., and the denial of women's agency in India. Both these erasures are necessary for the formation of "freedom" and "democracy" in the United States as well as in other First World nations. The discourse of "freedom" is essential to the consolidation and ongoing construction of Western state power structures, especially at the present time with the increase in the collection of information on citizens and noncitizens with new technologies, and the corresponding redefinitions of issues of privacy and personal freedoms. The ideology of American "freedom" constructs U.S. nationalism.

From *Our Feet Walk the Sky: Women of the South Asian Diaspora*. © 1993 by the Women of South Asian Descent Collective.

Jasmine supports and maintains this discourse of "Americanness" and "freedom" as connected and synonymous even while it can be consumed as a "multicultural" text. It supports the "multiculturalism" that is being embraced currently within liberal U.S. circles; this multiculturalism readily absorbs a text by a "minority" woman, that attacks one kind of racism practiced by the white working class, while remaining oblivious to the more subtle and powerful racism of the upper classes. Affiliating itself with the white upper classes, it speaks of "difference" and "diversity," though it presents diversity in the normative language of the dominant classes. An acceptable form of diversity is presented, within which upper-class minorities and whites align themselves on the basis of class; this version of "diversity" involves acceptance not only of middle and upper class minorities but also of state control by these classes. At present, this notion of "diversity" serves to formulate an image of the U.S. as a nation of "tolerance" that is a model for democratic rights around the world.

Unlike the *Sun*'s reviewer, many South Asians have been concerned with the novel's treatment of South Asian women, immigrants and minority groups, as well as other people of color in the U.S. In order to see such representations as linked to nationalist needs in both the U.S. and India, we need to look at the colonial discourses of essential identities based on gender, race and class within which texts about Asia and Asian women are produced and consumed. These are the global contexts that affect Asians living in the so-called First and Third Worlds, since it remains important for nations in the West to define themselves and their projects in opposition to what is termed the "Third World."

What is suggested by this Western subject formation is that all feminist opposition is defined in the West; for instance, it is believed that if there are feminists in India, they follow the same agendas as those in the U.S. This problematic formulation emerges from a Eurocentrism that ignores any discussion of Third World women's specific exploitations and agendas. For women of Asian origins in the U.S., progressive communities arise out of political coalitions and not from the national essence that is constructed through an authentic "tradition." Such a tradition, though seemingly protective, is often repressive and ineffective against the racist onslaught of white culture of "freedom" and "independence," and a European colonial history in which Asian societies were seen as exploitative and barbaric. This "tradition" colludes with the colonial stereotypes of Asian women as passive and affects both Asians and Asian Americans. It is therefore important to state that it is not America with its much vaunted freedom and equality that makes Asian women into "free" Americans, but that Asian women were active, oppositional, empowered and struggling, though their agendas and struggles were different from those of Western feminists. Alternate and specific histories and accounts of women's lives in Asia affects Asians living in North America for they enable oppositions that do not utilize the questionable structure of First World freedom and equality.

In the aftermath of the Los Angeles uprising in 1991 that followed from the Rodney King case, what we need to focus on are coalitions, within Asian American communities and between minority communities, against racism, homophobia, immigration law biases, sexism and other inequalities. In order to make these coalitions we need to understand the connected issues of state nationalism and cultural nationalism, i.e., how do those South Asians who belong to dominant communities within their nations of origins become politicized as minorities in the U.S.? On what basis do they construct themselves as separate and different? What form does their connection to their country of origin take?

Within the South Asian community and affecting its participation in the larger group of Asian Americans, are the connections between the nationalist politics since the independence of South Asian nations, and the formations of coalitions with other minority groups in the U.S. In the case of Indian immigrants, the effect of decades of nationalist struggle in India resulted in the hegemony of the middle and upper classes, which were English speaking and educated by colonial and Indian education to believe in modernization, development and progress. The dominant culture in India, constructed through such nationalist discourses, required the exclusion of minorities and a belief in the necessity of their assimilating. Power-hungry politicians, millions of disenfranchised peoples and the failure of the secularization project, all contributed to making the communal riots in India that resulted in the deaths of many hundreds of people. We now see the problems and dangers of this hegemonic culture that leaves out the poor religious minorities and the tribal groups in the construction of the Indian nation.

While for some the belief in modernization leads to a rejection of anything associated with what is seen as "tradition," for many South Asian immigrants (most of which comprised the professional, hence, modernized classes because of the nature of immigration laws after 1965) the belief in a tradition, supposedly static and authentic, remains important for struggles against racism and assimilation. Thus many immigrants to the U.S. who belong to the Indian upper classes are unable to jettison their nationalist luggage, keeping ties to a "home" that is, for them, free of discrimination, and where race seems not to matter. The Indian government, wishing for investments from U.S. immigrants, maintains and nurtures the ties to "home" by creating a category called the "Non-Resident Indian" (N.R.I.) that gives a special financial status to visiting immigrants. Yet this position of

dominance in India, together with acculturation in the U.S., where stereotypes of African Americans, Chicano/as and other minorities abound, often
prevents any coalitions with disenfranchised groups in the U.S., with other
Asian Americans, and with more recent Southeast Asian immigrant groups,
and often leads to an uncritical position on U.S. ideology of "democracy"
and "freedom."

In what follows, I compare the works of two South Asian women
writing in North America to examine how they restructure Indian colonial
and post-independence formations in order to align themselves to different
communities and different histories in diasporic situations.

In Meena Alexander's recent novel *Nampally Road*, the range of women
is impressive. The female characters include a professor and writer, a Muslim
woman, a laborer-activist and a doctor. Such a range prevents any simplistic
formulation such as oppressed Indian women versus independent American
women. The novel's complex representation of India in the Indira Gandhi
era, combined with the issue of inclusion and empowerment through affiliations on the basis of gender and class in both India and the U.S., effectively
dismantles simplistic colonial constructs of the monolithic Third World
woman as victim.

Not unlike some of Alexander's poems set in the U.S., this book is
about the relationships across classes: between those who have profited from
nationalism and those whose exploitation continues, not by the British, but
by neocolonial elites. The book is based on a famous case in which a Muslim
woman was raped in Hyderabad by several policemen in a police station.
This rape caused riots; the people of the town burnt down the station. In
Alexander's novel, they rescue the woman during the riot and try to burn
down the tents erected to celebrate the rule of the Chief Minister of the state
who sees the state as his private kingdom. The novel focuses on the politics
of gender and class, for it is not only about a rape but about the rape of a
woman without any power: a poor Muslim woman with no access to power
structures, for Muslims in contemporary India have become a disenfranchised minority. Commenting on nationalist politics, it speaks of the power
of the contemporary politicians in contemporary India, who are creating
little kingdoms for themselves, complete with coopted police and armed
secret henchmen. The henchmen wear "three-piece suits and black
sunglasses modelled on Papa Doc Duvalier's dreaded Tonton Macoutes"
(39); dictators in Haiti become models for repressive politics in other post-
colonies. For these politicians, the votes of the majority population are
obtained by increasing control over minorities and women.

In the meantime, the anger and protests against corruption and misuse of power by politicians and the state are seen to require a "containment" necessary to continue the celebrations that would proclaim Limca Gowda a "great leader," another Mahatma Gandhi or Krishna reborn. As the radio announcer says, in what the narrator describes as a "deep, clipped voice, well trained by the BBC Overseas Service people," the celebration is "a historic moment" and that "there is no doubt that all troublesome elements will be subdued. A new world will arise." (75–76) Here Alexander connects the power of such politicians to a neocolonialism that comes from lessons learnt from the British, exemplified by the radio announcer's news report, spoken in the BBC style, in which the poor and powerless are "troublesome elements." (76) Neocolonial elites in India are linked to those in other Third World countries; Papa Doc's terror squads are compared to Limca Gowda's Eveready Men.

While revealing right-wing affiliations, Alexander's narrator focuses also on affiliations between the oppressed. Yet the novel reveals not only the possibilities but also the problematics of these connections. Mira is concerned with the exploitation of the poor and of poor women in particular, but also with the relationship between the poor women and herself as a middle-class person. Although the novel suggests that she tries to understand Rameeza without turning her into a cipher for Otherness, the failure of this attempt in the novel is significant in its betrayal of class relations. Ironically, therefore, one can see the novel as successful in many ways in its examination of the location of the Indian middle-class intellectual and the process of decolonization even while its representation of the gendered subaltern subject, Rameeza Be, is much less convincing. As a college professor and writer, Mira Kannadical questions the lessons of British imperialism, her colonial education, her preoccupation with Wordsworth, and the utter difference between Wordsworth's Romantic Self, which requires an Other to complete its binary structure, and the lives of the poor around her. She questions the ideological effect of her writing, such that in the end her notebooks remain under her bed, her class on Wordsworth untaught, while she is occupied with the rescue of Rameeza Be and the protests that follow. Yet class differences between the elites with an English education and cosmopolitan ties and those disenfranchised minorities, exacerbated within nationalism, cannot be sutured easily.

Alexander constructs a web of struggle that includes India and England, which it necessarily must since the economic structures that give power and privilege to politicians and elites are themselves linked. As a student in London, Mira participates in anti-Thatcher marches. Even though the agenda is different in London, there is a link between the march against Thatcher and the riot against Limca Gowda. Both are concerned with redressing the rights of those without power and working against the politicians for whom people as individuals cease to exist and are linked in the common opposition to the rising power of global economic structures. Alexander presents a politics of location that has a continuity; struggle in India and struggle in London are linked through opposition to similar and connected structures of oppression.

Consequently, for Meena Alexander, the problems of Indian nationalism are very much uppermost, even while she writes poetry about crime and poverty in the streets of New York, for the problematic of nationalism is the creation of powerful elites and disenfranchised people. It is also about coalitions between the elites and coalitions that must be built in order to oppose the right-wing ones. New York and Hyderabad both have different versions of this nationalist problem; "home" and "abroad" are equally unsettling.

Another set of affiliations is set up by poet Surjit Kalsey. Very different from Alexander, Kalsey writes of the problems of immigrants who come to America because of economic necessity and the hope of bettering their lives, but are disappointed. While Alexander calls on commonalities on the basis of class and gender, Kalsey's work focuses more on race and class discrimination. Such work enables coalitions between people of color; coalitions that are becoming increasingly necessary in the economic recession that pits minorities against each other.

Kalsey, a South Asian Canadian, works on constructing an Indian and an immigrant heritage for poets living in North America. The heritage is not only of poets in India but of the early South Asian settlers in America. In an essay on Canadian Punjabi Literature, she cites as the founding texts the writings of the first immigrants from India. Kalsey's work focuses on the lives of undocumented and working-class immigrants to the U.S., revealing the harshness and difficulties of an existence that is common to many immigrants. In "Siddharta Does Penance Once Again," Kalsey describes the feelings of a young man who leaves his wife behind in order to come to America to make a living. What Kalsey fuses is the structures of experience in India (the traveler is Siddharta in a world of miseries), with the experience of the early Asian immigrants and more recent Asian and Mexican farmworkers. Many of these immigrants had to leave wives and families behind in search of a living. Travel is immigration here, but is also seen as a pilgrimage, leaving what is familiar in search of a mortal salvation. Kalsey portrays their loneliness, their longings to see their loved ones as well as their exploitation as itinerant workers. The worker/speaker of the poem is ironic in his use of the metaphor of pilgrimage for immigration, for this "pilgrimage" has "hermits" who exploit them, and the other "pilgrims" are the immigrant farmworkers: "Everyday they pack us into closed wagons/to dump us into the raspberry, strawberry or blueberry fields." His promises are the promises of many other immigrants, Chinese, Japanese, Filipino or South Asian:

> I'll come home very soon
> or I'll apply for your immigration very soon
> so that with you own eyes you can touch that "holy Tree"
> under which, doing penance,
> I've found the path to salvation from hunger . . . (26)

Kalsey presents the plight of the farmworker within the background of racism in America. The sad irony is that this search for a mortal salvation creates divided families, alienation and sorrow. Yet the experiences presented in this poem sets up affiliations across many communities of color, for many Asian and Mexican and African American's shared the same experience that the farmworker in the poem speaks of. These affiliations occur on the basis of race as well as of class. More importantly, the poem does not present India and America within the free-unfree binary, for such a binary does not exist for an immigrant who is a farmworker.

As shown by the work of Alexander and Kalsey, South Asian and South Asian American politics of location moves between nationalist politics of contemporary India, colonial discourses and new affiliations demanded by immigrant contexts. Despite different agendas in different locations, the transnational nature of these struggles implies a linkage among various contexts. Faced with neocolonial alliances between colonialists and elites, struggles for self-determination and against exploitation also form oppositional coalitions. Meena Alexander and Surjit Kalsey are two examples of South Asian women who bring to their work different but linked affiliations to the communities in which they live and move.

Bharati Mukherjee's novel *Jasmine*, on the other hand, makes distinctions rather than affiliations among the working classes and those who are not in privileged positions. Not only does this narrative participate in the problematic discourse of Indian nationalism, but it also prevents any coalitions on the basis of another kind of history: that of immigration to America, thus foreclosing the problematization of U.S. nationalist ideology. The characterization of other U.S. ethnic communities reveals that this text does not participate in any formation of Asian American communities struggling against racism, sexism and stereotypes of Asians as backward and barbaric. Moreover, the stereotyping of a minority community from India, the Sikhs, reveals a disinterest in participating in the formation of an Asian American anti-racism coalition for it ignores immigration history. Sikhs, who are described in the text as fanatics and terrorists, formed the majority among the first South Asians to come to the U.S. They and other South Asians were important in contributing to the struggle for Indian independence, as well as in providing a history of South Asian presence in the U.S. that can be built upon to provide coalitions with other Asian Americans.

Yet by ignoring such histories, *Jasmine* not only cannot connect newly arrived immigrant communities to the earlier ones, but it also cannot present the struggle against racism as one that has a history with all the communities that history created and can create. Mukherjee's protagonist, Jasmine, outside such a history, is consequently presented as an anomaly among Asians and Asian women and outside all preexisting contexts and communities of struggle. Without history and community, Jasmine's struggle is that of the Euro-American feminist striving for individuality. Thus the only "freedom" that *Jasmine* reveals is that of being part of and valorizing the dominant power structure. But more problematically, this so-called "freedom," gained at the expense of Asians and other people of color, is taken as empowerment. For Mukherjee, as she has said recently, insisting on being called "American" is political intervention, rather than seeing herself as Asian-American or even as Indo-American. Instead of dismantling the hegemony of the term, "American," she wants to be included within it.

In light of Mukherjee's statements, it is not surprising that what seems most important to the protagonist of the novel, *Jasmine*, is becoming part of the dominant, white, upper class group. This is done at the expense of Asian women, South Asian minorities, other Asian cultures and groups and other people of color. Such a formation testifies to the ways in which nationalisms, though seemingly in opposition, collude in order to become powerful; some Indian elites, gaining power through nationalist struggles in India, make alliances with the white, upper classes as immigrants in the U.S.

Moreover, Mukherjee's narrative of a simplistic religious conflict presents communalism as a manifestation of natural antipathies between people who follow different religions rather than as a colonial construct that is being redeployed for particular reasons by various politicians today. Communalism, as Gyan Panday has suggested in his important book, *Communalism and Nationalism in North India*, is a colonial construct that enabled state control in the guise of mediating religious divisions. According to Panday, "Communalism . . . is a form of colonialist knowledge . . . The paradox is that the nationalists have done more than anyone else to propagate its use." In effect, communalism as religious difference, was constructed as the Other of modernity and nationalism; therefore, it was necessary for the emergence of India as a nation. Indian nationalist claims for the Hindu character of the Indian nation and of Hindu nationalism (and conflicts in response to this claim) occurred concurrently with the positioning of the Indian nation-state as the keeper of law and order, just as the colonial state had been.

If we see "communalism" in this more complex light, we have to be aware of the way in which divisions on the basis of religion were much more than what they appeared to be, and to see religious differences as being utilized and mobilized for many reasons by many people in power and by the state. Class, caste, regional, gender divisions that are changing and historically specific reveal that these entities are as constructed as is the nationalist history of India. Without such complexities—which have to be ignored if a narrative is to be presented in terms of "freedom" and "unfreedom," in which the nation is unproblematized—we have a narrative of stereotypes. Thus, just as all Palestinians or Iranians are seen as terrorists in the West, all Sikhs are terrorists in Mukherjee's work. What is unproblematized is this Hindu nationalist structure of the innocent Hindu vs. the terrorist Sikh. This structure, and other similar ones, are currently being utilized by right-wing politicians in India to advance their own power much as the English used what they had termed "communal" divisions. Hundreds of people have died in this new mobilization of "communalism," and the Hindu vs. Sikh division is only one of many being utilized in India at the present time. Unfortunately, the nationalist legacy and the rhetoric of colonialism and Western "freedom" that enables the designation of certain groups as "terrorists" adds not only to the present ethnic strife in India, but it elides the way in which the unrest of the minorities in India is to a large extent the response to the consolidation of power in the hands of the dominant Hindu elites, to a greater centralization of state power, the diminution of the rights of minorities and to the unfulfilled promises of nationalism to the poor in India.

Consequently, to keep to an unquestioned discourse of communalism is to be faithful to the controlling right-wing power structures and to the extension of the power of the state in India. Such a narrative also extends the power of those in the U.S. who are all too ready to dismiss all nonChristians as fanatics and terrorists. Such racist discourses enable the extension of state power over minority and white working-class communities in the U.S. as well.

Jasmine's claim to the reader's interest and attention seems based on the notion that she is unlike other Indian women—that she is active, a risk-taker and adventurous. Mukherjee has called these qualities being "American," claiming that many "Americans" live in other parts of the world. Thus Jasmine is implicitly "American" from the very beginning, so that, unlike other Indian women, she has the sympathy of many American readers. Since she is supposedly an anomaly among Indian women, she is represented as a rebel, one who can act according to her desires. Such an agency is, however, miraculously unexplained, because what is revealed to the reader is that women are so oppressed in India that such an agency is impossible. Jasmine has the "scrubbed-rawest hands" because "I boiled the river water three and four times, when everyone else just let the mud settle before drinking." (39) She is also the only one with the courage to face a mad dog, while other women crawl away terrified. Since she is so anomalous, no one understands Jasmine. Infant girls are thrown in wells, others have various terrible fates. Jasmine is the survivor, unlike all the others who live miserable lives. This is clearly a First World fantasy of Third World women's lives. Thus Jasmine says, "My grandmother may have named me Jyoti, Light, but in surviving I was already Jane, a fighter and adapter." (35) In this text, a "Jyoti" cannot be a fighter. One has to be Jane, a European American, to be one.

Trinh T. Minh-ha has called this portrayal of an anomalous Third World woman as a representation of "specialness" rather than one of difference. Trinh suggests that this kind of formation creates a division "between I-who-have-made-it and You-who-cannot-make-it" and it has unfortunate consequences in the preservation of one's identity as special at the cost of other women; it leads to a "double game: on the one hand, (I shall) loudly assert my right, as a woman, and an exemplary one, to have access to equal opportunity; on the other hand, (I shall) quietly maintain my privileges by helping the master perpetuate his cycle of oppression." This representation of Jasmine's "specialness" seemingly enables a denunciation of racism in the U.S. (which is likely to lull criticism of the book from minorities and liberals who welcome other minority voices), at the same time as it suggests, problematically, that racism should not be directed against Jasmine because she is different from other women of color.

We search for what is called the "genuine foreignness" that makes all white men she meets fall in love with her. But all we find is submission and mystery in the guise of independence. Thus Jasmine's freedom simply implies her ability to change herself according to the wants of the dominant culture. Her power is to make people aware of her oriental mystery, to long for Otherness that she embodies, to make them want something Indian at their dinner table every day. Difference is reduced to curry—one that can be consumed by the dominant classes.

If this narrative is one of "specialness," then what is problematic is Mukherjee's own position within the U.S. and the agenda of liberal "multiculturalism" within which this novel is consumed. *Jasmine* works on the level of monolithic representations, for instance, of what it means to be an "Indian woman," or what it means to live in a "typical" Indian community in the

U.S., by focusing on what it means to be an "anomalous Indian woman." While many authors who are not writing about white America have to struggle against what has been called the "burden of representation," the success of this novel depends on it being seen as representative.

It is not surprising, therefore, that other nonwhite communities are also presented as representative, and Jasmine has little solidarity with them. For instance, when she arrives in the U.S. and is walking the road looking for help, it is not the Mexican farmworkers who help her, but a white woman. The men in the fields are "Short, thick, darkskinned men with vaguely Asian features" (115); a little boy among them points a toy gun at her, which looks similar to the Uzi carried by the so-called Sikh terrorists. He sprays her with imaginary bullets while she is gasping for water. Like the Sikhs, the Latinos in the fields seem violent and threatening to Jasmine.

It is the white woman, Lillian, who rescues her and who becomes the model of what Jasmine yearns to be. She is described as "a facilitator who made possible the lives of absolute ordinariness that we ached for" (117)— this ordinariness never available in Asia but present in an upper middle class white existence in Manhattan. The other refugees in Lillian's house are never described as individuals, nor are they named; they are "the Kanjobal women" who teach Jasmine how to make tortillas while she teaches them how to make chapatis. This is as far as we get in terms of solidarity with other people of color. Lillian, on the other hand, teaches them how to be domestics, but she too, amazingly enough, sees Jasmine as different from "the Kanjobal women." So in her "brisk, direct way," she says "Jazzy, you don't strike me as a picker or a domestic." (120) We wonder why the others were seen as appropriate for domestic work, while Jazzy is sent off to Lillian's daughter in New York as a "very special case." (120) After Lillian is busted for harboring undocumented persons, Jasmine sees this woman for whom the only future for women of color is as domestics, as a heroine: "She represented to me the best in the American experience and the American character." (121)

The lives of other South Asian immigrants are presented as empty and pathetic in comparison to Jasmine's, since she is full of hope and desire, and the South Asian immigrant family she stays with seem not to have such feelings. We are told they have "retired behind ghetto walls," because they chose to live there. (129) Flushing, New Jersey, seems like Punjab to her, and of course, this is a derogatory comparison. Jasmine, immured in the immigrant ghetto, is oppressed by the boredom of such an existence. Since this life does not qualify as that of the "absolute ordinariness" that occurs only in a white middle-class existence, she would often find herself "in the bathroom with the light off, head down on the cold, cracked rim of the sink, sobbing from unnamed, unfulfilled wants." (131) It is, of course, not possible to present the immigrant "ghetto" as a place of pleasure, comfort and community, one that immigrants would intentionally or actively seek out and prefer to live in. Nor does it even suggest, as in the case of Chinatowns, that in a climate of racism, the "ghetto" may be the only haven.

What the novel suggests is that since life in India equals violence, the "ordinary" life Jasmine searches for is only available within middle-class existence in New York. The text does not present the "ordinary" in India. This ordinary life, available within all classes and in many places, cannot be represented through the tourist's gaze. This is because the tourist can only see in comparison with the West, and within this comparison, places in Asia only can be situated in relation to modernity. A homogeneous Third World thus appears, where women seen are seen only as exploited and oppressed. What is not visible in touristic novels such as *Jasmine* is the representation of lives in the so-called "Third World" as normal, ordinary, with all the pleasures and pains that ordinary life contains. Mukherjee's work reveals the Third World as barbaric and the First as civilized; its success in the U.S. depends on keeping to this problematic assumption. In *Jasmine*, life in India is anomalous, strange, unnatural; none of its characters have any pleasures in the details of living. And it is not only India that is viewed through a tourist's lens, but also Vietnam, as becomes apparent in the section of *Jasmine* that concerns the young boy, Du, Jasmine's adopted son. Du is presented as the perfect Asian, because he has endured terrible privations and tragedies but survives to become a computer whiz. Thus, in seeing what they have in common, Jasmine says:

> "Du's doing well because he has always trained with live ammo, without a net, with no multiple choice. No guesswork: only certain knowledge or silence. Once upon a time, like me, he was someone else. We've been many selves. We've survived hideous times. I envy Bud the straight line and smooth planes of his history." (190)

To live in Asia is to live in a combat zone, a zone of warfare; consequently America, as its opposite, is the place where, in contrast, Lillian Gordon's "absolute ordinariness" can become possible. It is never possible in Asia.

Mukherjee's novel seems written for Euro-American audiences with the gaze of a Euro-American tourist, and not of one who has lived in India or comes from India. Like the work of V.S. Naipaul, *Jasmine* represents South Asia with the tropes and ideologies of Western hegemonic structures. Its portrayals of women in India are especially problematic because, without present the complexity of state formations, regional politics and contemporary power structures as they impact upon gender relations in India, the novel does not help in the formation of feminist agendas different from those of bourgeois feminists in Europe and North America

On the other hand, a reading of Meena Alexander's novel, *Nampally Road*, gains immensely from a knowledge of specific events that occurred in India in the eighties, from knowing well how politicians function there, as well as from a concern for lives of women in different classes and communities. Alexander's work is, unfortunately, not as well known as Mukherjee's. Its complexity prevents it from functioning as a representative text describing "the Indian woman" or "the South Asian immigrant experience," as does *Jasmine*. Perhaps it is for this reason, unfortunately, that it will not be a best-seller in the U.S.

JEANNE ROSIER SMITH

Monkey Business:
Maxine Hong Kingston's Transformational Trickster Texts

In her groundbreaking study on women writers of Chinese ancestry, *Between Worlds*, Amy Ling observes that "the feeling of being between worlds, totally at home nowhere," characterizes writing by Chinese American women. Because of the high value placed on feminine modesty and reticence in Chinese culture, Ling explains, a woman of Chinese ancestry who wants to publish in the United States "must be something of a rebel, for writing, an act of rebellion and self-assertion, runs counter to Confucian training. Also she has to possess two basic character traits: an indomitable will and an unshakeable self-confidence" (14). Kingston's trickster aesthetic affirms the importance of these traits in her work. The trickster Monkey, whose will, confidence, and outrageous rebellion disrupt heaven and win him battles with dragons and gods, inspires the crafting of Kingston's *Woman Warrior*, *China Men*, and *Tripmaster Monkey*. In all of her works, the trickster embodies Kingston's vision of identity and of the transformative power of narrative.

From *Writing Tricksters: Mythic Gambols in American Ethnic Literature.* © 1997 by The Regents of the University of California.

MONKEY MOTHERS AND OTHER PARADOXES:
THE WOMAN WARRIOR

Although Kingston does not introduce an overt trickster character into her works until *Tripmaster Monkey*, the formal and thematic concerns of *The Woman Warrior* and *China Men* show signs of the trickster's influence. Classified as "autobiography," and labeled as nonfiction on its cover, *The Woman Warrior* transgresses both of these restrictive definitions and offers a trickster-inspired model for narrative form and the construction of identity. As a trickster text, *The Woman Warrior* encourages a sense of truth as multifaceted, both through the example of the trickster mother, Brave Orchid, and through a narrative that demands and plays on reader involvement.

Though much of the criticism of *The Woman Warrior* focuses on the difficulties created by competing and often contradictory allegiances, such contradiction is not necessarily debilitating. Kingston's multivocal *Woman Warrior* redefines *autobiography* as a process of acknowledging and giving voice to contradictions and paradoxes within the self. The trickster, whose identity is not stable but always shifting, who speaks in many languages and challenges preconceived notions, embodies this process. The trickster's androgynous, multivocal, polyvalent identity reconciles or encompasses the "agonizing contradictions" that split women writers by their allegiance to various groups (Hunt 11). Like Han Suyin's avowal that "I shall be both" and Gloria Anzaldúa's assertion that "only your labels split me," Kingston's autobiography affirms a fluid, tricksterlike identity not bounded by restrictive definitions (Ling 115; Anzaldúa and Moraga 205). Kingston's conception of identity in *The Woman Warrior* challenges a predominantly male tradition in Asian American literature, which stresses a monolithic, unified identity. Robert Lee connects the form of the work to a political subversion of the status quo, suggesting one way in which *The Woman Warrior* plays a trickster role in relation to Asian American tradition: "It is precisely the discontinuities, dislocations, and erasures in the history of Chinese women in the United States that *The Woman Warrior* interrogates, thereby challenging both the silence imposed by Orientalism and the authoritarianism of a reasserted patriarchy that threatens to seal Chinese American women's experiences off in its masculinized revision of history" (55). In the spirit of the trickster, *The Woman Warrior* outrageously pokes holes in stereotypes and established hierarchies. The text uses trickster strategies both to challenge a stultifying patriarchy and to champion an ethnic Chinese American culture that, in the face of harsh discriminatory laws, has had to rely on trickster strategies for its continuity. It is "camouflage, subterfuge and surprise that enable the immigrant traditions to survive and [that] imbue them with power for resistance" (Lee 57).

Kingston's autobiography incorporates memoir, novel, myth, fantasy, legend, and biography and thus not only challenges an Asian American male tradition but also rejects a view of the self as an isolated individual. The author's remark that "I hope my writing has many layers, as human beings have layers," encourages us to read the self as composed of multiple stories ("Cultural Mis-Readings" 65). *The Woman Warrior* encompasses the voices and perspectives of the narrator's mother, her aunts, her sister, and her grandmother, as well as mythical forebears Fa Mu Lan and Ts'ai Yen, and thereby suggests a notion of identity that includes one's community and culture. "'I' am nothing but who 'I' am in relation to other people," Kingston explains ("Personal Statement" 23). This relational view of identity calls for a fluid conception of autobiography as a form that creates and preserves community as well as individuality. She feels compelled to invent a new auto-biographical form, she explains, because "we're always on the brink of disappearing. Our culture's disappearing and our communities are always disappearing" (Fishkin 786). Kingston's autobiography gives voice to the many women who have created community for her.

As a gathering of varied and often contradictory stories, *The Woman Warrior* explores a sense of truth that allows for paradox. The tricksterlike image of the elusive, ever-changing dragon appears throughout *The Woman Warrior*, suggesting the impossibility of a single all-encompassing perspective. The narrator, as Fa Mu Lan, learns about paradox through dragons: "I learned to make my mind large, as the universe is large, so that there is room for paradoxes. . . . The dragon lives in the sky, ocean, marshes, and mountains; and the mountains are also its cranium. Its voice thunders and jingles like copper pans. It breathes fire and water; and sometimes the dragon is one, sometimes many" (*WW* 29). Like truth, the dragon can never be seen in its entirety and therefore forms a central trope in the text for the indeterminacy of any one point of view. The idea that paradox may be the most accurate representation of truth becomes clear when the narrator speculates about her mother cutting her frenum. "She pushed my tongue up and sliced the frenum. Or maybe she snipped it with a pair of scissors. I don't remember her doing it. . . . I saw no scars in my mouth." The narrator is unsure not only about how but also whether and why her mother cut her frenum: "Sometimes I felt very proud that my mother committed such a powerful act upon me. At other times I was terrified— the first thing my mother did when she saw me was to cut my tongue." In the same act, the mother silences her daughter and frees her tongue "to move in any language" (*WW* 164). The passage captures the ambivalence of the narrator's relationship to her mother and the paradoxically debilitating and empowering effect Brave Orchid has on her.

As Brave Orchid teaches her daughter to value paradox, she passes on a trickster legacy, for Brave Orchid, whose very name is a paradox, is a trickster who undermines and upsets the injunctions that she delivers. The mother's legacy to her daughter is necessarily complex because she represents for her daughter the oppressive authority of Chinese culture, especially regarding acceptable female behavior. Yet through her actions and her stories, Brave Orchid sends vivid messages that subvert her authoritarian proclamations. The no name aunt's story dramatizes this tension between an oppressive overt message—"Don't humiliate us" (*WW* 5)—and a subtle message of rebellion; like the narrator, who flouts her mother's injunction not to tell, Brave Orchid herself has broken a taboo by telling the story of the no name aunt to her daughter. Though "You must not tell" carries the force of command, Brave Orchid's later request, "Don't let your father know that I told you," betrays her own sense of transgression and sets up a clandestine alliance with her daughter against the father (*WW* 5). Brave Orchid hands down a secret legacy of powerful stories to her daughter, who muses, "I have believed that. . . words [were] so strong and fathers so frail that 'aunt' would do my father some mysterious harm" (*WW* 15).

Contradiction and paradox, the trickster's hallmarks, define Brave Orchid. She slyly communicates trickster strategies to her daughter through the disparity between her words and her actions. Though she openly repeats misogynistic sayings like "'There's no profit in raising girls. Better to raise geese than girls,'" Brave Orchid sings the legend of Fa Mu Lan to her daughter, thereby giving her a means to fight against tradition. "She said I would grow up a wife and a slave, but she taught me the song of the warrior woman" (*WW* 20). Brave Orchid's life story, told in "Shaman," suggests that her example as a deserted wife turned doctor, who would cross the ocean to bear six children after the age of forty-five, provides another powerful antidote to her misogynist maxims.

As the protagonist struggles to come to terms with her cultural heritage, she must wrestle with her mother's confusing, contradictory, cryptic stories (*WW* 163). "'I don't want to listen to any more of your stories; they have no logic. They scramble me up. You lie with stories. You won't tell me a story and then say, "This is a true story," or "This is just a story."' . . . I can't tell what's real and what you make up'" (*WW* 202). The book records the process of the narrator's gradual acceptance that truth is multifaceted. Reality encompasses different, sometimes conflicting versions, and the enigmatic Brave Orchid, both woman and shaman, has trickily equipped not crippled her daughter by conveying this. Whereas the naive protagonist struggles with distinctions between "a true story" and "just a story," the narrator finally collapses these distinctions by presenting herself as a tricksterlike "outlaw knotmaker" whose story is a mix of actual, fictional, and mythic events (*WW* 163).

As *The Woman Warrior* works to subvert the protagonist's polarized thinking, it does the same for the reader. The narration of Moon Orchid's adventures in "At the Western Palace" provides a useful example of how the text questions the relative values of "a true story" and "just a story." Kingston will not allow her reader to rest comfortably with the separation of "fiction" and "fact," or with the idea that either possesses a higher claim to reality. "At the Western Palace," the fourth section of *The Woman Warrior*, is an extended third-person omniscient narrative, thoroughly grounded in the mundane details of modern life. With its classic short story structure, the chapter seems at first glance to be the most "realistic" and accessible and therefore the most reliable of the work's five sections. However, the opening words of the next section destabilize that comfortable trust in the narrator's omniscience: "What my brother actually said was" (*WW* 164). Not having witnessed most of the events herself, Kingston has embellished her brother's version of the story. She considers the relative worth of the two stories and concedes, "His version of the story may be better than mine because of its bareness, not twisted into designs" (*WW* 164). Yet although she suggests that her brother's story may be closer to the "facts," her inclusion of "At the Western Palace" implies that she is proud of her outlaw knotmaking. Indeed, although the brother drove Brave Orchid and her sister to Los Angeles and participated in some of the story's events, he is limited by his perspective. His brief statements highlight his absorption in his own role: "I drove Mom and Second Aunt to Los Angeles to see Aunt's husband who's got the other wife. . . . I don't remember [what Mom said]. I pretended a pedestrian broke her leg so he would come" (*WW* 163). The narrator's fictionalized version of the story, which imaginatively enters the minds of the participants ("Moon Orchid was so ashamed, she held her hands over her face. She wished she could also hide her dappled hands" [*WW* 153]), may be truer than a firsthand account.

In presenting alternative variations on stories, Kingston's tricksterlike narrative acts upon her reader in much the same way as Brave Orchid's stories act upon the narrator. Vicente Gotera records student responses to *The Woman Warrior* that sound much like Kingston's narrator: "I had trouble determining whether a particular storyline was truth or fantasy," one student writes (65). Like Brave Orchid's story of the no name aunt, Kingston tells us "once and for all the useful parts" (*WW* 6), leaving gaps and blanks in her story that test the reader's "strength to establish realities" (*WW* 5). Kingston explains, "I meant to give people those questions so that they can wrestle with them in their own lives. You know, I can answer those questions, but then . . . I just answer [them] for me. . . . When people wrestle with them and struggle with them in their own minds and in their own lives, all kinds of exciting things happen to them" (Fishkin 785). Kingston implies that there is no definitive way to fill the gaps in the text—the answers to the questions that the text raises change according to the reader. Kingston's comments suggest that she sees reading as an interactive process. When readers encounter a trickster text, "all kinds of exciting things happen to them," as they, like Kingston's narrator, wrestle with unresolved contradictions and perhaps begin to question their own comfortable way of viewing the world.

TRICKSTER HISTORY: *CHINA MEN*

If *The Woman Warrior*'s narrator is a trickster-in-training who grows up learning to distrust received truths, *China Men*'s narrator steps even further outside of her own point of view to tell the fathers' stories. *China Men* combines history, biography, autobiography, myth, fiction, and fantasy to reclaim and recreate Chinese American history as a multilayered story. "What I am doing is putting many kinds of stories and people right next to one another, as they are in real life. Each character is viewed from the vantage point of the others" (Pfaff 26). The work celebrates Kingston's ancestors, and by extension all China men, as tricksters who survived and triumphed despite unjust immigration laws and labor practices.

Like *The Woman Warrior*, *China Men* has proved a difficult work to classify under traditional genre categories. Primarily viewed as "biography" or "history," it also contains autobiographical vignettes, western and Chinese myths and legends, and multiple versions of a single life. If *The Woman Warrior*'s structure reflects a multilayered self, *China Men*'s structure reflects a multilayered community, culture, and history. To truly tell the story of China men, Kingston creates a communal chronicle, which reminds us that history is composed of many lives and many stories—not *his* story but *their* stories. She includes an eight-page section composed of U.S. immigration laws, which she calls "pure history," in order to combat mainstream readers' ignorance of the Chinese American immigrant experience, but the section's dry, official tone emphasizes the limitations of the history genre (Pfaff 25). The collective mode of *China Men* subverts a traditional, monologic history that—as Kingston's need to include "The Laws" implies—has all but erased Chinese Americans (Goellnicht 196).

In addition to challenging conventional written history, Kingston's work fights to recover an oral legacy that she senses has already been lost. Unlike Kingston's mother, who passes on a rich oral tradition to her daughter, her father remains silent, and she must invent his stories herself. *China Men* is Kingston's talk-story to her father: "I'll tell you what I suppose from your silences and a few words, and you can tell me that I'm mistaken. You'll just have to speak up with the real stories if I've got you wrong" (*CM* 15) This narrative stance recalls trickster Nanapush's direct address to Lulu in Louise Erdrich's *Tracks*, but here the roles are reversed: rather than a grandfather passing down an oral legacy to his granddaughter, here the daughter must reimagine her father's and grandfathers' stories, underscoring the precariousness of the oral tradition.

That Kingston had to separate the stories of her family into two volumes to reflect the historical and geographic split between Chinese American men's and women's experiences accounts in part for the breach in the oral tradition from father to daughter. Additionally, one incident in *China Men* suggests that Kingston's own fear and resentment of her male relatives' misogyny has prevented her from hearing the men's stories in the past. It involves Kau Goong, her grandmother's adventurous brother: "My brothers remember him as a generous old man; he took them to a smoking place where men with silver and wood pipes gave them presents and praised them. The only times he spoke to me were to scold and to give orders. 'Bad girl,' he said" (*CM* 180). When Kau Goong comes in the house looking for her one day, his loud shouts send her scurrying to the cellar to avoid "his bossy presence" (*CM* 180). Though she successfully avoids a confrontation that day, years later at his funeral she muses, "I listened to find out more about Kau Goong's pillages, his plunders, and sackings . . . but they did not mention his crimes though he was safe from deportation now. I should have yelled questions at him. I shouldn't have hidden from him" (*CM* 185). Kingston imaginatively retells the stories of China men to recover a history silenced by missed communication. As the Kau Goong episode ironically implies, patriarchal misogyny has nearly extinguished this heroic tradition by squelching the female voice that can pass it on.

China Men's introductory chapter, "On Discovery," foregrounds issues of gender and discovery by adapting an incident from the eighteenth-century Chinese novel *Flowers in the Mirror*. The segment demonstrates Kingston's trickster techniques: adaptation, invention, and defamiliarization. In Kingston's version, Tang Ao, a male scholar and traveler, "discovers" the "Land of Women" and is forced to endure the pain and humiliation of becoming a traditional female courtesan, with bound feet, plucked brows, pierced ears, and painted face. Though Kingston preserves the essential details of the eighteenth-century story (Cheung, *Articulate* 102), she switches some characters (in the original version the tortures are inflicted on Tang Ao's brother-in-law) and relocates the Land of Women to North America.

Several critics have noted the double-edged commentary Kingston's trans-
position of this story allows, as both a sympathetic allegory for the emasculation of Chinese men in America and (as in the original version) a
critique of patriarchy that has subjected Chinese women to similar treatment for centuries.

Kingston's prominent placement of the Tang Ao myth in a chapter
titled "On Discovery" in a book that questions the monologic voice of
history raises crucial questions about the nature of historic discoveries.
Traditional myths of American history begin with its "discovery" by Christo-
pher Columbus. Kingston's adaptation ends by suggesting that the Land of
Women (or North America) was discovered by the Chinese as early as A.D.
441 (*CM* 5). This casually mentioned "fact" challenges the legitimacy and
primacy of western myths of discovery by predating them and claiming the
discovery of America for the Chinese, but it also questions the motives of
such discovery. *Discovery* is a primary imperialist euphemism, designed to
obscure the issue of prior inhabitancy in order to appropriate land for one's
own purposes. When Tang Ao "discovers" the Land of Women, he remains
unthreatened even though they immediately capture him: "if he had had
male companions, he would've winked over his shoulder" (*CM* 3). As Tang
Ao's fate makes abundantly clear, discovery does not equal possession; in
fact, Tang Ao's ignorance of the civilization he "discovers" and his entrap-
ment in his own sexist ideas of women prevent him from seeing them as
potentially dangerous and result in his becoming *their* possession. By desta-
bilizing the term *discovery*, Kingston prepares readers to consider the alternative viewpoints and potential threats that lie behind their unexamined
preconceptions.

Kingston not only relocates Chinese stories in North America but also
recasts western myths as Chinese tales, most notably pirating Daniel Defoe's
enormously popular novel *Robinson Crusoe* as "The Adventures of Lo Bun
Sun." As David Leiwei Li has observed, Kingston faithfully preserves the
original story, changing only outward details such as Lo Bun Sun's cultiva-
tion of rice ("American Canon" 489). The effects of this transformation are
manifold. Defamiliarizing the story forces readers to consider the assumptions underlying this master narrative of western imperialism. Kingston's
adaptation reveals Crusoe's justification as "one of protocolonizer, imposer of
Western norms. . . . Kingston's creative reproduction of the Robinson myth
lays bare the device that rationalizes almost all Western colonization, the
workings of language and culture that presuppose the inherent supremacy of
European civilization and the barbarous wretchedness of the native" (Li,
"American Canon" 489). Exposing the motives of Robinson Crusoe (and by
extension western colonization) through parody is a primary trickster

strategy. As in *The Woman Warrior*, where Brave Orchid's view of all whites as ghosts and Moon Orchid's view of America as a "wilderness" of barbarians speak: for Kingston's view of ethnocentrism as a human tendency not limited to westerners (*WW* 158), Kingston wields her trickster critique of ethnocentrism in *China Men*. By so easily recasting Defoe's tale as the story of a Chinese "Lo Bun Sun," Kingston shows that racism and ethnocentrism are not exclusively western but are fundamentally human foibles. Thus, like the double-edged Tang Ao myth that cuts at both racist treatment of China men in America and sexist treatment of women in China, Kingston's "Adventures of Lo Bun Sun" parodies the myth of European supremacy while hinting that such blind self-aggrandizement is not exclusive to the western world.

The lives and stories of men of Chinese ancestry in America might easily lend themselves to tragic forms: exploited workers, unwilling bachelors, mocked and degraded "Chinamen" in a racist society. Yet rather than suggesting a history of victimization, Kingston presents the stories of her fathers and grandfathers in a comic mode. They are dauntless, irrepressible tricksters, outwitting a system stacked against them. King-Kok Cheung describes the trickster spirit that pervades *China Men*: "A subversive imagination and a sense of play enable both the dispossessed natives and the exploited Chinese immigrants to survive despite the odds. The author's own transformation of tragedy into comedy exemplifies the characteristics she attributes to China Men and engages the reader in a way no straight-faced account of peonage could" (*Articulate* 105). With her own "subversive imagination," Kingston has clearly inherited her trickster sensibility from a long line of trickster ancestors, female and male.

Kingston's father emerges as trickster in *China Men* in the sheer multiplicity of his life stories. "In the course of the book, I have him coming into this country in five different ways. I'm very proud of that," Kingston comments (Pfaff 26). The early chapter "On Fathers" radically questions a child's ability to know her parent at all. One evening she and her siblings, waiting at the gate for their father to come home, think they see him coming and run to greet him, only to be told that they are mistaken. "Looking closely, we saw that he probably was not [our father]," Kingston remembers. The man walks away, looking "from the back, almost exactly" like their father, and moments later their own father appears and acknowledges them. Placed prominently as *China Men*'s second chapter and appearing before any stories of real fathers and grandfathers, "On Fathers" destabilizes the notion of "father" as a fixed, recognizable identity. That his children look to recognize him by his expensive suit and wingtip shoes, and so easily mistake him for someone else, suggests how little they know of the man inside. In a way, both men in this incident are Kingston's father: the one who denies her and walks away and the one who salutes her.

The two chapters dedicated to her father's life, "The Father from China" and "The American Father," presented as if they concerned different people, reflect the father's multiple identities. Both chapters present him as a man of resilience and invention. Despite Kingston's ambivalence toward his misogyny and stony silence, her portrayal of her father as a heroic trickster speaks for her admiration of him. Like the Chinese trickster Monkey, he studies rigorously for years, successfully passes his examinations (Monkey's earn him the knowledge of immortality), grows dissatisfied with the mediocrity and bureaucracy that surround him, and makes his own "Journey to the West." In America the father renames himself Edison, claiming for himself the cunning and resourcefulness of the famous inventor. After being duped out of the laundry business by his friends in New York, dodging arrest as manager of a gambling house, and enduring a depression that keeps him rooted to his chair as immovably as Monkey trapped for five hundred years under a mountain, Ed springs back to life and builds a new laundry in California, a self-made man many times over.

Kingston's other male ancestors are also heroic tricksters. Kingston's "crazy" grandfather, Ah Goong, shares the trickster's traditional position at the bottom of the social ladder, scorned by a family who calls him "Fleaman" and disregarded as crazy by many of his fellow railroad workers. Filled with the trickster's comic and arrogant sexuality, aloft in a basket blasting into the side of a cliff, Ah Goong shouts "I am fucking the world" (*CM* 133). Though discredited as crazy, Ah Goong wisely recognizes that his work on the railroad makes him an American. He tells the men who die building the railroad, "This is the Gold Mountain. We're marking the land now. The track sections are numbered, and your family will know where we leave you" (*CM* 138). Ah Goong helps organize the railroad workers, passing along the encoded message to strike by tying holiday food bundles with a "special pattern of red string" (*CM* 140). Kingston uses Ah Goong to subtly challenge stereotyped images of Chinese men and replace them with images of strength and heroism: "Ah Goong acquired another idea that added to his reputation for craziness: The pale, thin Chinese scholars and the rich men fat like Buddhas were less beautiful, less manly than these brown muscular railroad men, of whom he was one. One of ten thousand heroes" (*CM* 142). With their strike, Ah Goong and his compatriots overturn the oppressive power structure, demanding and securing a measure of freedom and respect. Bak Goong, the "Great Grandfather of the Sandalwood Mountains," is also a trickster . He fights a no-talking rule at the Hawaiian labor camp by singing subversive messages to his compatriots, a trickster technique often used by

African American slaves. After he is whipped for singing, he eventually finds his solution in the less articulate but equally effective technique of coughing out his thoughts. Like Nanapush of Erdrich's *Tracks*, Bak Goong soon discovers that his life depends on talking. He becomes the camp storyteller, a "talk addict" who inspires the men with stories of trickster Chan Moong Gut. During one comic episode, Bak Goong and his friends mock female missionaries, making lewd comments in a dialect they don't understand and offering them more and more tea to force them to urinate. Later, Bak Goong explains to the men that they have reenacted a trickster story, "Chan Moong Gut and the Gambling Wives," which connects them to a comic, subversive trickster tradition. In a hilarious defamiliarization of one of western culture's most sacred images, Bak Goong observes the "Jesus demonesses" hand out "grisly cards with a demon nailed to a cross, probably a warning about what happened to you if you didn't convert" (*CM* 112).

When Bak Goong becomes ill, he attributes it to pent-up speech: "His tongue was heavy and his throat blocked. He awoke certain that he had to cure himself by talking whenever he pleased. . . . 'Uncles and Brothers, I have diagnosed our illness. It is a congestion from not talking. What we have to do is talk and talk'" (*CM* 115). He then tells them a story that "cannot be left unsaid," about a king who relieves himself by shouting his secret into the ground (*CM* 116). The story inspires the men to dig an "ear into the world," into which they shout all their secrets, frustrations, joys, and sorrows (*CM* 117). A trickster who invents and creates culture, Bak Goong tells the men, "That wasn't a custom. We made it up. We can make up customs because we're the founding ancestors of this place" (*CM* 117). Their new custom has the positive effects of a trickster strategy: their show of anger, rage, despair, and joy wins them more freedom and independence from the intimidated whites.

Like Bak Goong's shouting party, Kingston's art is collaborative, and it simultaneously expresses rage at her forefathers' mistreatment and joy at their victories. One of the few women's stories recounted in *China Men*—the singing and crying ritual performed before her mother's wedding—perhaps best captures the novel's trickster spirit. Since the trickster opposes entrenched oppression of all kinds, it is not surprising to find feminist critique alongside tribute to male ancestors. The women gather to listen to the bride's lament, a litany of anger, sorrow, and hope at the prospect of a new life with her husband and his family: "The women punctuated her long complaints with clangs of pot lids for cymbals. The rhymes made them laugh. MaMa wailed, her eyes wet, and sang as she laughed and cried, mourned, joked, praised, found the appropriate old songs and invented new songs in melismata of singing and keening. She sang for three evenings. The length of her laments that ended in sobs and laughter was wonderful to hear" (*CM* 31). Balancing sobs and laughter, finding appropriate old songs and inventing new ones, Kingston's *China Men* continues this dynamic, self-renewing, trickster-inspired tradition.

THE MONKEY AND HIS COMMUNITY: *TRIPMASTER MONKEY*

Whereas *The Woman Warrior* and *China Men* employ trickster strategies in themes and form—challenging genre labels, evoking a paradox-rich reality, tricking and teaching with numerous story versions—Kingston's 1989 novel, *Tripmaster Monkey*, confirms the centrality of the trickster to Kingston's work, not only by employing a trickster aesthetic formally but also by introducing a trickster protagonist as a model for personal and cultural identity. A full-blown trickster novel, *Tripmaster Monkey* is a groundbreaking, boundary-breaking work that revises and reinvents cultural myths, resists conventional plotting, and unsettles the reader's comfortable assumptions. The novel's protagonist, Wittman Ah Sing, is a Berkeley beatnik and modern American incarnation of the Monkey King of Chinese legend, whose adventures were crystallized in Wu Ch'eng-en's sixteenth-century novel, *Journey to the West*. Monkey attains immortality through his perseverance and audacity and repeatedly disrupts bureaucratic order in Heaven and on earth until he finally embarks upon a journey to bring the Buddhist Scriptures to China from India. Thus he combines temerity with grace and commands our laughter and our respect.

Wandering in and around San Francisco, negotiating cultural border-lines, crusading against racism and questioning the American dream, Wittman interweaves Chinese mythic history and American Romantic values as he works out his identity as a Chinese American man. Wittman's wander-ings culminate in his final creation, a "combination revue-lecture" designed, Kingston tells us, to "entertain and educate the solitaries which make up a community" (*TM* 288). A metaphor for the novel's storytelling process, the play's multiple-voiced presentation and culturally mixed audience constitute Kingston's vision of communal unity in storytelling. As both clown and savior, Wittman the Monkey trickster gathers a new American community to participate in his play, which wages a war against racism and celebrates the community as a place of healing.

Wittman's scars from racism are deep: on the first page of *Tripmaster Monkey* he contemplates suicide. While he fights against the alienation, racism, and stereotyping he finds both within himself and in others, he creates an identity of interwoven cultural strands. Kingston emphasizes the worldwide roots of Wittman's identity with her encyclopedic allusions. An English major at Berkeley in the sixties, Wittman is steeped in Shakespeare, Rilke, Woolf, Beckett, Whitman, Thoreau, Ginsberg, Kerouac, and countless others, as well as in American popular culture and the Chinese classic novels *The Water Margin, Journey to the West, and Romance of the Three Kingdoms*. Like the quintessentially American poet for whom he is named, Wittman celebrates the diversity of America and strives for integration of himself and the world in the face of racism and a disintegrating community. Kingston comments in an interview that Wittman sees integration "on simple levels, such as integrating the busses and the bathrooms. . . . But he also has to work on integrating himself. And then there's that large integration between him and the rest of the universe. And America" (M. Chin 60). To Kingston, "integration" does not mean melting down differences, but harmonizing diverse and conflicting elements, whether within the self or in a larger community. The monkey trickster, "man of a thousand faces," master of seventy-two transformations, is an ideal trope for an integrated selfhood (*TM* 25).

As a monkey, Wittman remains always on the radical fringe even while he galvanizes the community to action. His long hair, beard, and eccentric clothes signal his defiance of communal norms: "people who wear black turtleneck sweaters have no place. You don't easily come home, come back to Chinatown, where they give you the stink-eye and call you a saang-hsu lo, a whisker-growing man, Beatnik" (*TM* 11). Wittman exists on the margins not only of Chinatown but also of an explicitly American consumer culture; he dresses in shoes left on beaches and ties found on trees, decorates his room from India Imports garbage dumpsters, and eats the last piece of pizza others leave behind. Combining the legacy of Benjamin Franklin with that of the trickster, he declares himself "self-made. . . out of dregs and slags" (*TM* 207). Wittman announces his own mythic status in American superhero terms: "Listen, Lois," he says to Nanci, "underneath these glasses . . . I am really: the present-day U.S.A. incarnation of the King of the Monkeys" (*TM* 33). The pairing of Superman and Monkey signals Wittman's dual cultural inheritance yet emphasizes his Americanness. By allowing Wittman to be both mythic and realistic, Kingston treads a thin line between fantasy and reality in *Tripmaster Monkey*, much as she does in *The Woman Warrior*. Wittman himself insists on the reality of his mythic identity: "Not 'supposed to be.' I *am*" a monkey, he says to Taña (*TM* 191). As an American Monkey, Wittman uses his "Monkey powers—outrage and jokes" to "spook out prejudice," bust through stereotypes, and finally create a community (*TM* 241, 332).

Because his culture is, in Kingston's words, "on the brink of disappearing", Wittman's search for identity ultimately involves recreating his community (Fishkin 786). The new community he envisions consists not only of other American-born Chinese Americans but also of everyone he meets: "Do the right thing by whoever crosses your path," he decides. "Those coincidental people are your people" (*TM* 223). This is why he searches out PoPo, the mysterious pseudo-grandmother who arrived one day on his parents' doorsteps and whom his parents finally abandon in the mountains when she becomes a burden to them. Although Wittman never determines the truth of his blood relationship to PoPo, the mystery is ultimately irrelevant; she is his relative if only by virtue of coincidence. PoPo's abandonment signals the breakdown of the community that Wittman must rebuild, mainly through an accretion of stories.

Communities survive by their stories, and tricksters are consummate storytellers. "Got no money. Got no home. Got story," Wittman says (*TM* 175). Wittman uses stories to preserve and renew his Chinese American culture and community, persuading an old man at the Benevolent Association to let him stage his play by enacting a Monkey episode from *Journey the West*. His story secures a stage for the building of community. In addition to being a plot device that moves the action of the novel forward, storytelling forms the substance of the narrative itself. In picaresque trickster fashion, the novel resists linear development with its loose anecdotal construction and frequent talk-story forays. The reader must give up a search for plot in a narration whose very substance is interruptions, sidetrips, and verbal fireworks to be enjoyed for their own sake, even as their abundance threatens to overshadow those who relay them. The novel's narrator teases the reader about the trappings of traditional plotting and calls attention to its artificiality. "If there is a plot to life, then his setting out in search of her will cause PoPo to appear" (*TM* 207). Rather than finding her when he sets out on his quest, Wittman runs into PoPo anticlimactically, on the street while doing his laundry. Like Wittman, who is writing a "play that continues like life," with *Tripmaster Monkey* Kingston appears to be deliberately writing an antifiction, flaunting her own ability to invent or not invent an exciting moment in order to render life more truthfully (*TM* 169).

Critics have noted the postmodern quality of Kingston's writing. Pointing to the novel's "disjunctured, decentralized perspective," Patricia Lin describes *Tripmaster Monkey*'s narrative structure as a "pastiche" of "prescripted texts" that Wittman gathers because "there are no new stories" (Lin 337). Though *Tripmaster Monkey* does indeed share many important aspects of postmodernism, its focus on a culturally based trickster injects a positive sense of exuberance, enthusiasm, and possibility into Kingston's writing that contradicts the ennui characteristic of much postmodern writing. Rather than producing a sense of incoherence or meaninglessness, Kingston's pastiche can be read as multivocality, designed to evoke the richness of a diverse culture. The multiple and conflicting voices in *Tripmaster Monkey*, as well as its borrowings from sources such as Rilke, *Journey to the West*, Chang and Eng, American movies, and Beat generation poetry, define the diverse cultural milieu against which and out of which Wittman must create an identity and forge a community.

Wittman's, and Kingston's, cultural inheritance is both eastern and western. In fact, as "postmodern" as Kingston's narrative technique is, it also shares many of the aspects of traditional Chinese novels. As C. T. Hsia explains, because classic Chinese novels evolved in part from a tradition of oral storytellers, who would parcel out the story in sessions at a tea house for a year or more, the narratives tend to be rambling, lengthy, and episodic. Hsia's description of these narratives is strikingly reminiscent of *Tripmaster Monkey*: "In such elaborate retelling, the plot as such becomes almost irrelevant; at each session the storyteller attends to a fraction of an episode with vivid impersonations of characters and free-ranging comments on manners and morals" (Hsia 9). Hsia's assessment of *Journey to the West*, that it is too long and repetitive though "invariably narrated with gusto," echoes many readers' reactions to *Tripmaster Monkey* (Hsia 113).

Tripmaster Monkey is multivocal not only in its extensive use of other texts but also in its exploration of the heteroglossia of contemporary American life. In order to describe Wittman's experience adequately, the novel creates an American vernacular language that mixes elements of various social worlds in which Wittman moves. Kingston's use of idiomatic, spoken American language captures the tones of a broad range of diverse social groups from tripping "hippy-dippies" to slick retail advertising campaigns, from his mother's swift, clacking mah-jongg table to his father's gruff poker group, from Mrs. Chew's warnings about "molly-see-no cherries" to the bureaucratic platitudes of the Unemployment Office. Kingston's interest in inventing a new American language places her, as she puts it, "in the tradition of American writers who consciously set out to create the literature of a new culture. Mark Twain, Walt Whitman, Gertrude Stein, the Beats all developed an ear for dialect, street language" (Li, "American Canon" 496). In Bakhtinian terms, a new language means a new worldview. Wittman's search for a new language connects language with social force and ultimately with the possibility of social change. "Where's our ain't-taking-noshit-from-nobody street-strutting language?" Wittman asks, adding, "I want so bad to be the first bad-jazz China Man bluesman of America" (*TM* 27). Nanci's reaction to Wittman's poetry, "you sound black," is upsetting to him primarily because it suggests imitation rather than invention (*TM* 32).

For an ethnic group often stereotyped as quiet and polite, it is especially important, Wittman feels, to generate a bold, creative, distinctive voice. Wittman's movement from poetry to theatrical performance significantly relates to defining an ethnic identity; because his appearance, unlike his poetic voice, cannot be mistaken as "black," when Wittman appears in the theater his difference gains center stage.

Chronology

1887   *When I Was a Boy in China*, autobiography by Lee Yan Phou. (China)

1897   *Buddha, a Drama in Twelve Scenes*, by Sadakichi Hartmann. (Japan)

1899   *Miss Numè of Japan: A Japanese-American Romance*, novel by Onoto Watanna / Winnifred Eaton. (Japan)

1901   *A Japanese Nightengale*, novel by Onoto Watanna.

1907   *The Diary of Delia*, novel by Onoto Watanna.

1909   *My Life in China and America*, autobiography by Wing Yung. (China)

1910   *Tama*, novel by Onoto Watanna. (Japan)

1912   *Mrs. Spring Fragrance*, novel by Sui Sin Far / Edith Eaton. (Japan)

1923   *Tanka: Poems in Exile*, by Jun Fujita. (Japan)

1926   *The Bandit Prince*, novel by Sessue Kintaro Hayakawa. (Japan)

1927   *Passport to Immortality*, essays by Sadakichi Hartmann.

1929   *The Hanging on Union Square*, novel by H.T. Tsiang. (China)

1930   *Hidden Flame*, poems by Bunichi Kagawa. (Japan)

1931   *The Grass Roof*, novel by Younghill Kang. (Korea)

1937   *East Goes West*, autobiography by Younghill Kang.

1942   *Chorus for America*, poems by Carlos Bulosan. (Philippines)

1943   *Father and Glorious Descendant*, biography by Pardee Lowe. (China)
        The Voice of Bataan, poems by Carlos Bulosan.

1944   *The Laughter of My Father*, stories by Carlos Bulosan.

1946   *Citizen 13660*, personal narrative by Mine Okubo. (Japan)
        America Is in the Heart: A Personal History, by Carlos Bulosan.

1949   *Yokohama, California*, short stories by Toshio Mori. (Japan)
        Poems, by José García Villa. (Philippines)

1950   *Fifth Chinese Daughter*, autobiography by Jade Snow Wong. (China)
        The Silent Traveler in New York, travel book and poems by Chiang
        Yee. (China)

1953   *Nisei Daughter*, novel by Monica Sone. (Japan)

1954   *Children of the Ash-Covered Loam and Other Stories*, by N.V.M.
        Gonzalez. (Philippines)
        September Monkey, novel by Induk Pahk. (Korea)

1955   *The Diplomat and Other Poems*, by Dominador I. Ilio. (Philippines)
        You Lovely People, stories by Bienvenido Santos. (Philippines)

1956   *A Season of Grace: a Novel*, by N.V.M. Gonzalez.

1957   *No-No Boy*, novel by John Okada. (Japan)
        The Full Circle, novel by Yoshiko Uchida. (Japan)
        Flower Drum Song, novel by Chin Yang Lee. (China)

1958   *La Via: A Spiritual Journey*, poems by Ricaredo Demetillo.
        (Philippines)

1959   *All I Asking For Is My Body*, novel by Milton Murayama. (Japan)
        The Flaming Lyre, poems by Amador T. Daguio. (Philippines)
        The Bamboo Dancers: a Novel, by N.V.M. Gonzalez.

1960   *Love Songs and Other Poems*, by Oscar de Zuniga. (Philippines)
        Sound of Falling Light: Letters in Exile, by Carlos Bulosan, edited
        by Delores S. Feria.

1961   *Eat a Bowl of Tea*, novel by Louis Chu. (China)

1962   *The Arid Year*, poems by Oscar de Zuniga.

1963   *A Stun of Jewels*, poems by Carlos A. Angeles. (Philippines)
        The House That Tai Ming Built, novel by Virginia Lee. (China)

1964   *The Peninsulars*, novel by Linda Ty-Casper. (Philippines)
        The Martyred, novel by Richard Kim. (Korea)

1965   *The Volcano* and *Villa Magdalena*, novels by Bienvenido N. Santos.
        (Philippines)
        Lucky Come Hawaii, novel by Jon Shirota. (Japan)

1966   *Takao and Grandfather's Sword*, juvenile fiction by Yoshiko Uchida.

1967   *The Day the Dancers Came: Selected Prose Works*, by Bienvenido N.
        Santos.

1968   *Crossings*, novel by Chuang Hua. (China)

1970   *Autobiography of a Chinese Woman*, by Buwei Yang Chao. (China)
        Lost Names, novel by Richard Kim. (Korea)

1971   *Journey to Topaz*, biography by Yoshiko Uchida.

1972   *Pineapple White*, novel by Jon Shirota.

1973   *Farewell to Manzanar*, novel by Jeanne Wakatsuki Houston (Japan)
        and James D. Houston.
        Bataan Harvest: War Poems, by Amador T. Daguilo.
        We Do Not Work Alone: The Thoughts of Kanjiro Kawai, biography by
        Yoshiko Uchida.

1974   *Eye to Eye*, stories by Diana Chang. (China)
        Chickencoop Chinaman, play by Frank Chin. (China)
        A Choice of Dreams, poems by Joy Kogawa. (Japan)

1975   *Dragonwings*, novel by Laurence Yep. (China)
        Dangerous Music, poems by Jessica Tarahata Hagedorn. (Japan)
        The Sandalwood Mountains: Readings and Stories of the Early Chinese in Hawaii, by Tin-Yuke Char. (China)

1976   *Camp Notes and Other Poems*, by Mitsuye Yamada. (Japan)
        The Woman Warrior: Memories of a Girlhood Among Ghosts, biography by Maxine Hong Kingston. (China)

1977   *Dreams in Harrison Railroad Park: Poems*, by Nellie Wong. (China)
        Sea Demons: A Novel, by Laurence Yep.
        Jericho Road, novel by Joy Kogawa.

1978   *Woman From Hiroshima*, novel by Toshio Mori. (Japan)
        The Buddha Bandits Down Highway 99: Poetry, by Garrett Kaoru Hongo (Japan), Alan Chong Lau (China), and Lawson Fusao Inada.
        The Philippines Is in the Heart: A Collection of Stories, by Carlos Bulosan.

1979   *His Native Coast, A Novel*, by Edith L. Tiempo. (Philippines)
        Scent of Apples: A Collection of Stories, by Bienvenido N. Santos.
        The Three-Cornered Sun, novel by Linda Ty-Casper.

1980   *China Men*, biography by Maxine Hong Kingston.

1981   *Obasan*, novel by Joy Kogawa.

1982   *Dictée*, novel by Theresa Hak Kyung Cha. (Korea)
        The Horizon is Definitely Speaking, poems by Diana Chang.
        Desert Exile: The Uprooting of a Japanese-American Family, personal narrative by Yoshiko Uchida.
        The Praying Man, novel by Bienvenido N. Santos.

1983   *Blue Dragon, White Tiger: A Tet Story*, novel by Tran Van Dinh. (Viet Nam)
        Corpse and Mirror, poems by John Yau. (China)
        Distances In Time, novel by Bienvenido N. Santos.

1984   *Memories of Our Paik Family's Life in the New World*, biography by
        Mary Paik Lee. (Korea)
        Barter in Panay: an Epic, by Ricaredo Demetillo.
        Death of Long Steam Lady, poems by Nellie Wong.

1985   *Seventeen Syllables: 5 Stories of Japanese American Life*, by Hisaye
        Yamamoto. (Japan)

1986   *Clay Walls*, novel by Kim Ronyoung. (Korea)
        Wings of Stone, novel by Linda Ty-Casper.

1987   *Dwarf Bamboo*, poems by Marilyn Chin. (China)
        Picture Bride, novel by Yoshiko Uchida.
        What the Hell For You Left Your Heart in San Francisco, novel by
        Bienvenido N. Santos.
        Ten Thousand Seeds, novel by Linda Ty-Casper.

1988   *Chickencoop Chinaman / The Year of the Dragon: Two Plays by Frank
        Chin*. (China)
        State of War, novel by Ninotchka Rosca. (Philippines)
        Balikbayan: A Filipino Homecoming, stories by Michelle Cruz Skinner.
        (Philippines)
        Woman With Horns and Other Stories, by Cecilia Manguerra-
        Brainard. (Philippines)
        Nostalgia, poems by Genny Lim.
        Desert Run: Poems and Other Stories, by Mitsuye Yamada.

1989   *Sushi and Sourdough*, novel by Tooru J. Kanazawa. (Japan)
        When Heaven and Earth Changed Places, novel by Le Ly Hayslip.
        (Viet Nam)
        Fallen Leaves, novel by Nguyen Thi Thi-Lam. (Viet Nam)
        The Joy Luck Club, novel by Amy Tan.
        Tripmaster Monkey: His Fake Book, novel by Maxine Hong Kingston.

1990   *Dogeaters*, novel by Jessica Tarahata Hagedorn. (Philippines)
        Power of Money and Other Stories, by Carlos Bulosan.
        Quiet Odyssey: A Pioneer Korean Woman in America, biography by
        Mary Paik Lee.

1991   "Talking to the Dead," short story by Sylvia A. Watanabe (Japan),
        wins an O. Henry Award.

Cebu, stories by Peter Bacho. (Philippines)
Now You Are Still, and Other Poems, by Carlos Bulosan.
Paper Angels and Bitter Cane: Two Plays, by Genny Lim.
The Invisible Thread, autobiography by Yoshiko Uchida.
The Kitchen God's Wife, novel by Amy Tan.

1992   *The Alien Corn*, novel by Edith L. Tiempo.

1993   *Shizuko's Daughter*, novel by Kyoko Mori. (Japan)
Guerilla Memoirs, novel by Dominador I. Ilio.
A Bruise of Ashes: Collected Poems, 1940–1992, by Carlos A. Angeles.
The Bread of Salt and Other Stories, by N.V.M. Gonzalez.
The Frontiers of Love: a Novel, by Diana Chang.

1994   *Visions of a Daughter, Foretold: Four Poems (1980–1993)*, by Jessica Tarahata Hagedorn.
Postscript to a Saintly Life, autobiography by Bienvenido N. Santos.

1995   *Transient: Stories 1977–1994*, by Connie Jan Maraan. (Philippines)
One, Tilting Leaves: a Novel, by Edith L. Tiempo.
The Cry and the Dedication, historical fiction by Carlos Bulosan.
The Dream of Water and *One Bird*, novels by Kyoko Mori.
The Hundred Secret Senses, novel by Amy Tan.

1996   *The Gangster of Love*, novel by Jessica Tarahata Hagedorn.

1997   *Drawing the Line: Poems*, by Lawson Fusao Inada.
Stolen Moments, poems by Nellie Wong.

Contributors

HAROLD BLOOM is Sterling Professor of Humanities at Yale University and Professor of English at New York University. In 1987–88 he was Charles Eliot Norton Professor of Poetry at Harvard University. He is the author of *The Anxiety of Influence*, *Poetry and Repression*, and many other volumes of literary criticism. His forthcoming study, *Freud: Transference and Authority*, considers all of Freud's major writings. A MacArthur Prize Fellow, Professor Bloom is general editor of five series of literary criticism published by Chelsea House.

DOROTHY RITSUKO MCDONALD is a professor in the Department of American Thought and Language at Michigan State University. Her essay, "Introduction to Frank Chin's *Chickencoop Chinaman* and *The Year of the Dragon*" is included in an MLA anthology.

AMY LING is Professor of English and Director of Asian American Studies at the University of Wisconsin. She is coeditor of *Imagining America: Stories From the Promised Land* and author of *Between Worlds: Women Writers of Chinese Ancestry*.

KATHARINE NEWMAN is the author of *The American Equation: Literature in a Multi-Ethnic Culture*.

S(AMMY).E(DWARD). SOLBERG is the author of *The Nim Thui Chimmuk (Your Silence) of Han Yong-un, a Korean Poet*, and coeditor of *Peoples of Washington: Perspectives of Cultural Diversity*.

RICHARD R. GUZMAN is a critic of Filipino literature. His essay is included in *Work on the Mountain / N.V.M. Gonzalez*, with an introduction by Oscar V. Campomanes.

ZENOBIA BAXTER MISTRI is an associate professor at Purdue University, where she teaches International Literature and Writing. She has published articles and reviews in *Studies in Short Fiction*, *Modern Fiction Studies*, and *The Old Northwest*.

SHIRLEY GEOK-LIN LIM is Professor of Asian American Studies at the University of California, Santa Barbara. She is the author of three books of poetry, a collection of short stories, and is coeditor of *The Forbidden Stitch: An Asian American Women's Anthology*.

ELAINE H. KIM is professor of Asian American Studies in the Ethnic Studies Department at the University of California, Berkeley. She is the author of *Asian American Literature, An Introduction to the Writings and Their Social Context*, *A Survey of Asian American Literature: Social Perspectives*, and *With Silk Wings: Asian American Women at Work*.

QUI-PHIET TRAN is associate professor of English at Schreiner University, Kerrville, Texas, and the author of *William Faulkner and the French New Novelists* as well as articles on the modern Vietnamese writer and artist.

RUTH Y. HSAIO is an instructor of English at Tufts University, Boston.

OSCAR V. CAMPOMANES received his Ph.D. from Brown University and is a scholar of Filipino American literature.

CHUNG-HEI YUN is professor of English and Humanities at Shawnee State University, Portsmouth, Ohio.

INDERPAL GREWAL is the author of *Home and Harem: Nation, Gender, Empire, and the Cultures of Travel*, *The Political Aesthetic of Victorian Travel*, and coeditor of *Scattered Hegemonies: Postmodernity and Transnational Feminist Practices*.

JEANNE ROSIER SMITH teaches American literature at Seton Hall University.

Bibliography

Alexander, Meena. *Nampally Road*. San Francisco: Mercury House, Inc., 1991.

Alquizola, Marilyn. "The Fictive Narrator of *America Is in the Heart*," in *Frontiers of American Studies*, ed. Gail M. Nomura et al. Washington: Washington State University, Pullman, 1989.

Amirthanayagam, Guy, editor. *Asian and Western Writers in Dialogue: New Cultural Identities*. London: Macmillan, 1982.

Baker, Houston, Jr., editor. *Three American Literatures: Essays in Chicano, Native American, and Asian-American Literature for Teachers of American Literature*. Introduction, Walter J. Ong. New York: Modern Language Association, 1982.

Brienza, Susan. "Telling Old Stories New Ways: Narrative Strategies in the Novels of Contemporary American Women." Paper delivered at symposium, Creating Women, University of California, Los Angeles, March 8, 1986.

Bruchac, Joseph, editor. *Breaking Silence: An Anthology of Contemporary Asian American Poets*. Greenfield Center, NY: Greenfield Review Press, 1983.

Bulosan, Carlos. *America Is in the Heart: A Personal History*. Seattle: University of Washington Press, 1981.

———. *If You Want to Know What We Are: A Carlos Bulosan Reader*. Minneapolis: West End, 1983.

———. *Sound of Falling Light: Letters in Exile*. Editor, Dolores Feria. Quezon City, Philippines: University of Philippines Press, 1960.

Bushnell, O.A. *The Return of Lono*. Reprint. Honolulu: University of Hawaii Press, 1979.

Cha, Theresa Hak Kyung. *Dictée*. New York: Tanam Press, 1982.

Chan, Jeffrey Paul et al. "Resources for Chinese and Japanese American Literary Traditions," *Amerasia* 8:1 (1981): 19–31.

Chang, Diana. *The Frontiers of Love*. New York: Random House, 1956.

———. *Woman of Thirty*. New York: Random House, 1959.

———. *The Only Game In Town*. New York: Random House, 1963.

———. *A Passion for Life*. New York: Random House, 1961.

————. *A Perfect Love*. New York: Jove Publishers, 1978.

————. *Eye to Eye*. New York: Harper & Row, 1975.

Cheung, King-kok. Introduction to *"Seventeen Syllables" and Other Stories* by Hisaye Yamamoto. Latham, NY: Kitchen Table Press, 1988. xi–xxv.

————. "The Woman Warrior vs. The Chinaman Pacific: Emasculation, Feminism, and Heroism," *Conflicts in Feminism*. Editor, Marianne Hirsch and Evelyn Fox Keller. New York: Routledge, 1990. 234–51.

————and Stan Yogi. *Asian American Literature: An Annotated Bibliography*. New York: Modern Language Association, 1988.

Chin, Frank. "The Most Popular Book in China," *Quilt* 4 (1970): 6–12.

————. "Don't Pen Us Up in Chinatown," *New York Times* (October 8, 1972): 1.

————. "Confessions of the Chinatown Cowboy," *Bulletin of Concerned Asian Scholars* 4:3 (1972): 58–70.

————. *Chickencoop Chinaman and the Year of the Dragon: Two Plays by Frank Chin*. Seattle: University of Washington Press, 1988.

———— and Jeffrey Paul Chan. "Racist Love," *Seeing through Shuck*. Editor, Richard Kostelanetz. New York: Ballantine books, 1972. 65–79.

————, et al., editors. *Aiiieeeee! An Anthology of Asian-American Writers*. Washington, DC: Howard University Press, 1975.

Chin, Marilyn. *Dwarf Bamboo*. Greenfield Center, NY: Greenfield Review Press, 1987.

Chock, Eric, and Darrell H.Y. Lum, editors. *The Best of Bamboo Ridge: The Hawaii Writers' Quarterly*. Honolulu: Bamboo Ridge Press, 1986.

————et al., editors. *Talk Story: An Anthology of Hawaii's Local Writer*. Honolulu: Talk Story, Inc. and Petronium Press, 1978.

Chu, Louis. *Eat a Bowl of Tea*. 1961. Seattle: University of Washington Press, 1979.

Chua, Cheng Lok. "Golden Mountain: Chinese Versions of the American Dream in Lin Yutang, Louis Chu, and Maxine Hong Kingston," *Ethnic Groups* 4:1–2 (1982): 33–59.

Crow, Charles L. "Home and Transcendence in Los Angeles Fiction," *Los Angeles in Fiction*. Editor, David Find. Albuquerque: University of New Mexico Press, 1984. 189–203.

————. "The *Issei* Father in the Fiction of Hisaye Yamamoto," *Opening Up Literary Criticism: Essays on American Prose and Poetry*. Editor, Leo Truchlar, Salzburg: Verlag Wolfgang Neugebauer, 1986. 34–40.

————. "A MELUS Interview: Hisaye Yamamoto," *MELUS* 14:1 (1987): 73–84.

Dasenbrock, Reed Way. "Intelligibility and Meaningfulness in Multicultural Literature in English," *PMLA* 102 (1987): 10–19.

Far, Sui Sin. "Leaves from the Mental Portfolio of an Eurasian," *Independent* (January 21, 1909): 125–32.

————. *Mrs. Spring Fragrance*. 1912. Urbana: University of Illinois Press, 1995.

Fernandez, Doreen and Edilberto Alegre. *The Writer and His Milieu*. Manila: De La Salle University Press, 1982.

Fujita, Gayle K. " 'To Attend the Sound of Stone': The Sensibility of Silence in *Obasan*," *MELUS* 12:3 (1986): 33–42.

Galdon, Joseph, editor. *Philippine Fiction*. Quezon City, Philippines: Ateneo de Manila University Press, 1972.

Goellnicht, Donald C. "Father Land and/or Mother Tongue: The Divided Female
    Subject in *The Woman Warrior* and *Obasan*," *Redefining Autobiography in
    Twentieth Century Women's Fiction*. Editors, Colette Hall and Janice Morgan.
    New York: Garland, 1991. 119–34.

Gonzalez, N.V.M. *Kalutang: A Filipino in the World*. Manila: Kalikasan Press, 1990.

———. *Mindoro and Beyond: Twenty-One Stories*. Quezon City, Philippines: University
    of Philippines Press, 1979.

———. "Drumming for the Captain," *World Literature Written in English* 15:2
    (November 1976): 415–21.

———. "The Filipino and the Novel," *Daedelus* 95:4 (Fall 1966): 961–71.

———. *Seven Hills Away*. Denver: Alan Swallow, 1947.

Guzman, Richard. " 'As in Myth, the Signs Were All Over': The Fiction of N.V.M.
Gonzalez," *Virginia Quarterly Review* 60:1 (Winter 1984): 102–18.

Haslam, Gerald W., editor. *Forgotten Pages of American Literature*, Boston: Houghton
    Mifflin, 1970.

Him Mark Lai, Genny Lim, and Judy Yung, editors and translators. *Island: Poetry and
    History of Chinese Immigrants on Angel Island, 1910–1940*. San Francisco:
    HOC DOI, 1980.

Hiura, Arnold, Stephen Sumida, and Martha Webb, editors. *Talk Story Big Island
    Anthology*. Honolulu: Talk Story, Inc. and Bamboo Ridge Press, 1979.

Hom, Marlon K. *Songs of Gold Mountain: Cantonese Rhymes from San Francisco China-
    town*. Berkeley: University of California Press, 1987.

Hsu, Kai-yu and Helen Palubinskas, editors. *Asian-American Authors*. Boston:
    Houghton Mifflin, 1972.

Hua, Chuang. *Crossings*. New York: Dial Press, 1968.

Islas, Arturo. "Interview with Maxine Hong Kingston," *Women Writers of the West
    Coast Speaking of Their Lives and Careers*. Editor, Marilyn Yalom. Santa
    Barbara: Capra, 1983. 11–19.

Johnson, Diane. "Ghosts," review of *The Woman Warrior*, by Maxine Hong Kingston,
    New York Review of Books (February 3, 1977).

Kagawa, Joy. *Obasan*. Boston: Godine, 1981.

Kageyama, Yuri. "Hisaye Yamamoto—Nisei Writer," *Sunbury* 10: 32–42.

Kang, Younghill. *East Goes West*. New York: Charles Scribner's Sons, 1937.

———. *The Grass Roof*. New York: Charles Scribner's Sons, 1931.

Kim, Elaine. *Asian American Literature: An Introduction to the Writings and Their Social
    Context*. Philadelphia: Temple University Press, 1982.

———. "Asian American Writers: A Bibliographical Review," *American Studies Inter-
    national* 22:2 (October 1984): 41–78.

Kingston, Maxine Hong. *The Woman Warrior: Memoirs of a Girlhood Among Ghosts*.
    New York: Knopf, 1976.

———. *China Men*. New York: Knopf, 1980.

———. *Tripmaster Monkey: His Fake Book*. New York: Random House, 1989.

———. *Hawaii One Summer, 1978*. San Francisco: Meadow Press, 1987.

Kramer, Jane. "On Being Chinese in China and America," review of *The Woman
    Warrior*, by Maxine Hong Kingston *New York Times Book Review*
    (November 7, 1976).

Lee, Virginia Chin-lan. *The House That Tai Ming Built*. New York: Macmillan,1963.

Leong, Russell. "Poetry within Earshot," *Amerasia Journal* 15:1 (1989): 165–93.

Lim, Shirley Geok-lin. "Assaying the Gold: or, Contesting the Ground of Asian American Literature." Paper presented at the Modern Language Association Convention, 1990.

Lin-Blind, Patricia. "The Icicle in the Desert: Perspective and Form in the Works of Two Chinese American Women Writers," *MELUS* 6:3 (1979): 51–71.

Ling, Amy. "I'm Here: An Asian American Woman's Response," *New Literary History* 19 (1987): 151–60.

———. *Between Worlds: Women Writers of Chinese Ancestry.* New York: Pergamon Press, 1990.

———. "Edith Eaton: Pioneer Chinamerican Writer and Feminist," *American Literary Realism, 1870–1910* 16:2 (1983): 287–98.

Lowe, Pardee. *Father and Glorious Descendant.* Boston: Little, Brown, and Company, 1943.

McDonald, Dorothy Ritsuko. "After Imprisonment: Ichiro's Search for Redemption in *No-No Boy*," *MELUS* 6:3 (1979): 19–26.

———and Katharine Newman. "Relocation and Dislocation: The Writings of Hisaye Yamamoto and Wakako Yamauchi," *MELUS* 7:3 (Fall 1980): 21–38.

Mirikitani, Janice, editor. *Time to Greez!: Incantations from the Third World.* San Francisco: Glide Publications, 1975.

———, editor. *Ayumi.* San Francisco: The Japanese Anthology Committee, 1980.

Morante, P.C. *Remembering Carlos Bulosan.* Quezon City, Philippines: Manlapaz, 1971.

Mori, Toshio Mori. *Yokohama, California.* 1949. Seattle: University of Washington Press, 1985.

Mukherjee, Bharati. *Jasmine.* New York: Fawcett Crest, 1989.

Mura, David. *After We Lost Our Way.* New York: Dutton, 1989.

Murayama, Milton. *All I Asking For Is My Body,* 1959. San Francisco: Supa Press, 1975.

Neubauer, Carol, E. "Developing Ties to the Past: Photography and Other Sources of Information in Maxine Hong Kingston's *China Men*," *MELUS* 10:4 (Winter 1983): 17–36.

Nunes, Susan. *A Small Obligation and Other Stories of Hilo.* Honolulu: Bamboo Ridge Press, 1982.

Okada, John. *No-No Boy.* San Francisco: Combined Asian American Resources Project, Inc., 1976.

Olney, James, editor. *Autobiography: Essays Theoretical and Critical.* Princeton: Princeton University Press, 1980.

Pfaff, Timothy. "Talk with Mrs. Kingston," *New York Times Book Review* (June 15, 1980).

Quemada, David. "The Contemporary Filipino Poet in English," *World Literature Written in English* 15:2 (November 1976): 429–37.

Rabine, Leslie W. "No Lost Paradise: Social Gender and Symbolic Gender in the Writings of Maxine Hong Kingston," *Signs: Journal of Women in Culture and Society* 12 (1987): 471–92.

Rainwater, Catherine and William Scheick, editors. *Contemporary American Women Writers: Narrative Strategies.* Lexington: University Press of Kentucky, 1985. 173–89.

Rustomji-Kerns, Roshni. "Expatriates, Immigrants, and Literature: Three South Asian Women Writers," *Massachusetts Review* 29:4 (1988): 655–65.

San Juan, Epifanio, Jr. "Mapping the Boundaries, Inscribing the Differences: The Filipino in the U.S.A.," *Journal of Ethnic Studies* 19:1 (Spring 1991): 117–31.

———. "Farewell, You Whose Homeland is Forever Arriving As I Embark: Journal of a Filipino Exile," *Kultura* 3:1 (1990): 34–41.

———. "Reflections on U.S.-Philippine Literary Relations," *Ang Makatao* (1988): 43–54.

———. "To the Filipino Artist in Exile," *Midweek* (August 19, 1987).

Santos, Bienvenido. "Philipino Old Timers: Fact and Fiction," *Amerasia* 9:2 (1982): 89–98.

———. *Scent of Apples.* Seattle: University of Washington Press, 1979.

———. "The Personal Saga of a 'Straggler' in Philippine Literature," *World Literature Written in English* 15:2 (November 1976): 398–405.

———. "The Filipino Novel in English," *Brown Heritage: Essays on Philippine Cultural Tradition and Literature.* Editor, Antonio Manuud. Quezon City, Philippines: Ateneo de Manila University Press, 1967.

Sledge, Linda Ching. "Maxine Hong Kingston's *China Men*: The Family Historian as Epic Poet," *MELUS* 7:4 (Winter 1980): 3–22.

Solberg, S.E. "Sui Sin Far/Edith Eaton: First Chinese-American Fictionalist," *MELUS* 8:1 (1981): 27–40.

Sone, Monica. *Nisei Daughter.* 1953. Seattle, University of Washington Press, 1979.

Sullivan, Rosemary. "Who Are the Immigrant Writers and What Have They Done?" *Globe and Mail* (October 17, 1987): E1.

Sumida, Stephen H. *And the View from the Shore: Literary Traditions of Hawai'i.* Seattle: University of Washington Press, 1991.

———. "Place as History in Hawaii's Literatures," *Defining a Sense of Place: A Humanities Guide.* Honolulu: Hawaii Committee for the Humanities, 1990. 12–15.

———. "Waiting for the Big Fish: Recent Research in the Asian American Literature of Hawaii." In Chock and Lum *The Best of Bamboo Ridge*, 302–21.

Tachiki, Amy, et al. *Roots: An Asian American Reader.* Los Angeles: Continental Graphics, 1971.

Tan, Amy. *The Joy Luck Club.* New York: Putnam, 1989.

———. *The Siamese Cat.* New York: Macmillan, 1994.

———. *The Hundred Secret Senses.* New York: G.P. Putnam's Sons, 1995.

———. *The Kitchen God's Wife.* New York: Putnam, 1991.

———. *The Moon Lady.* New York: Macmillan, 1992.

———. *The Old Woman Remembered a Swan She had Bought.* Berkeley: Black Oak Books, 1989.

Tran, Qui-Phiet. "Vietnamese Artists and Writers in America: 1975 to the Present," *Journal of the American Studies Association of Texas* 20 (1989): 101–10.

Trinh T. Minh-ha. *Woman, Native, Other.* Bloomington, IN: Indiana University Press, 1989.

Wand, David Hsin-Fu, editor. *Asian-American Heritage: An Anthology of Prose and Poetry.* New York: Washington Square Press, 1974.

Wang, Alfred S. "Maxine Hong Kingston's Reclaiming of America: The Birthright of the Chinese American Male," *South Dakota Review* 26:1 (Spring 1988): 18–29.

Watanna, Onoto. *The Diary of Delia*. New York: Page, 1907.

———. *Marion: A Story of an Artist's Model by Herself and the Author of Me*. New York: Watt, 1916.

———. *A Japanese Nightengale*. New York: Harper, 1901.

———. *Me, A Book of Remembrance*. New York: Century, 1915.

———. *Miss Numè of Japan*. Chicago: Rand, McNally, 1899.

White-Parks, Annette. "Sui Sin Far: Writer on the Chinese-Anglo Borders of North America, 1885–1914." Ph.D. dissertation, Washington State University, Program in American Studies, 1991.

Wong, Cynthia Sau-ling. "Necessity and Extravagance in Maxine Kingston's *Woman Warrior*," *MELUS* 15:1 (1988): 3–26.

Wong, Jade Snow. *Fifth Chinese Daughter*. 1945. Seattle: University of Washington Press, 1989.

Wong, Sau-ling C. "Tales of Postwar Chinatown: Short Stories of The Bud, 1947–1948," *Amerasia* 14:2 (1988): 61–79.

Yalom, Marilyn, editor. *Women Writers of the West Coast: Speaking of Their Lives and Careers*. Santa Barbara: Capra, 1983.

Acknowledgements

"After Imprisonment: Ichiro's Search for Redemption in *No-No Boy*" by Dorothy Ritsuko McDonald from *MELUS: The Journal of the Society for the Study of the Multi-Ethnic Literature of the United States*, Vol. 6, No. 3 (Fall 1979). Copyright © by the University of Southern California.

"Writer in a Hyphenated Condition: Diana Chang" by Amy Ling from *MELUS: The Journal of the Society for the Study of the Multi-Ethnic Literature of the United States*, Vol. 7, No. 4 (Winter 1980). Copyright © 1980 by the University of Southern California.

"Relocation and Dislocation: The Writings of Hisaye Yamamoto and Wakako Yamauchi" by Dorothy Ritsuko McDonald and Katharine Newman from *MELUS: The Journal of the Society for the Study of the Multi-Ethnic Literature of the United States*, Vol. 7, No. 3 (Fall 1980). Copyright © by the University of Southern California.

"Sui Sin Far / Edith Eaton: The First Chinese-American Fictionist" by S.E. Solberg from *MELUS: The Journal of the Society for the Study of the Multi-Ethnic Literature of the United States*, Vol. 8, No. 1 (Spring 1981). Copyright © 1981 by the University of Southern California.

"Winnifred Eaton: Ethnic Chameleon and Popular Success" by Amy Ling from *MELUS: The Journal of the Society for the Study of the Multi-Ethnic Literature of the United States*, Vol. 11, No. 3 (Fall 1984). Copyright © 1984 by the University of Cincinnati.

" 'As In Myth, the Signs Were All Over': The Fiction of N.V.M. Gonzalez" by Richard R. Guzman from *The Virginia Quarterly Review*, Vol. 60, No. 1 (Winter 1984). Copyright © 1984 by The Virginia Quarterly Review.

Index